Picabia Inside Out

Philip Pearlstein

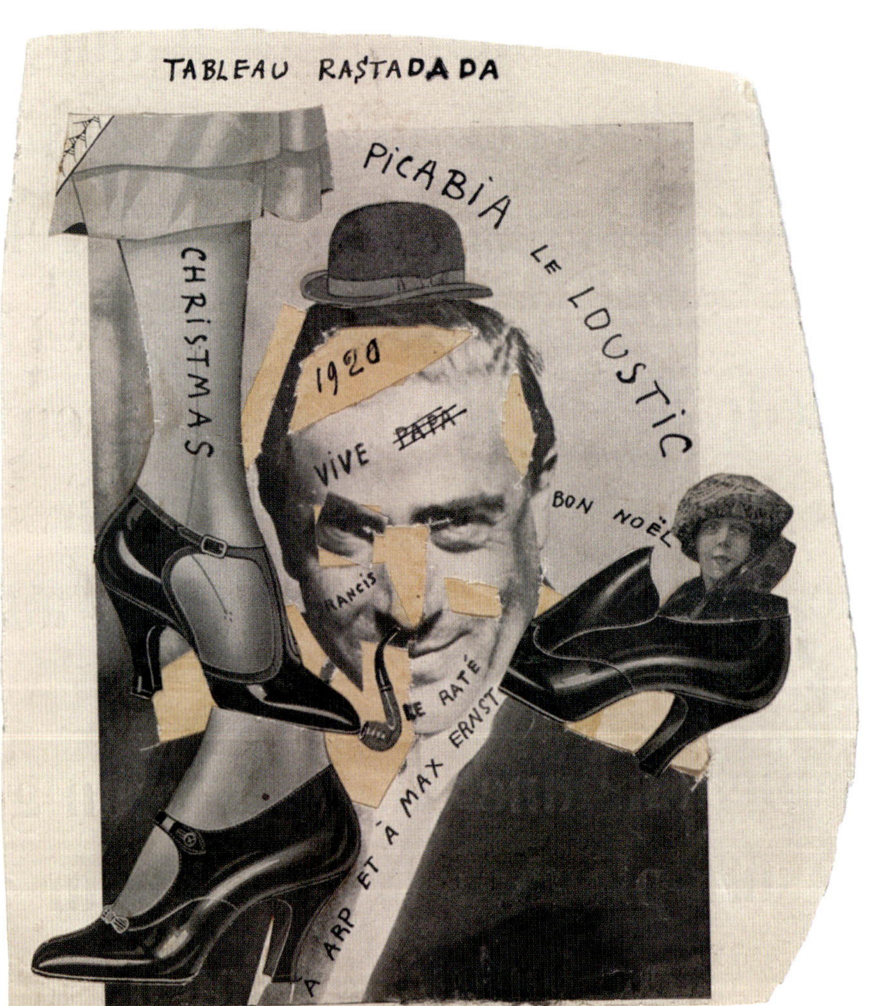

TABLEAU RASTADADA
PICABIA LE LOUSTIC
CHRISTMAS
1920
VIVE PAPA
BON NOËL
RANCIS
LE RATÉ
À ARP ET À MAX ERNST

Picabia Inside Out

Philip Pearlstein

HENI Publishing, London

Frontispiece: Francis Picabia
Tableau Rastadada (Rastadada Painting), 1920
Cut-and-pasted printed paper on paper with ink, 19 × 17.1 cm (7 ½ × 6 ¾ in.) © ADAGP, Paris and DACS, London 2023. Gift of Abby Aldrich Rockefeller (by exchange). The Museum of Modern Art, New York/Scala, Florence.

The back section of this book is a faithful reproduction of an original manuscript written in 1955 and is published here without any modifications to the text.

ISBN 978-1-912122-64-6

Designed by Sylvia Ugga
Edited by Kirsty Watling
Printed and bound in China by Toppan Leefung
Typeface: Vaud

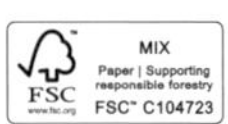

Contents

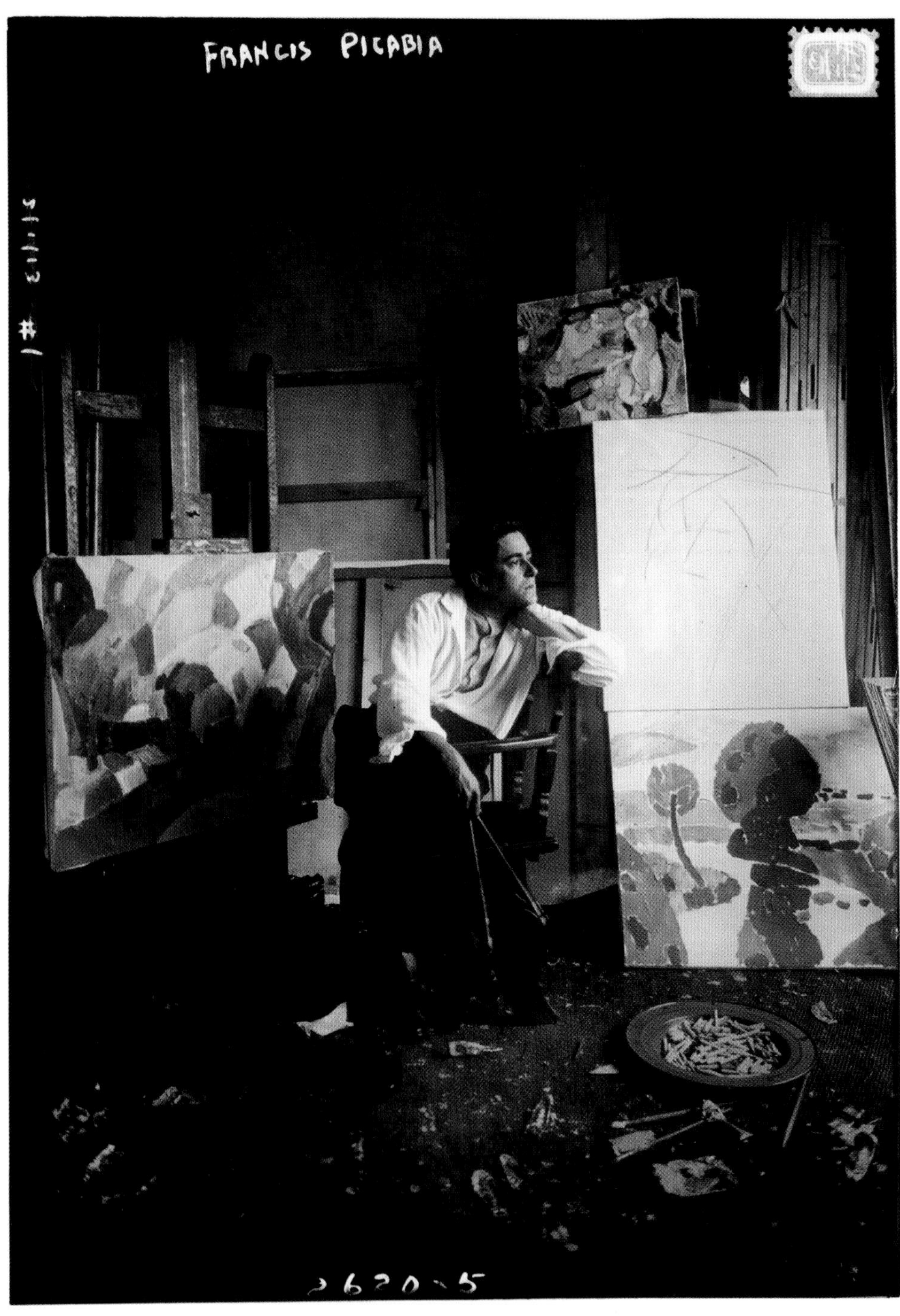

George Grantham Bain
Francis Picabia, *c.*1910–15

Pearlstein and Picabia: The Odd Couple?

Foreword by Robert Storr

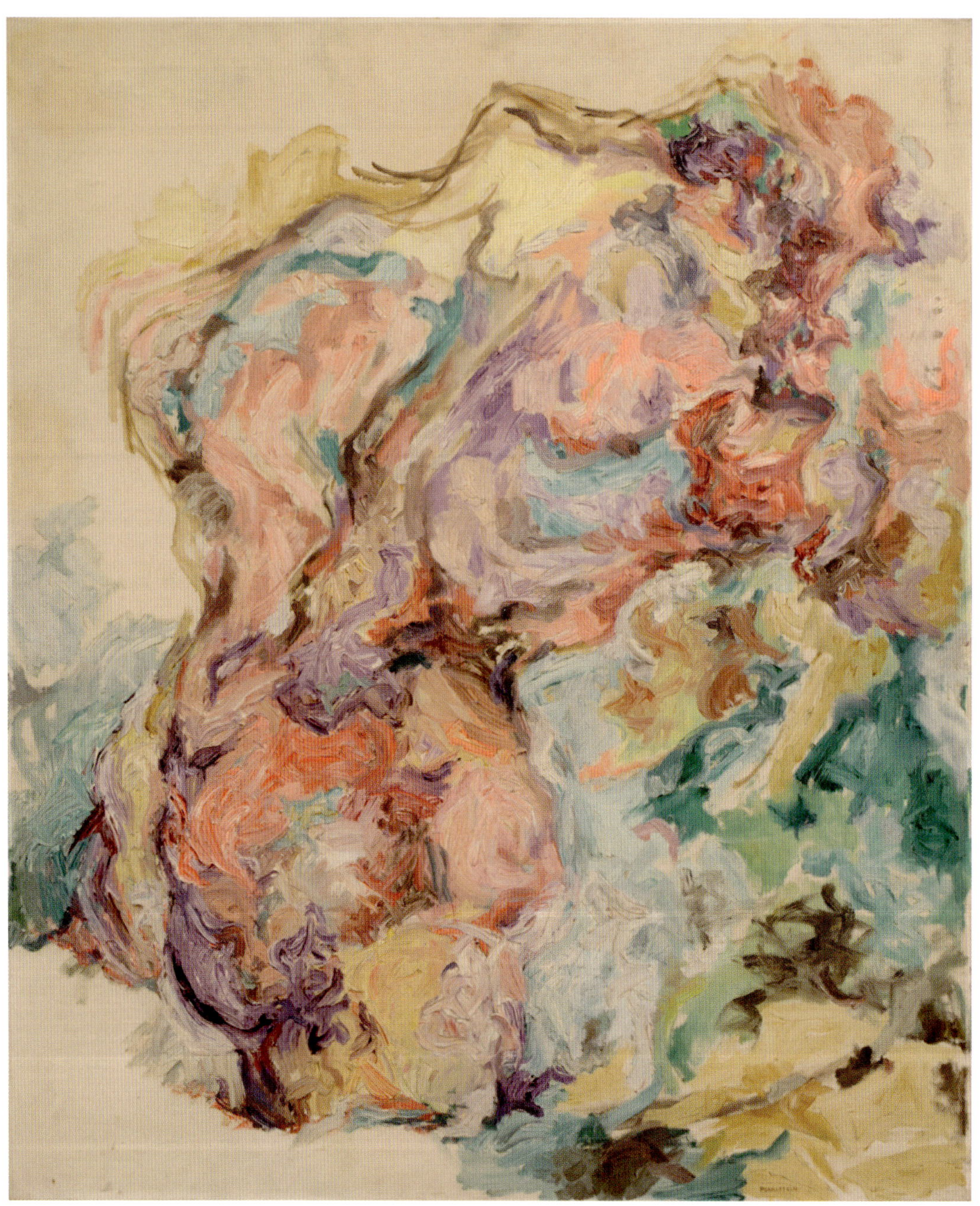

Philip Pearlstein
Torso, 1953

For over seven decades, Philip Pearlstein has been the most reliably yet perversely enlightening misfit on the North American art scene, the quintessential odd man out of the New York School. Even so he has been a certified member of that School, starting shortly after its postwar formation and for as long as it lasted into the 1970s. Not to mention his singular public presence ever since it dissolved, after the 1980s and on, into the amorphous "global" art world we now inhabit – or at least visit online.

These are all exceptional distinctions, but being the exception to any rule much less several – even the one that proves the rule – comes at a price. For Pearlstein that has resulted in his long occupying a dubious kind of "also ran" position. The fact that he has stayed in the race for nearly 80 years is in and of itself a unique measure of his role in art history. But the more one takes stock of his endurance and wide-ranging accomplishment, and the more attentively one studies his art, the more he stands apart from his contemporaries of several generations.

First consider the qualities frequently and readily ascribed to his work: figurative, realist, cool. Indeed, Pearlstein's work has been closely if not obsessively observed, in the main studio-based, and overall diligently, unapologetically descriptive. To the point of an aggressive psychological as well as social neutrality that has thrown many critics off because it borders on an anti-painterly "Just the Facts Ma'am" Jack Webb-like approach to his medium. All of these elements run hard against the grain of the emotionally charged, accident-prone gesturalism of New York School Painting in its 1950s and 1960s heyday, although he practiced a variant of that at the outset of his career while on a Fulbright Fellowship in 1958 in Rome where he painted the ruins of that city in lively, overtly liquid strokes. Ironically, none of the deliberate, mimetic qualities ascribed to his way of working prevented the critic Clement Greenberg from singling Pearlstein's early, awkward, yet painterly landscapes out for special attention before the artist consolidated his strictly factual orientation and embarked on his Wrong-Way Corrigan detour from "mainstream" aesthetics as Greenberg's formalism uncompromisingly mandated them.

But, then, nothing about Pearlstein's preparation for his future inclined him to accept such orthodoxies as predicates for art making. And no reading of the art historical record, much less any projection of its future based on such readings, could dissuade him from following through on first-hand insights he had gained from early struggles with the contradictions of lived experience and the fully articulated paradoxes of art as he had encountered it in the world. In his hometown of Pittsburgh, P.A. – with its spectacular river gorges and Dark Satanic Mills, not to mention its uniquely endowed universities and museums, one of North America's most beautiful yet rawest monuments to the Industrial Revolution – Pearlstein was a high school art prodigy. Thereafter he studied at the Carnegie Institute alongside the equally talented Andrew Warhola, who regularly took refuge from his own straitened circumstances in the Pearlsteins' relatively more spacious and prosperous household.

Thereafter, they set off together to New York to seek their fortunes as artists. For a time, during which both earned their livings as illustrators, they lived together until Pearlstein moved out to marry Dorothy Cantor, also a painter as well as another Carnegie graduate. Prepared by his on-the-job U.S. Army training making signs and drawing soldiers from life while stationed in Italy during World War II, Pearlstein found steady employment as a mail order catalogue artist in the studio of modernist Czech graphic designer, Ladislav Sutnar. A preternaturally gifted and inventive graphic stylist, Warhol, in turn, rapidly became the darling of high-end art directors at agencies and glossies throughout New York. Yet if, of the two, Warhol was the first to find success in his "day job," Pearlstein was the first to find himself as a painter.

Pearlstein's distinctly skewed take on "high art" was apparent from the paintings he made to blow off steam from the pressure of his work in advertising. One was a straightforwardly cheeky send-up of the ads he drew – it shows a nude in the shower being attacked by plumbing fixtures (p.51). Call it a premonition of Alfred Hitchcock's *Psycho* (1960) and an over-the-shoulder aside to Marcel Duchamp's *The Bride Stripped Bare by Her Bachelors, Even* (1915–23) (p.55), as well as an allusion to the anomalous sculpture *God* (*circa* 1917) by the pioneer New York Dadaists, Morton Livingston Schamberg and Elsa von Freytag-Loringhoven. If the initial parallel seems far-fetched, the latter two were – improbably for a mid-twentieth century realist – right in Pearlstein's bailiwick. But I'll explain that in a moment...

Two other early Pearlsteins, dating 1949–50 and 1952 respectively, were, in basic ways, singularly ahead of their time. The first was dominated by a dollar sign on which children are impaled. He created this tragicomic caricature within a few years of his military service taking back the major cities of the Italian boot, during which period the painter saw a lot of Renaissance art and architecture first hand but must also have witnessed his share of horror and destruction. It is noteworthy that Pearlstein conjured this garishly grotesque insignia over a decade before Warhol made the first of his many emblematic riffs on the same universal symbol of wealth.

The second such seminal "one off" – which I as a curator had a hand in ushering into the Museum of Modern Art in New York – was Pearlstein's quasi-Mannerist rendition of Superman flying above the clouds over Manhattan. It wasn't until a decade on, in the year that he painted his first

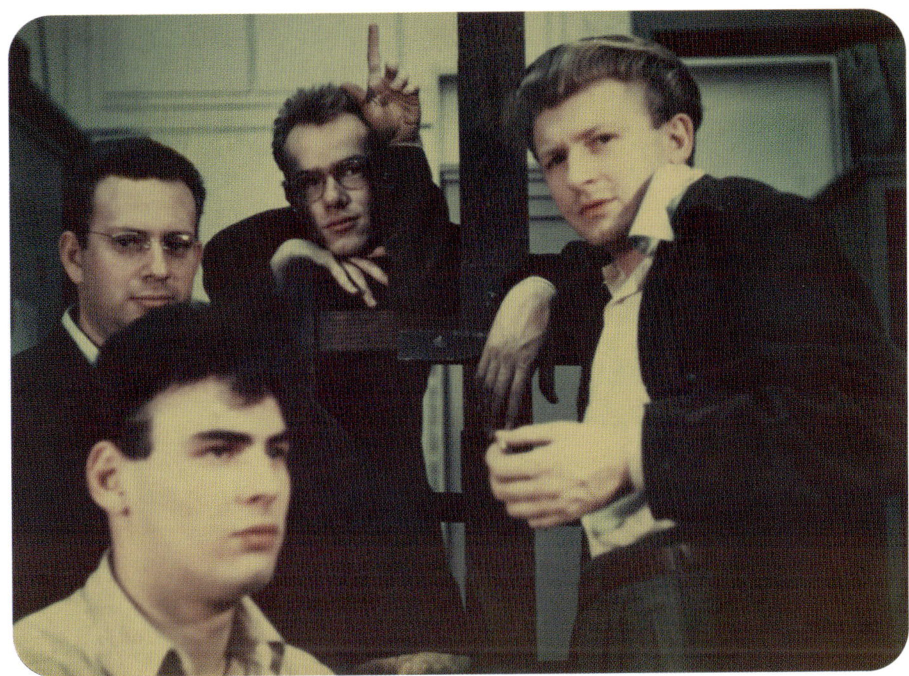

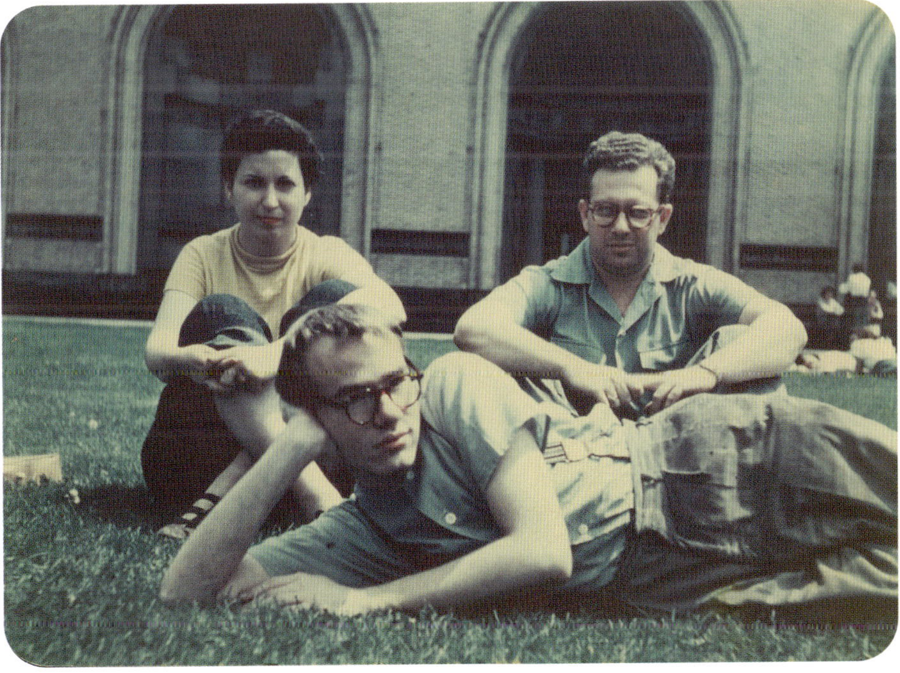

top: Philip Pearlstein, Andy Warhola, Arthur Elias, and Leonard Kessler at Carnegie Tech, *c.*1948

bottom: Dorothy Cantor, Philip Pearlstein, and Andy Warhola at Carnegie Tech, *c.*1948

$ sign, that Pearlstein's Pittsburgh classmate become New York roommate, Warhol, baffled by his lack of success in the gallery world with his fey, often gold-ground depictions of alluring young men, would make his iconic Pop and "butch" version of the all-American Superhero in 1961.

By the end of their first year in New York, Pearlstein had married Dorothy Cantor and had parted company with Warhol. Eager to follow-up on his exposure to Classical and Renaissance culture while in uniform, Pearlstein decided to use the remainder of the educational benefits granted by the G.I. Bill to enroll in the master's degree program in art history at the prestigious Institute of Fine Arts where he studied with the likes of Warburg Institute scholar, Erwin Panofsky, whose portrait he eventually painted, and attended lectures sitting next to another veteran taking advantage of the same opportunity, Ad Reinhardt.

It was as a student at the I.F.A. that Pearlstein became aware of the work of one of early Modern Art's greatest "bad boys," the peripatetic Parisian avant-gardist Francis Picabia, who, with his fellow expatriate French Dandy and Anti-Art co-conspirator, Duchamp, had invented New York Dada, along with Schamberg, von Freytag and a motley assortment of confederates. It was a curious choice for a young artist of Pearlstein's era and background, inasmuch as neither Picabia nor Duchamp were well-known outside of inner circles of the modernist *cognoscenti,* although they *were* nevertheless notorious for the scandals they had created in the Teens and Twenties of the century. The revival of Duchamp's reputation in Europe and the United States didn't begin before Pop art – sometimes called Neo-Dada both by "progressive" admirers and "reactionary" detractors – flourished in the mid-1960s. The piety-defying practices for which Duchamp was infamous at least had some revolutionary cachet, whereas Picabia's lapses in modernist as well as traditional "good taste" – paintings crudely derived from movie posters, sheet music illustrations, pin-ups and still more vulgar sources – were deemed unforgivable, if not unspeakable for a majority of dedicated "art lovers." Pearlstein's thesis advisor, Dr. José López-Rey, was, ironically, a renowned Velázquez scholar.

So, what possessed Pearlstein to devote so much attention to such a widely shunned modernist precursor? Why did he want to give voice to Picabia's corrosively irreverent ideas and dive into such polluted waters to retrieve them? That will take an essay of far greater length or depth than this foreword can afford. Suffice it for the purposes of introducing Pearlstein's own texts setting forth his research into the subject, and, along the way elucidating his interest in it, to say that the cluster of early paintings previously cited shows him well disposed to aesthetic anomalies and improprieties. Although sometimes disguised by his generally

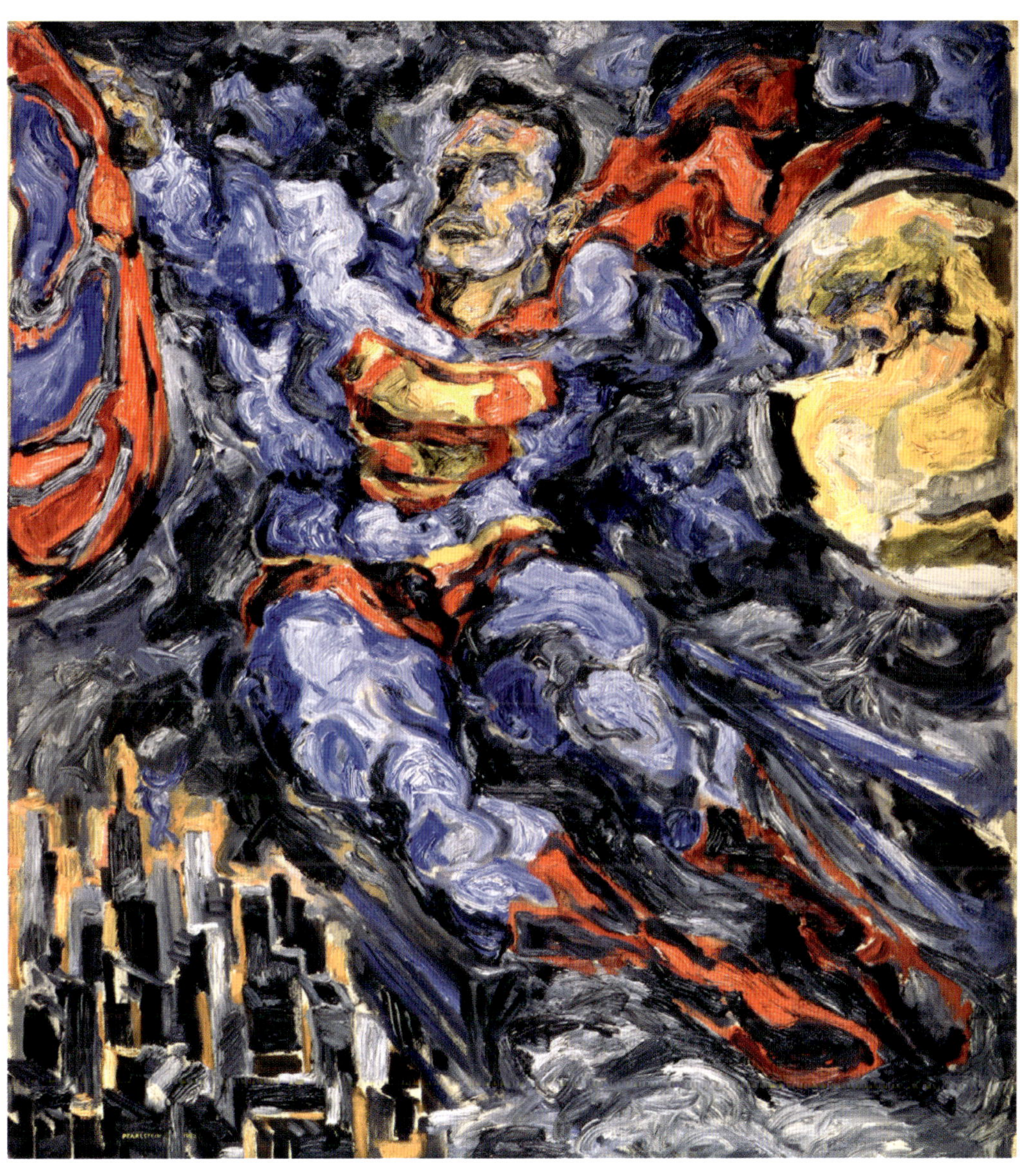

Philip Pearlstein
Superman, 1952

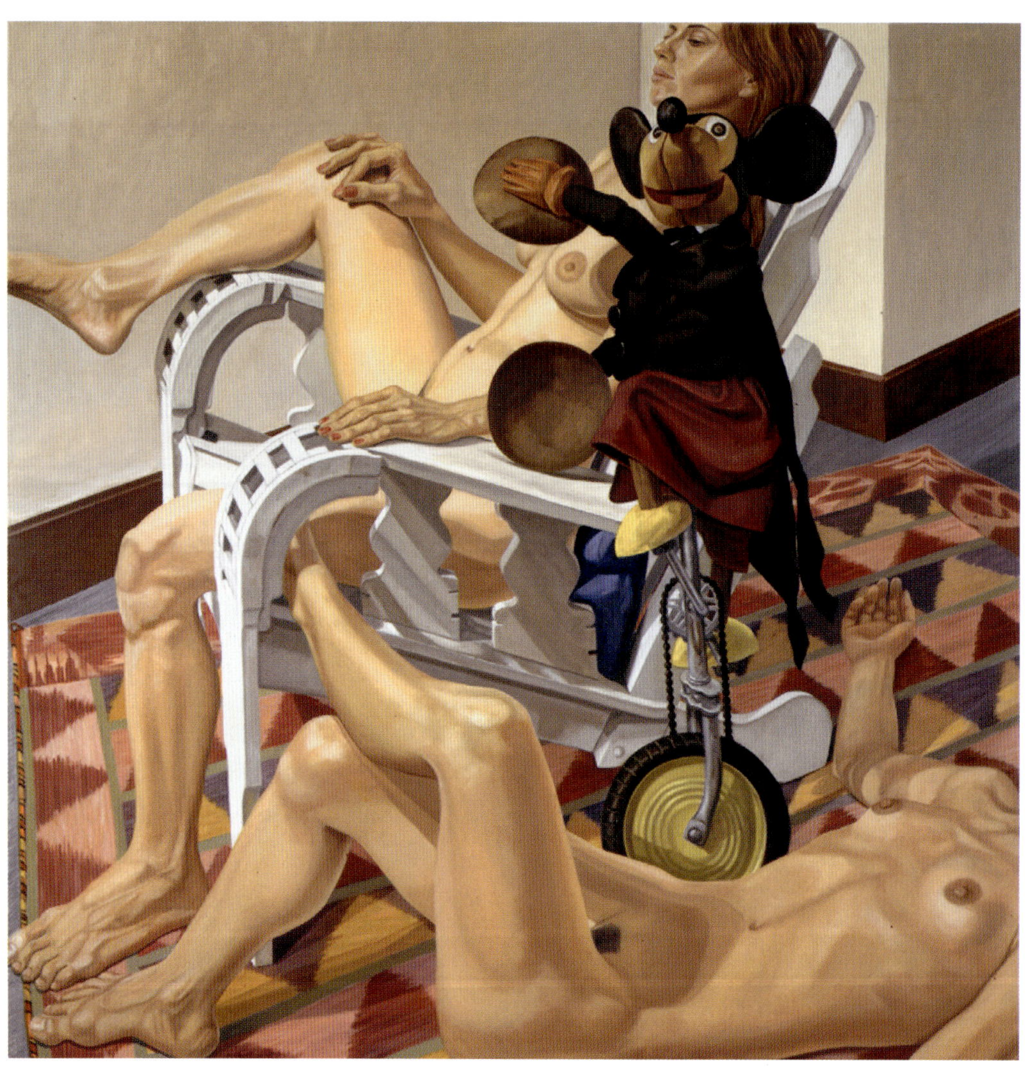

Philip Pearlstein
Two Female Nudes and Mickey Mouse, 2001

subdued tonal palette and sober-sided, unhurried, and uninflected way with a brush.

Indeed, over the long haul, Pearlstein never abandoned his Picabian roots and of late has, with increasing regularity and openness, given free rein to his proclivity for a pictorial strangeness totally at odds with the traditional conventions of the genres he has devoted his life to – the nude and still life – as if he was affirming his faith in their abiding relevance and intrinsic value and teasing them at the same time. Witness the incongruous "collectibles" that have been the main event and/or sideshows of so many of his paintings – Godzilla dolls and Mickey Mouse toys that he juxtaposes to wan bodies or exquisite antiques. Or consider the ways he has used wildly distorting reflections in the casing of an industrial fan or a transparent plastic inflatable chair, to mirror his models and himself, thereby satirizing the dynamics between artist and muse, that Lucian Freud went to such self-serious pains to dramatize, while scooping Jeff Koons when it comes to appropriating the most risible kitsch.

Thus, in retrospect Pearlstein can be clearly seen as a precursor to "postmodernism," and a bellwether of the widespread resistance to "avant-garde" orthodoxy that weighed so heavily on the imagination of artists at the point of that dogma's greatest hegemony from 1960 through the 1970s. Other notable painters who recognized in Picabia's work an irresistible example of mocking defiance of the "laws of art history" include Gerhard Richter and Sigmar Polke. There are more still. So read these texts not only for their scholarly account of Picabia's weird achievement but as a declaration of independence from modernist doctrine, a document of fundamental dissent at a time when the sentiment of rebellion was growing but very few were ready, willing and able to make the case for "doing the wrong thing" as Picabia had done, and as Pearlstein did in bringing him back to public attention.

Robert Storr
Brooklyn, 2023

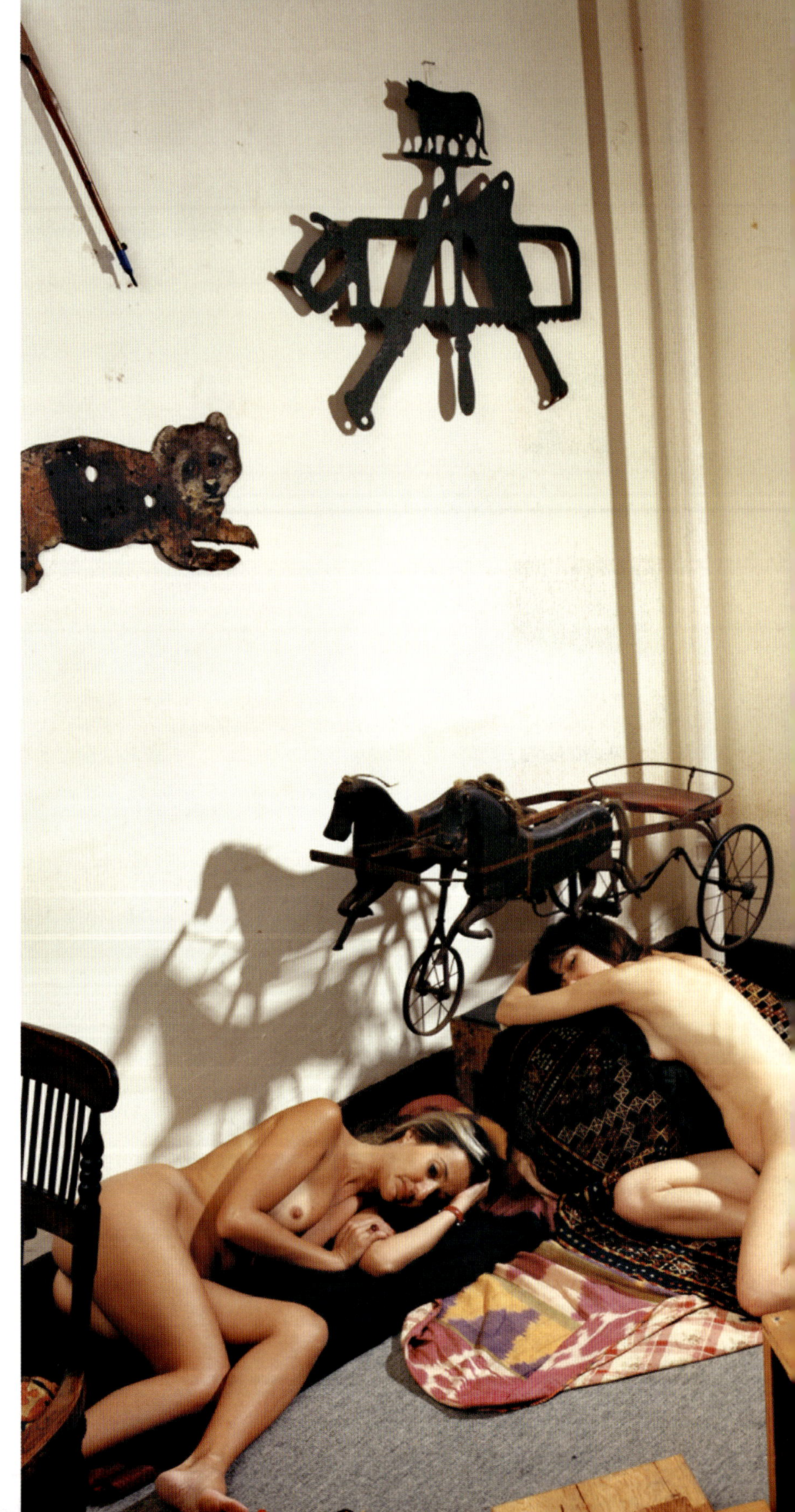

Philip Pearlstein, New York, 2007
Photo by Jason Schmidt

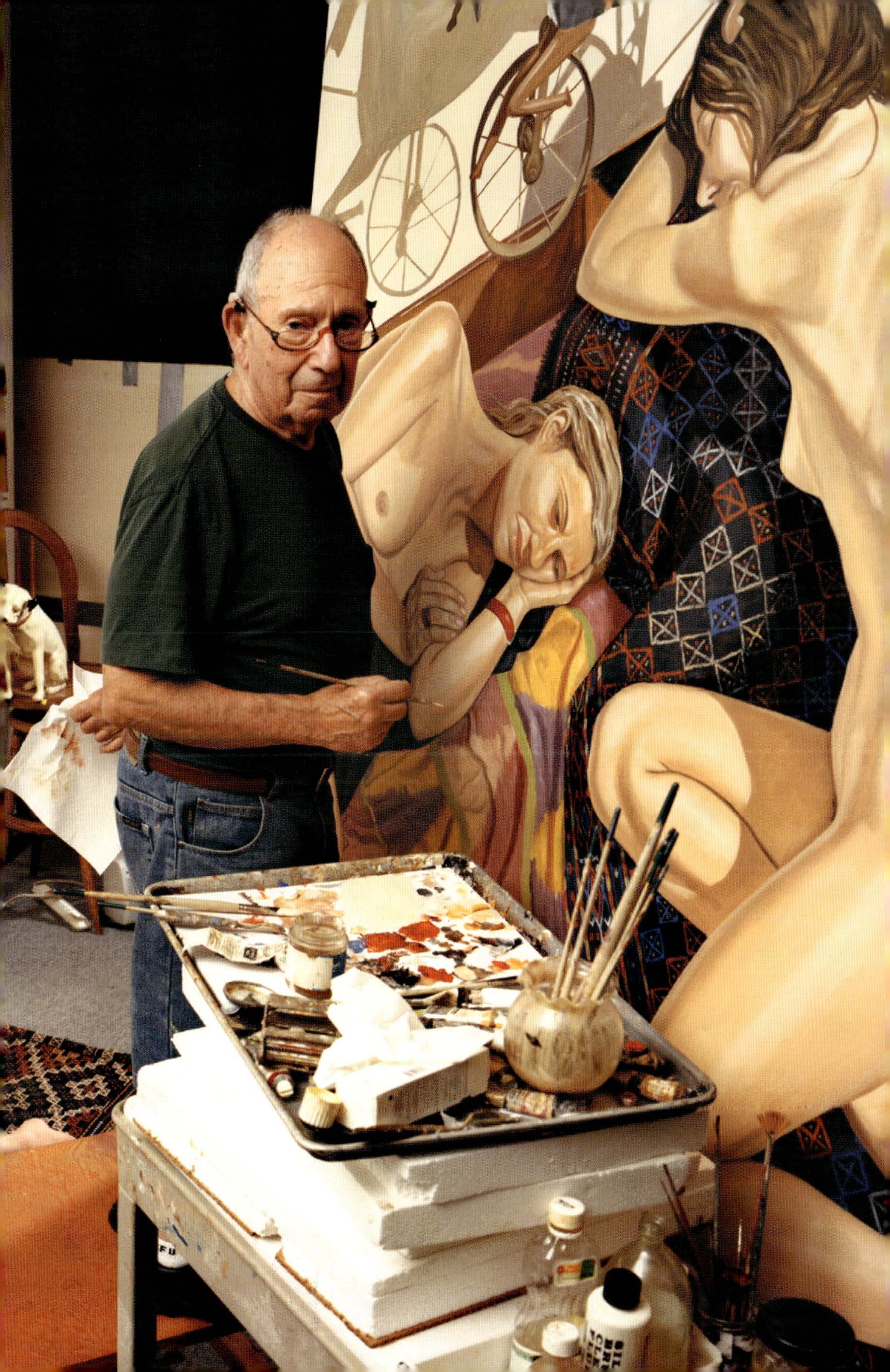

Pearlstein, Picabia and Duchamp: A Timeline

1879 Francis Picabia is born in Paris.

1887 Marcel Duchamp is born in Normandy.

1909 Picabia paints *Caoutchouc* (Rubber), considered to be one of the first abstract works in Western painting. Marries Gabrielle Buffet.

1911 Picabia and Duchamp meet at the Salon d'Automne in Paris, where Cubism is officially introduced.

1913 Picabia travels to New York to exhibit at the Armory Show. *Danses à la source* (Dances at the Spring) (1912), *Procession à Séville* (Procession in Seville) (1912), and Duchamp's *Nude Descending a Staircase (No. II)* (1912) are shown.

Alfred Stieglitz exhibits Picabia's watercolor studies of New York at his gallery, 291. *Chanson nègre* (Negro Song) (1913) is shown.

1915 Duchamp arrives in New York. Begins work on *The Large Glass*.

1914 Outbreak of World War I. Duchamp is exempt from military service. Picabia is drafted to the French Army, secures an assignment in Cuba, but stays in New York.

1917 Duchamp creates *Fountain*. His readymades anticipate the Dada movement, which Picabia introduces to New York in the magazine *391*.

1919 Duchamp creates *L.H.O.O.Q.*

1920 Picabia creates *Tableau Rastadada* (Rastadada Painting), and *L'Œil cacodylate* (The Cacodylic Eye) in 1921.

1924 Philip Pearlstein is born in Pittsburgh.

1927 Picabia starts to paint the "Transparencies."

1939 Outbreak of World War II. Duchamp takes voluntary exile in New York. Picabia moves to the South of France, paints nudes from magazines.

1942 Pearlstein enrolls at Carnegie Institute of Technology in Pittsburgh (now Carnegie Mellon University).

1943 Pearlstein is drafted to the U.S. Army, assigned to the infantry replacement unit. Serves in Italy and works as an illustrator, painting road signs, training manuals, and other designs.

1949 Pearlstein graduates from Carnegie Tech. Moves to New York with Andy Warhola (now Warhol).

1950 Pearlstein begins graduate work at New York University's Institute of Fine Arts. Starts collecting research material for his master's thesis on Picabia. Marries Dorothy Cantor.

1953 Francis Picabia dies in Paris, aged 74.

Pearlstein is approached by major art publications to write an article on Picabia. Starts attending "The Club" with Willem de Kooning and other Abstract Expressionists later known as the New York School.

1954 Clement Greenberg selects Pearlstein for the *Emerging Talent* show at Kootz Gallery, New York. *Torso* (1953) is shown (p.8). Duchamp marries Alexina Sattler.

1955 Pearlstein completes his master's thesis, "The Paintings of Francis Picabia, 1908–1930."

1956 Pearlstein publishes "The Symbolic Language of Francis Picabia" in *ARTS* magazine.

1958 Pearlstein travels across Italy painting landscapes on the Fulbright–Hays Fellowship, through 1959.

1962 Pearlstein begins to paint directly from the model in his studio. Leads a revival of realism, cited by critics as the preeminent figure painter of the late twentieth century.

1968 Marcel Duchamp dies in Neuilly, near Paris, aged 81.

1970 Pearlstein publishes "Hello and Goodbye, Francis Picabia" in *ARTnews*.

1977 Pearlstein is appointed Distinguished Professor at Brooklyn College, New York. Retires 1988.

2017 Pearlstein publishes "When the Dada Daddies Got Real; Or, How I Turned Picabia Inside Out" in *Brooklyn Rail*.

2022 Philip Pearlstein dies in New York, aged 98.

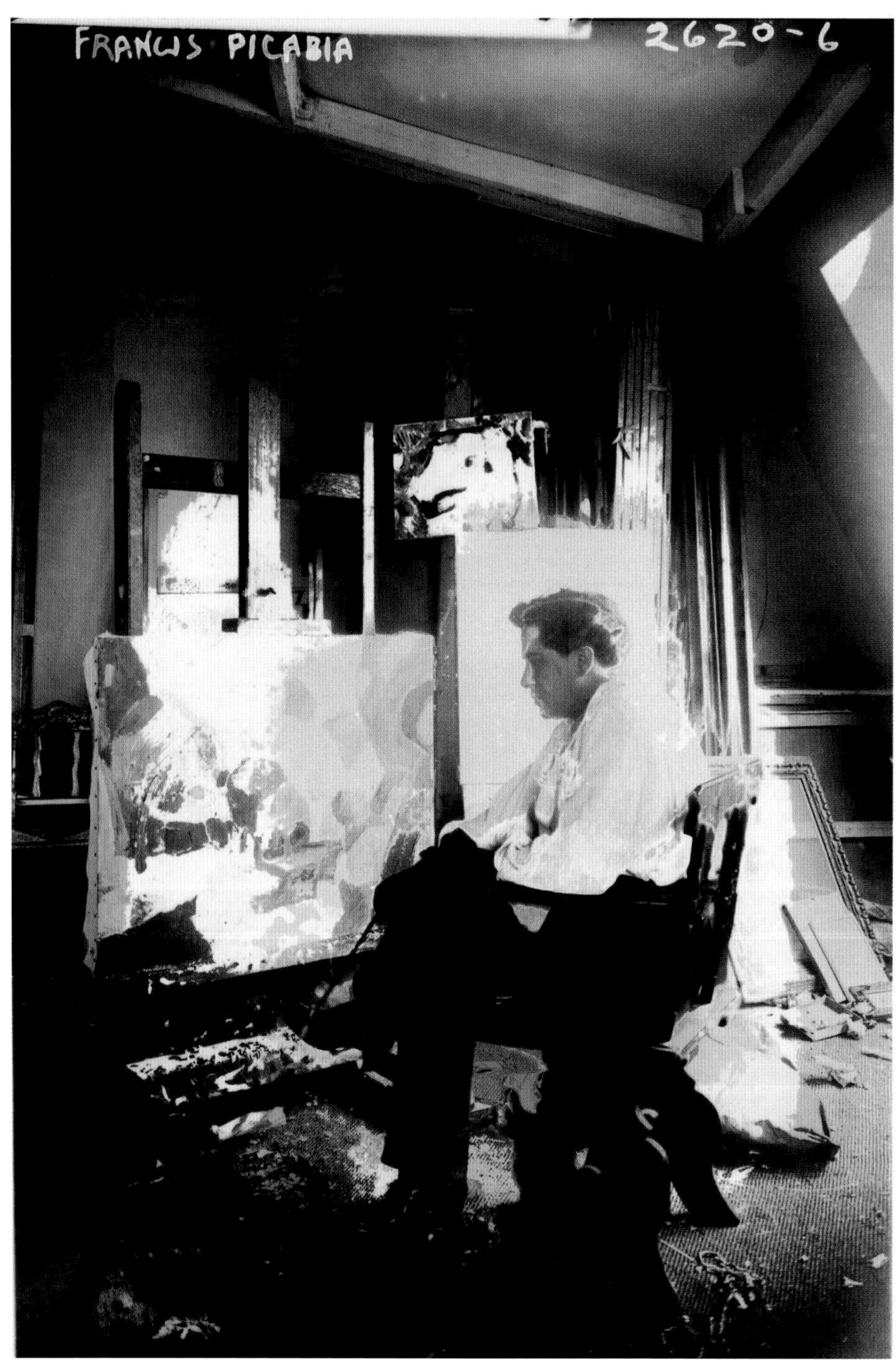

George Grantham Bain
Francis Picabia, *c.*1910–15

The Symbolic Language of Francis Picabia*

* First published in *ARTS* magazine, January 1956.

PART II. EIGHT PAGES.

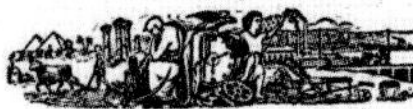

MISCELLANY AND ART.

NEW-YORK, SUNDAY, MARCH 9, 1913.

A POST-CUBIST'S IMPRESSIONS OF NEW YORK

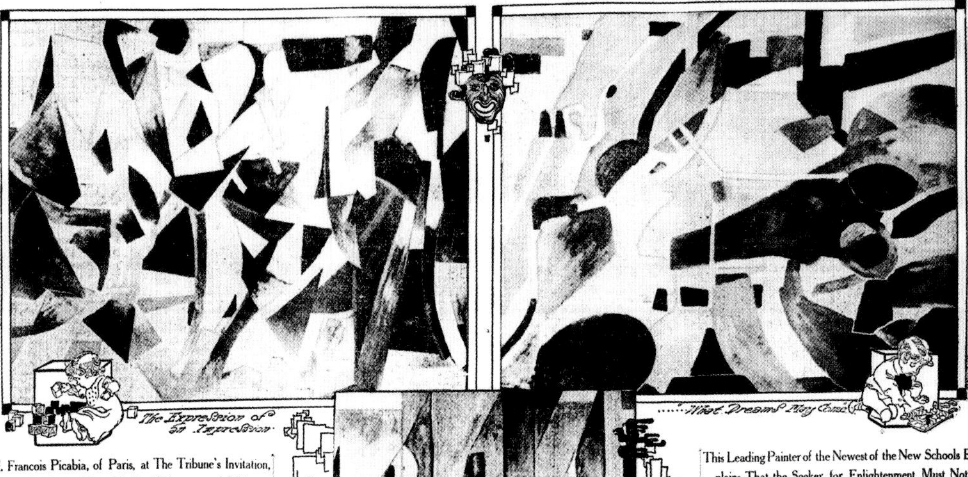

The Expression of an Expression

"What Dreams May Come"

M. Francois Picabia, of Paris, at The Tribune's Invitation, Fares Forth into New York's Highways and Makes a Mental Collection of Impressions of the Great City of the Western World—The Moods Which These Impressions Cause He Expresses Here in Line and Form.

This Leading Painter of the Newest of the New Schools Explains That the Seeker for Enlightenment Must Not Seek for Depiction or Objective Presentation in These or Any Other Pictures Which He Makes—He Will Find Many Who Will Cordially Agree with Him.

Skyscrapers and Infinity from the River?

M. Francois Picabia in his Studio

Francis Picabia paintings published in the *New York Tribune*, March 9, 1913

The most publicized painter in New York at the time of the 1913 Armory Show was Francis Picabia. Of Cuban nationality, but a lifelong resident of France, Picabia travelled from Paris to be in New York when the show opened – and the press seized upon him as the representative of the modern painters of Europe. The tabloid writers had their fun at his expense, but the serious writers of the art columns treated his pronouncements about the new art with respect.

In June 1913, Alfred Stieglitz featured Picabia in a special number of his publication *Camera Work*, and when he held an exhibition at his gallery, 291, of the drawing and watercolor studies of New York that Picabia made during his six-month stay, Stieglitz later devoted part of *Camera Work, Number XLII–XLIII*, to reprinting the press reviews along with the introduction Picabia wrote for the exhibition catalogue. In these printed interviews and statements, Picabia made an earnest effort to educate the public in what he felt were the fundamental premises of his painting, and he repeatedly expressed the hope that the public would soon learn to understand abstract art.

Picabia's compulsion to explain himself at this time is curious in view of the desire to keep art exclusive – to keep it for the few sensitive persons capable of appreciating its subtleties – which prevailed in the intellectual avant-garde circles of Paris and New York to which he was attached. It even more strikingly contradicts the burgeoning Dada spirit in Picabia which made him, a few years later, hurl insults at the public who came to hear him lecture on Dada.

Picabia's ideas about painting were unique for a member of the Parisian Cubist milieu of 1913. Most Cubists followed the lead of Braque and Picasso by placing little or no importance on the subject matter of their paintings, and concentrated on the problems of painting per se. They gave the still life or human figure used as their subject a minimum of associational overtones. Picabia, on the other hand, placed the greatest importance on the subject matter of his paintings, and the plastic elements of the paintings exist in order to convey the subject. This aspect of Picabia as rebel to the Cubists' depreciation of literary values in painting is the Picabia that holds our interest at present, rather than the debonair sportsman of Cubism, or the cosmopolitan high clown of Dadaism.

Picabia was never a Cubist in the sense that Braque and Picasso were in their work from 1908 to 1912. He was not concerned with the analysis of the forms of real objects. Rather, he was drawn to explore abstract painting, yet he was not interested in abstract forms and colors solely for the sake of their formal relationships. For him, abstract forms were vehicles serving to carry onto the canvas the "emotional, temperamental, subjective states" of mind resulting from his experiences in life (a concept similar to Futurism).

Before 1908, Picabia's paintings had been in the tradition of Monet and Sisley, with a few experiments influenced by the Fauves. Between 1908 and 1909, however, Picabia completed a number of landscape drawings and paintings that abstracted the forms and colors seen in nature, and he was among the first artists to conceive the hypothesis that painting is simply an arbitrary organization of forms and colors. To this hypothesis he added another: that abstract shapes and colors are as capable of arousing emotions as are the sounds of music. (This concept was debated between Picabia and Guillaume Apollinaire, the poet, who questioned its validity, but recognized that it was generating creative effort. In *The Cubist Painters*, published in 1913, Apollinaire, after terming the productions of Braque and Picasso "Scientific Cubism," gave the name "Orphic Cubism" to the work of painters in the Cubist orbit, including Marcel Duchamp and Robert Delaunay, who, like Picabia, made use of extra-painterly concepts. Their work, wrote Apollinaire, "must offer simultaneously pure aesthetic pleasure, a clearly perceptible construction, and a meaning, the subject, which is sublime."[1]

A further evolution in his ideas on abstract painting led Picabia, by 1913, to conceive of shapes and colors as a syntax capable not only of arousing emotions, but even of conveying subtleties of thought. With this language he wished to state ideas rather than describe scenes or objects.

In his pronouncements at the time of the Armory Show, Picabia expressed belief in the ability of the subconscious to invent the symbols of this new visual language and minimized the role of naturalistic representation in painting. He asserted that "pure art cannot reproduce a material fact. It can only make real the immaterial or emotional fact... Art can express the fourth dimension of the soul, but not the third dimension of actuality." In setting down his impressions of New York, Picabia declared: "I do not paint these things which my eye sees. I paint that which my brain, my soul, sees.... I absorb these impressions [of the city's activity]. I am in no hurry to put them on canvas. I let them remain in my mind, and then when the spirit of creation is at flood tide, I improvise my pictures as a musician improvises music."[2]

To illustrate these ideas he painted *Procession à Séville* (Procession in Seville), one of the works exhibited at the Armory. Composed of abstract shapes which he used to refer to the forms in nature, the painting seems close in style to those 1908 works of Braque and Picasso in which the solid forms are literally cubed. But Picabia used the cubed forms simply as a convention; his cubes did not result from an analysis of forms in nature.

1 From Guillaume Apollinaire, *The Cubist Painters*, 1913. Also discussed in "When the Dada Daddies Got Real; Or, How I Turned Picabia Inside Out" (p.68).

2 See "Hello and Goodbye, Francis Picabia" for an extended quotation of Picabia's impressions of New York (pp.43–4).

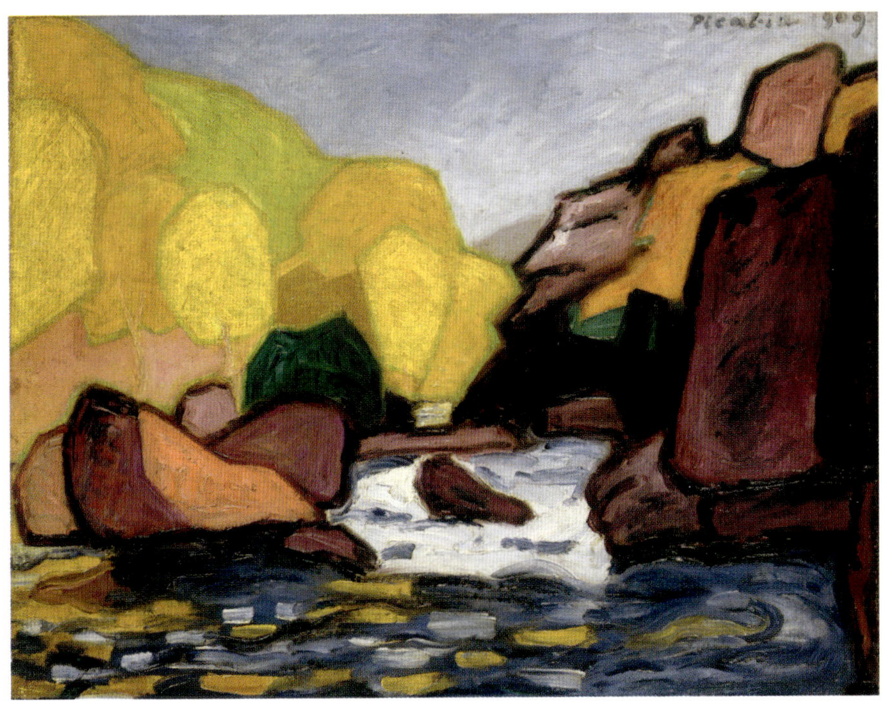

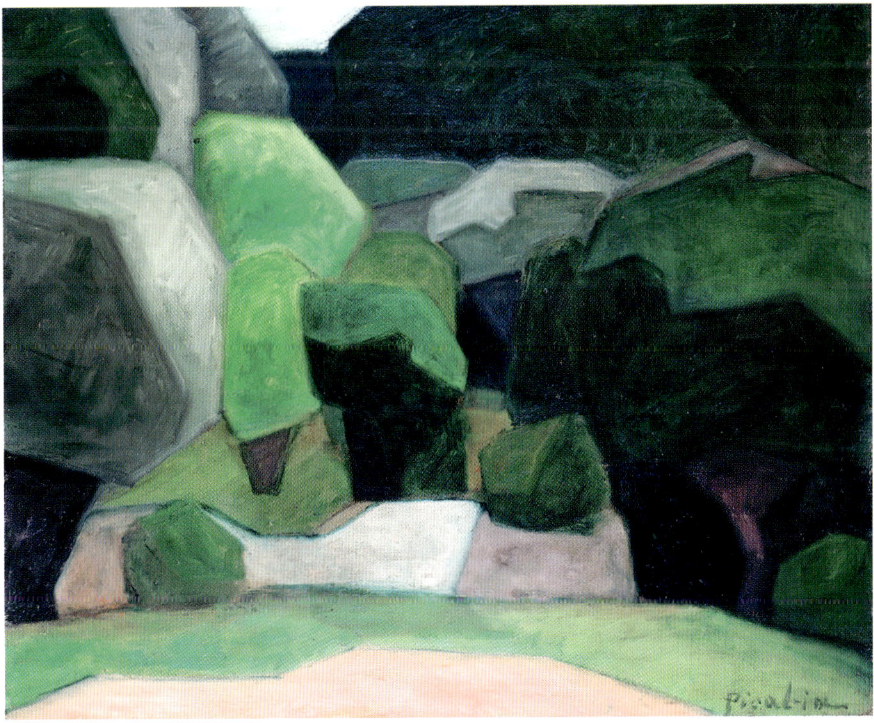

top: Francis Picabia
Bords de la Sédelle
(Banks of the Sedelle), 1909

bottom: Francis Picabia
Paysage à Cassis
(Landscape in Cassis), *c.*1909–10

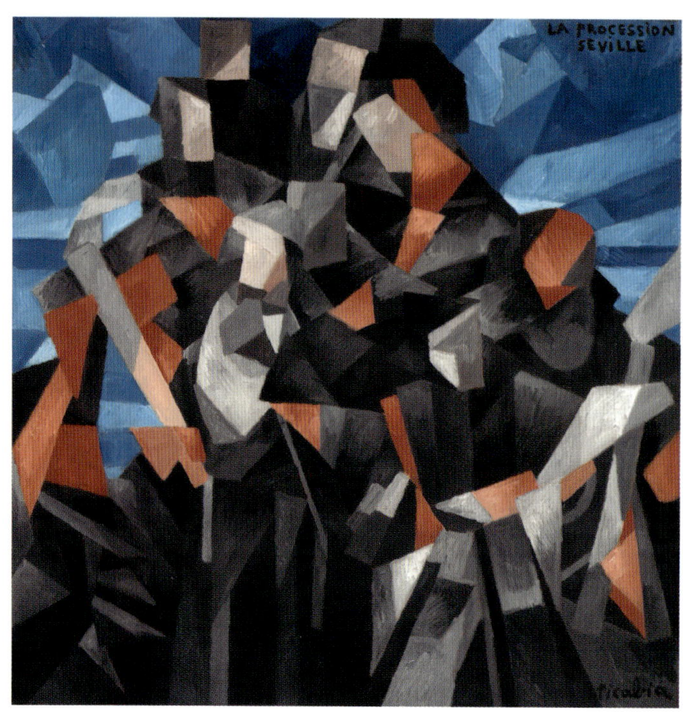

Francis Picabia
Procession à Séville
(Procession in Seville), 1912

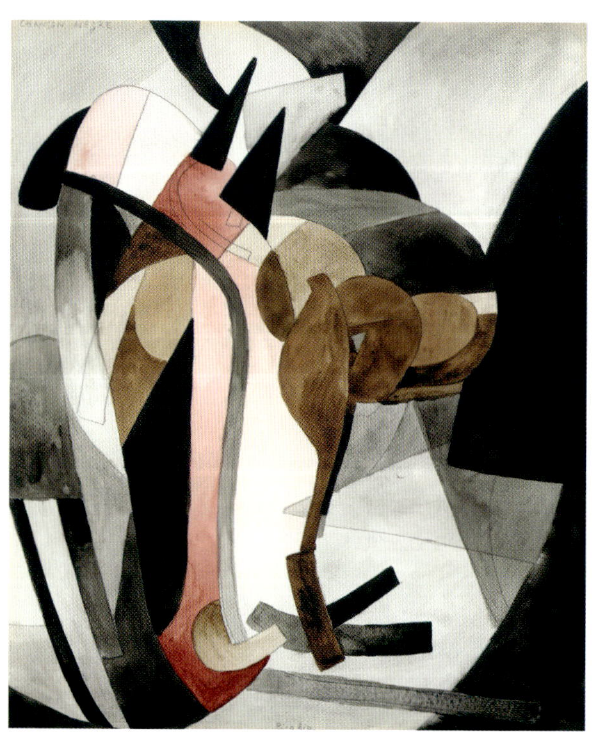

Francis Picabia
Chanson nègre (I) (Negro Song [I]), 1913

He spoke of having left the plane of the five senses, which he called "*matière pensée*" (material thought), and of being concerned solely with psychic perception, which he called "*pensée pure*" (pure thought). Picabia explained that, had he painted *Procession à Séville* through "*matière pensée*," he would have produced a more or less photographic interpretation, which would have been limited. But he had evolved his interpretation to the idea of a religious procession, which evoked emotions from his aesthetic nature, and these materialized in a harmony produced through arrangement of color and form – "the language which the evolutive art imposes upon itself." A canvas that originates in "*pensée pure*" is without limitation; it blends with the infinite.

Of the watercolors Picabia did during his stay in New York, *Chanson nègre* (Negro Song)[3] was the one that most successfully demonstrated the capacity of his psychic perception, his "*pensée pure*," to invent the proper symbols. Picabia reported that purple was the inevitable and dominating color that sprang to his consciousness when he heard the songs of jazz musicians in Harlem. The subject of this painting is made up of the cluster of curvilinear shapes in the upper right center of the painting. These shapes form only an ambiguous, elemental symbol of a human being. Its sensuous quality is enhanced by the colors, which are burnt umber, black, the white of the paper in untouched areas, and one long line of violet, that of the linear element curving up on the left side of the figure. The singer seems to stand in a darkened room, illuminated by a spotlight.

Radical as they may have seemed in 1913, Picabia's ideas on the capacity for painting to speak as directly as music and literature were part of the twentieth-century painters' inheritance from nineteenth-century French art. The idea of the direct expressiveness of the aesthetic elements, that specific sensations received by any of the senses can arouse specific emotional responses, was commonly accepted in the nineteenth century and was elaborated in the concept of "Correspondances." The academician Charles Blanc wrote of the affinity between emotion and color, and of the secret relation that all lines have to emotion. Charles Henry, Director of the Laboratory of the Psychology of Perception at the Sorbonne, attempted to establish a scientific basis for the idea, and the Symbolist poets and painters accepted the theory as fact. Baudelaire, in his poem entitled "Correspondances," stated that "Scents, colors and sounds answer to one another."

3 Among the works presented in the exhibition at 291 were two watercolors Picabia made in reaction to hearing African American music, both exhibited with the title *Negro Song* (I and II). This title incorporates a now outdated and derogatory term to denote a person of Black African heritage, though it was common at the time.

Picabia's statement, "We must devote ourselves to setting down on our canvas not things, but emotions produced in our minds by things,"[4] has its nineteenth-century parallel in Mallarmé's formula that the artist must "paint not the thing itself but the effect it produces."[5] Picabia's favorite analogy of painting and music probably has its immediate origin in the high regard the Symbolists showed for music as a pure expression of the ideal essence of reality itself, divorced from contaminating materiality – the attribution of direct emotional expressiveness to music was made by Plato.[6]

After Picabia's visit to Paris in 1913, a significant shift occurred in the subject matter of his work. The themes of his paintings until then had derived from his personal experiences – his impressions of activity in cities, of visits to nightclubs, of seeing people dance, and so on. But thereafter, for the next decade, his subject matter was drawn from, and determined by, his attitude towards society at large.[7]

This attitude, which Picabia nurtured in company with his friends Marcel Duchamp and Apollinaire, was the same that later motivated the Dada movement. It consisted of observing the futility and contradictions inherent in all aspects of human life, together with a sort of social protest against the degradation of human values that resulted from industrialization. The values of "high art" were mocked, along with the deplorable taste of the masses. Nothing remained sacred. The Dadaists' predecessors in negativity were the bohemians of the nineteenth century, and the Italian Futurists of the early twentieth century. But the bohemians expressed their revolt chiefly by devotion to the concept of "art for art's sake"; they had not directly attacked the values held sacred by society. The Italian Futurists had political aims, while the Dadaists, except the communists among them, had no positive program.

Picabia and Duchamp were truly Dada in spirit from the time they first met in 1910; they were joined by Apollinaire in 1912. The historical Dada movement was formed in Zurich, Switzerland in 1916. Picabia and Duchamp were unaware of it until later in 1918 when Picabia, after extended stays in New York, and Barcelona during the war years, met and joined the group in Zurich. The Dadaists expressed their observations in terms of wit, buffoonery, and irrationality (for example, the machinery Picabia pictured is always incapable of motion). One of the most famous examples of Dada art is the reproduction of the *Mona Lisa* on which Duchamp drew a moustache and added the letters "L.H.O.O.Q.," which, when given the French pronunciation, make an obscene pun. Picabia printed this oeuvre

4 In an interview with the *New York Times*, date unknown.

5 In a letter to Henri Cazalis, 1864.

6 The concept of "Correspondances" is explored along with other aspects of the influence of nineteenth-century thought on the Cubist painters by Christopher Gray in *The Cubist Aesthetic Theories*, 1953.

7 Also discussed by Pearlstein in "When the Dada Daddies Got Real; Or, How I Turned Picabia Inside Out" (p.71).

391

Au pluriel

" Une définition n'a jamais été qu'un mot pour un autre — et le commun des mortels l'appelle erreur ".

De plus en plus, de moins en moins, Trois cent quatre vingt onze est un oiseau à poils, la Vierge satisfaite le tient dans ses bras, la pluie des grands jours, un biceps bien tendre, une ombre à plusieurs, les paupières comme des ongles ou les ongles comme des heures ou.

Petit, petit trois cent quatre vingt onze de ma mère et des liqueurs de dessert, de plus en plus, de moins en moins, une lumière derrière un coup de poing, un coup de poing sur une lumière.

Je suis comme les autres, je vais au café. Aussitôt, j'entends : " Garçon un 391 des dimanches ". Je suis discret, je ne répète jamais ce que j'écoute dans les water-closets.

Un aimable désordre simili or n'étant qu'un effet de l'art, j'ai pu enjamber deux ou trois fois dans ma vie une belle religieuse aux cornes d'ivoire, une belle, très belle.

Le livre sur lequel j'écris est ouvert à la page 202.

En le lisant, les Cubistes ont bien pleuré.

PAUL ELUARD.

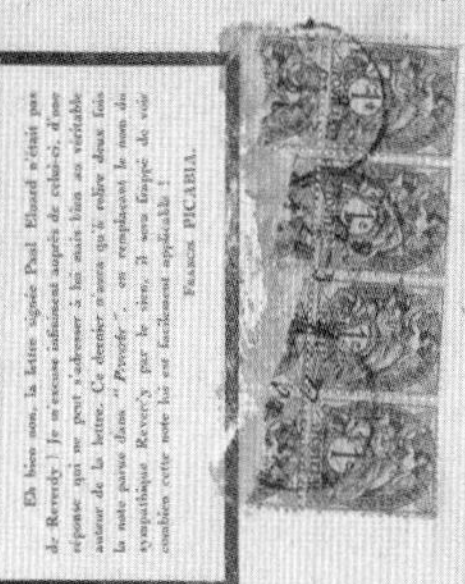

Eh bien non, la lettre signée Paul Eluard n'était pas de Reverdy ! Je m'excuse infiniment auprès de celui-ci, d'une réponse qui ne peut s'adresser à lui mais bien au véritable auteur de la lettre. Ce dernier n'aura qu'à relire deux fois la note parue dans " *Proverbe* ", en remplaçant le nom du sympathique Reverdy par le sien, il sera frappé de voir combien cette note lui est facilement applicable !

FRANCIS PICABIA.

TABLEAU DADA par MARCEL DUCHAMP

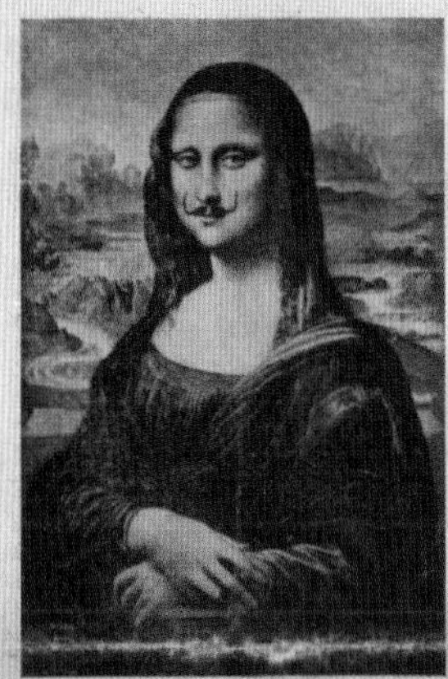

L H O O Q

Manifeste DADA

Les cubistes veulent couvrir Dada de neige ; ça vous étonne mais c'est ainsi, ils veulent vider la neige de leur pipe pour recouvrir Dada.

Tu en es sûr ?

Parfaitement, les faits sont révélés par des bouches grotesques.

Ils pensent que Dada peut les empêcher de pratiquer ce commerce odieux : Vendre de l'art très cher.

L'art vaut plus cher que le saucisson, plus cher que les femmes, plus cher que tout.

L'art est visible comme Dieu ! (voir Saint-Sulpice).

L'art est un produit pharmaceutique pour imbéciles.

Les tables tournent grâce à l'esprit ; les tableaux et autres œuvres d'art sont comme les tables coffres-forts, l'esprit est dedans et devient de plus en plus génial suivant les prix de salles de ventes.

Comédie, comédie, comédie, comédie, comédie, mes chers amis.

Les marchands n'aiment pas la peinture, ils connaissent le mystère de l'esprit..........

Achetez les reproductions des autographes.

Ne soyez donc pas snobs, vous ne serez pas moins intelligents parce que le voisin possèdera une chose semblable à la vôtre.

Plus de chiures de mouches sur les murs.

Il y en aura tout de même, c'est évident, mais un peu moins.

Dada bien certainement va être de plus en plus détesté, son coupe-file lui permettant de couper les processions en chantant " Viens Poupoule ", quel sacrilège !!!

Le cubisme représente la disette des idées.

Ils ont cubé les tableaux des primitifs, cubé les sculptures nègres, cubé les violons, cubé les guitares, cubé les journaux illustrés, cubé la merde et les profils de jeunes filles, maintenant il faut cuber de l'argent !!!

Dada, lui, ne veut rien, rien, rien, il fait quelque chose pour que le public dise : "nous ne comprenons rien, rien, rien". " Les Dadaïstes ne sont rien, rien, rien, bien certainement ils n'arriveront à rien, rien, rien ".

Francis PICABIA

qui ne sait rien, rien, rien.

Marcel Duchamp's *L.H.O.O.Q.* printed on the cover of Francis Picabia's magazine *391*, 1919 on the cover of his own publication, *391*. But though *391* is often hilariously funny, as is most of Dada, it is an angry publication, and Picabia printed the picture of the moustached Mona Lisa in a spirit of genuine iconoclasm.[8]

The works with which Picabia expressed his attitude towards society were created in terms of his language of visual symbols. This language could operate only in analogies – in the resemblance of individual invented abstract shapes and colors to others in the known visual sphere, or else in the suggestiveness of the overall grouping and character of the shapes in a picture. The title of a painting offers a clue to interpreting the puns, either visual or verbal. To a great extent, of course, every painting is made up of such visual symbols. Until this time, however, the meanings of the symbols were usually established by long tradition, but Picabia, and Duchamp as well, invented the symbolic language anew for each work. While some of the puns are more or less self-evident, pictorial elements were often arbitrarily assigned meanings, which unaided spectators could not possibly guess. It does not seem to have mattered to Picabia that only an initiated few were capable of reading his works.

At the same time as Picabia made his attitude towards society the subject of his paintings, the abstract shapes that compose them began to suggest the world of machinery. His earlier paintings, such as *Danses à la source* (Dances at the Spring) (p.73), already had the reduction of forms to simplified, sharp-edged shapes that gave many paintings created between 1908 and 1912 (those of Braque and Picasso, as well as Léger and Duchamp) their "mechanical" look, though they were not of machine forms. In his new paintings Picabia purposefully exploited this characteristic, and the forms – while remaining abstract in the sense of having been invented by the artist, and abstract in their color – were, in effect, pictured machine elements. These elements, some of which resembled parts of the human body, were made to masquerade as personages in specific social situations. As the symbol of twentieth-century society, the machine was shown in mocking charades of that society. The machine became the constant term in the language of symbols, whatever else was added by way of qualification, inflection, or nuance. A similar transformation had already taken place in Duchamp's work, as in his 1912 *Mariée* (Bride).

The full realization of Picabia's ideas at this time can be seen in *Je revois en souvenir ma chère Udnie* (I See Again in Memory My Dear Udnie). Here the machine elements are analogous to the inner organs of the female body and the external organs of the male. As this painting has its compositional origin in the drawing *Fille née sans mère* (Daughter Born without a Mother), it may be assumed that the "*fille*" of the drawing is implicit in the

8 Also discussed in "When the Dada Daddies Got Real; Or, How I Turned Picabia Inside Out" (p.72).

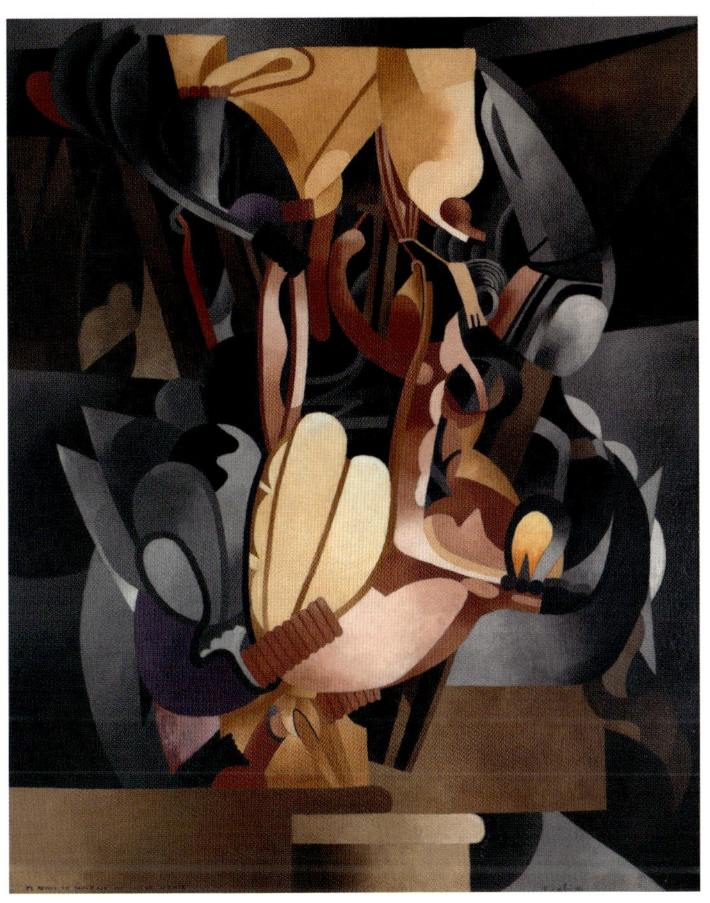

Francis Picabia
Je revois en souvenir ma chère Udnie
(I See Again in Memory My Dear Udnie), 1914

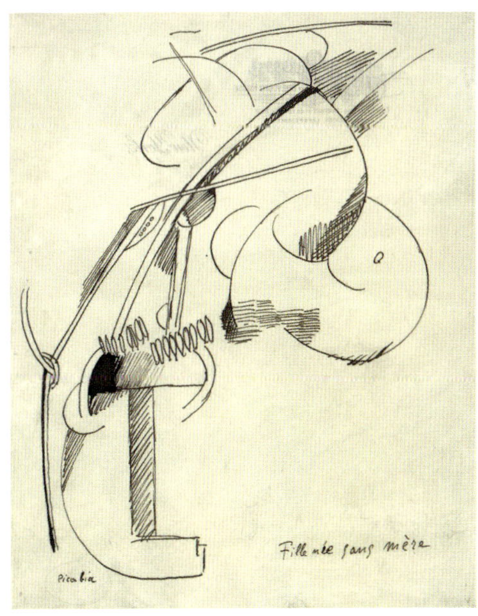

Francis Picabia
Fille née sans mère (Daughter Born without a Mother), 1913

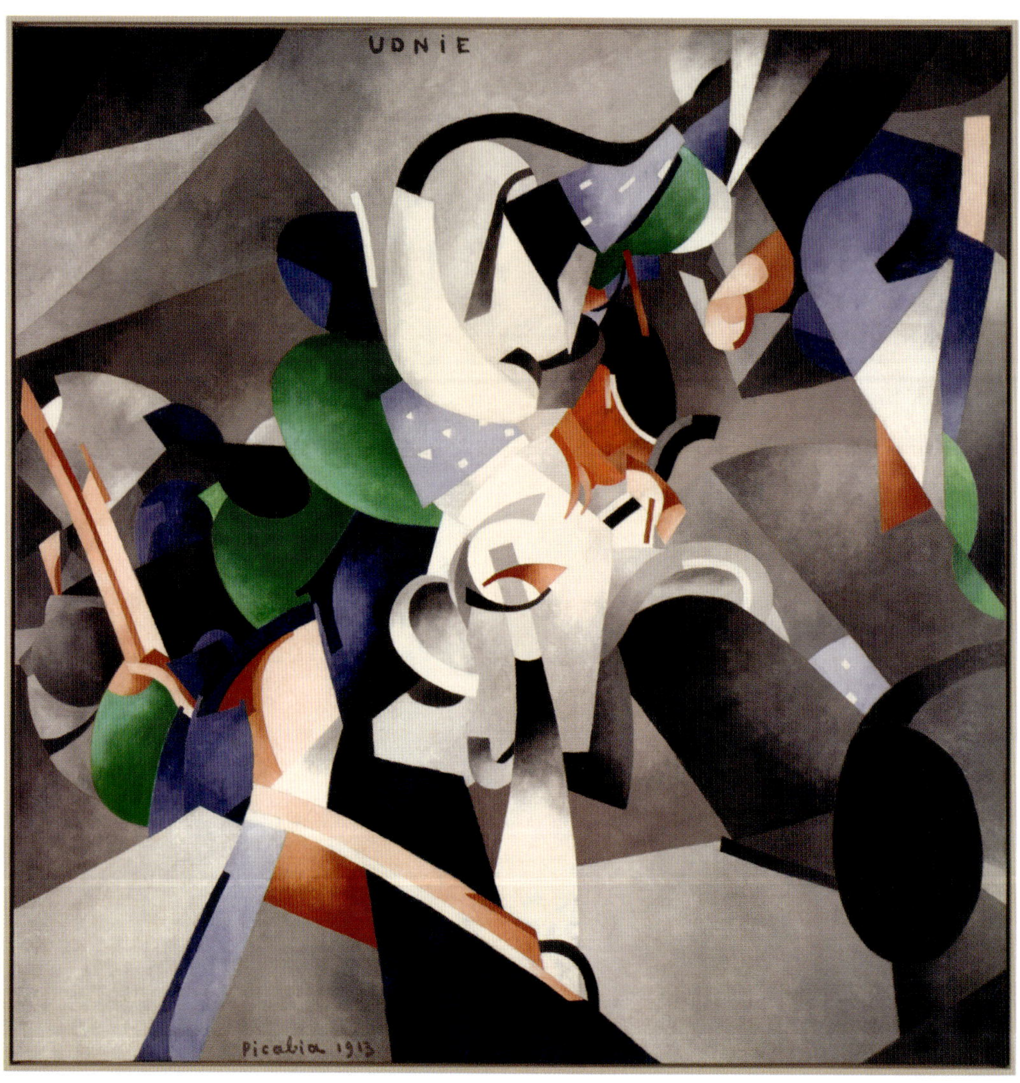

Francis Picabia
Udnie (Jeune fille américaine; danse)
(Udnie [Young American Girl; Dance]), 1913

painting.[9] According to Gabrielle Buffet-Picabia, behind Picabia's imagery of the "daughter born without a mother" is the idea that the machine was conceived in the mind of man, born into the world through the efforts of his body, like Athena from the forehead of Zeus. That this child of man's intellect should be feminine is due partly to the fact that in French the noun "machine" is feminine; reference to a machine as "she" is common usage throughout the world. Having created this female being, man uses her body: she becomes his mistress. And it is in this role, in which she mimics a human mistress, that Picabia had painted her as Udnie. The bourgeois sentiment of the title conjures up the vision of a middle-aged businessman recalling a former love. The actual subject of the painting is his memory of sexual intercourse with her, which is represented in ideographic terms; both the male and female principles are clearly represented.

Another of the paintings done in late 1913 is a large work entitled *Edtaonisl (ecclésiastique)* (Edtaonisl [Ecclesiastical) (p.56), whose subject matter, when deciphered, is the beating heart of a clergyman who watches a star dancer and her troupe rehearsing on the deck of a transatlantic liner. Also dating from 1913 is a simple portrait of *Udnie (Jeune fille américaine; danse)* (Udnie [Young American Girl; Dance]); in this appearance the heroine can be recognized as fully clothed.

Picabia painted very little from the end of 1913 to 1920, the years of World War I. Most of his creative efforts went into literary activity. He published several small volumes of his poetry, and became involved in the writing and publishing of periodicals expressing the Dada attitude. He liberally illustrated these with graphic works that present a new phase in his machine representation and symbolism.

Hitherto he had exploited the resemblance of machine forms to the human physiology. Now he, as did Duchamp, began to use forms that were unequivocally mechanical, that bore no visual resemblance to the human body. In these graphic works words are given an importance often equal to that of the lines. This may have been prompted by the example of Apollinaire's calligraphic poems.

Among the earliest works in this manner is the 1915 *Portrait d'une jeune fille américaine dans l'état de nudité* (Portrait of a Young American Girl in the State of Nudity). Here Picabia once more peeks at his "*fille née sans mère*," represented in the drawing as a spark plug – as a "kindler of flame," Gabrielle Buffet-Picabia suggests. The spark plug is hopefully

9 *Fille née sans mère* is a drawing Picabia made in New York in 1913. Drawn on the reverse side of stationery bearing the letterhead of the Hotel Breevort, it is his specific reference to machine forms. This drawing was the basis for the composition of the painting *Je revois en souvenir ma chère Udnie*.

labelled, in the style of American advertising, "for-ever." The "*nudité*" in the title suggests the possibility that "Udnie" of the earlier paintings is a pig-Latin version of the word.[10]

In 1918 Picabia endowed his "*fille*" with an intellect and published the book she wrote, *Poèmes et dessins de la fille née sans mère* (Poems and Drawings of the Daughter Born without a Mother) – 18 drawings and 51 poems. Until now the machine had been viewed by man. This book was her opportunity to view man in turn. And she did so with deep feeling, expressing her thoughts, most of the time quite as incoherently as Picabia in his own poems, but suggestively nonetheless, on what she saw of man's anguish and doubts on such subjects as war, religion, love, the senselessness of life, and the nature of man himself. Her drawings of machine elements were more delicate and tentative than those Picabia had drawn earlier.

A number of Picabia's graphic works are in the nature of Duchamp's readymades, objects found by the artist and designated by him as works of art, and sometimes signed with his name. The anti-social implications of the "readymade" lie chiefly in the "desanctification" of the traditional artistic means of expression, and often in the choice of objects which insult bourgeois taste. Picabia's readymades are usually drawings of photographs either copied or actually cut out from catalogues and advertisements. The *Portrait d'une jeune fille américaine dans l'état de nudité* is an example. A more sensational readymade is the 1920 stuffed monkey pulling at his tail which sticks out from between his legs. It is titled *Natures Mortes: Portrait de Cézanne, Portrait de Rembrandt, Portrait de Renoir* (Still Life: Portrait of Cézanne, Portrait of Rembrandt, Portrait of Renoir) – a blasphemy against the values of "high art." An ink blot entitled *La Sainte Vierge* (The Holy Virgin) is a gesture of anti-religion, anti-sentiment iconoclasm.[11]

Precedents for many of the techniques utilized by Picabia exist in nineteenth-century literature, in the works of Sade, Baudelaire, Rimbaud, and others, who emphasized the importance of the imagination, experimented with automatism, and appreciated the element of surprise in chance juxtapositions, who used words according to sound as much as meaning, and even invented words when necessary for their purposes. Picabia and the other Dada painters took up these literary techniques, and transposed them to the graphic plane. Examples are in Picabia's belief in the ability of the subconscious to invent the symbols of a new visual language, his and Duchamp's "readymades," and his scattering of unrelated words and phrases over the surface of drawings and paintings. Beyond these are Duchamp's experiments with chance, Hans Arp's compositions "arranged according to the laws of chance," the abstract "Merz" collages

10 See also "When the Dada Daddies Got Real; Or, How I Turned Picabia Inside Out" (p.74).

11 See also "When the Dada Daddies Got Real; Or, How I Turned Picabia Inside Out" (p.75).

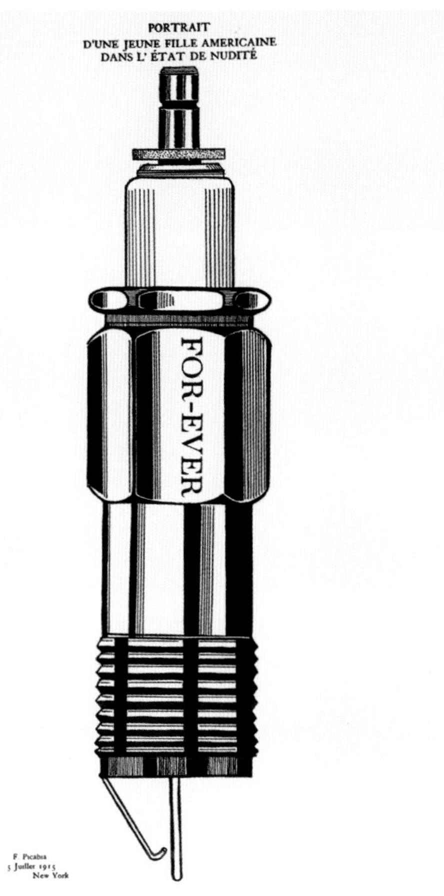

Francis Picabia
Portrait d'une jeune fille américaine dans l'état de nudité (Portrait of a Young American Girl in the State of Nudity), 1915

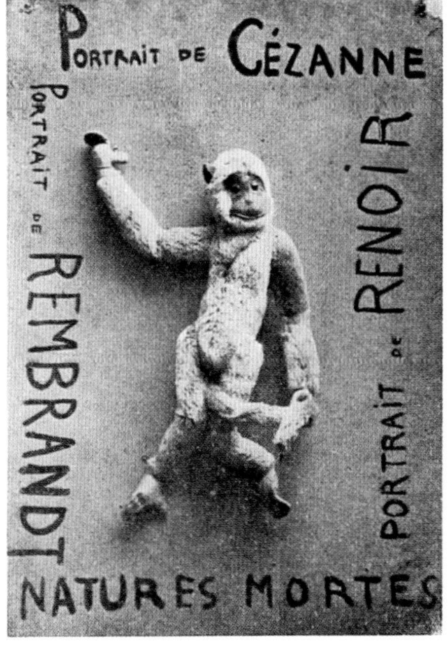

Francis Picabia
Natures Mortes: Portrait de Cézanne, Portrait de Rembrandt, Portrait de Renoir (Still Life: Portrait of Cézanne, Portrait of Rembrandt, Portrait of Renoir), 1920

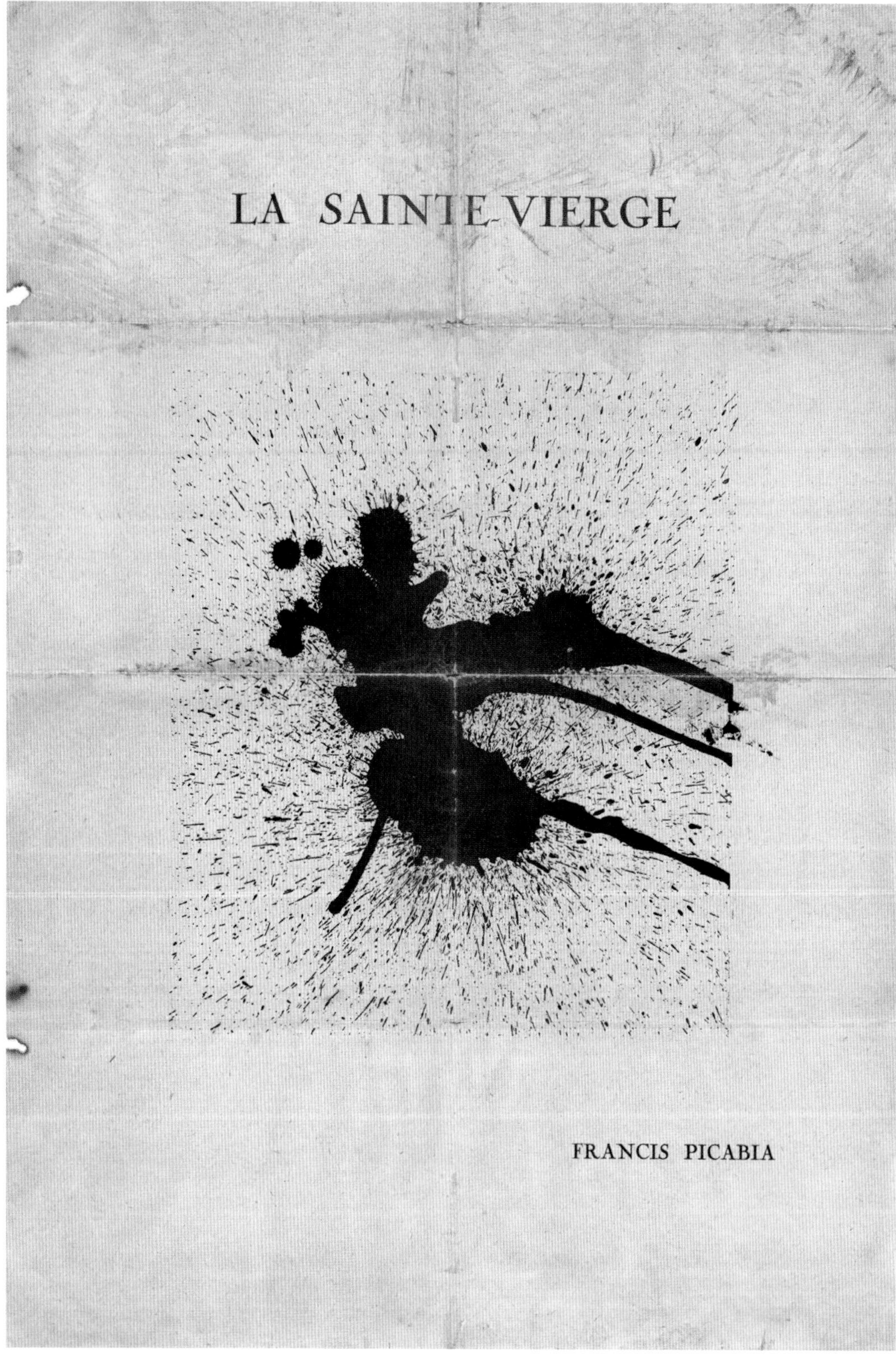

Francis Picabia
La Sainte Vierge (The Holy Virgin), 1920

of Kurt Schwitters, and the fantastic representational collages which Arp and Max Ernst produced in collaboration called "*fatagaga*." (The Italian Futurists had anticipated the Dadaists in some of these techniques.)

When it was apparent that Dada had become a successful art movement and had outlasted its inherent purpose of negation and destruction of all values, Picabia announced his withdrawal from the movement by a series of insults to those who had been his friends. This withdrawal brought to an end his experiments with abstract art and the invention of new visual symbols – and brought to an end that phase of his career with which we are concerned.

During the following decades, until his death in 1953, Picabia completely ignored the world of machinery as a source of ideas. He painted in several different styles, but always clearly represented human figures and the natural world. An exception was a brief period at the close of World War II when he painted brightly colored dots on dark backgrounds, dots that were abstract, but suggestive of stars in outer space. This break in the pattern of his work troubled him no more than his earlier shifts. He swept aside all charge of inconsistency with: "our heads are round so our thoughts can change direction."[12]

12 See also in "When the Dada Daddies Got Real; Or, How I Turned Picabia Inside Out" (p.78).

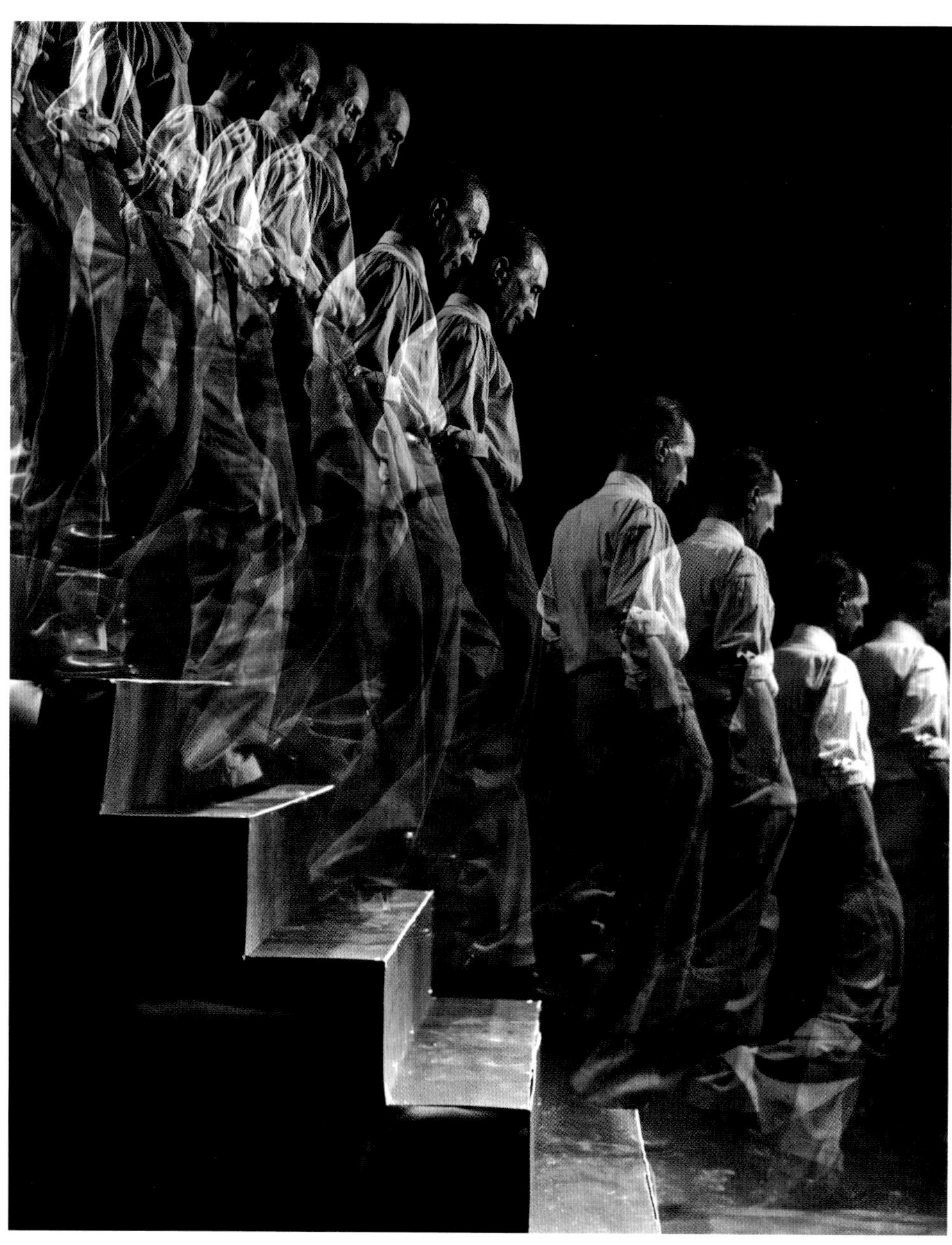

Eliot Elisofon
Marcel Duchamp descending a staircase,
1952

Hello and Goodbye, Francis Picabia*

* First published in *ARTnews*, September 1970.

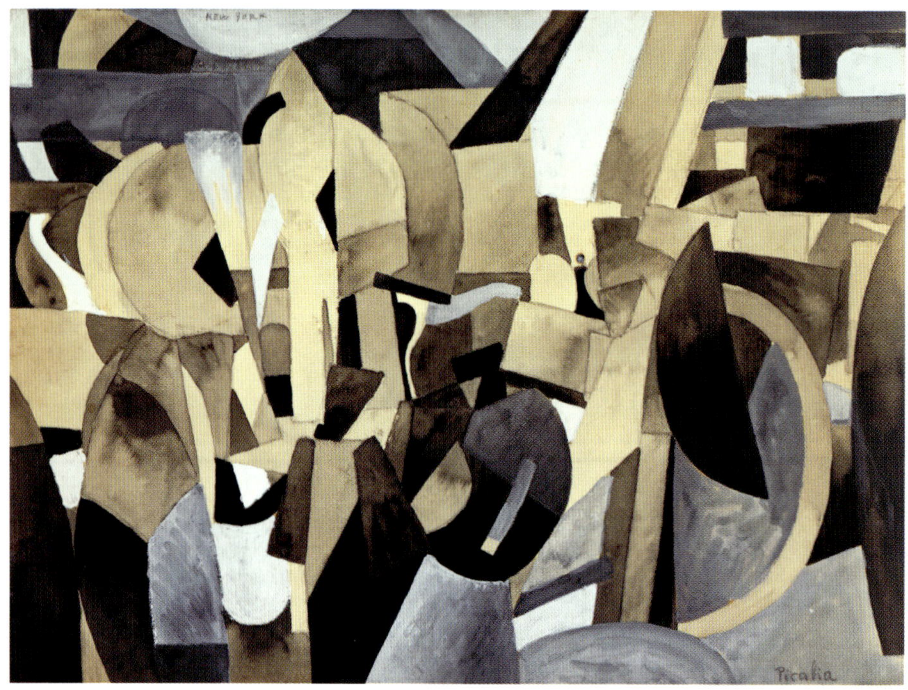

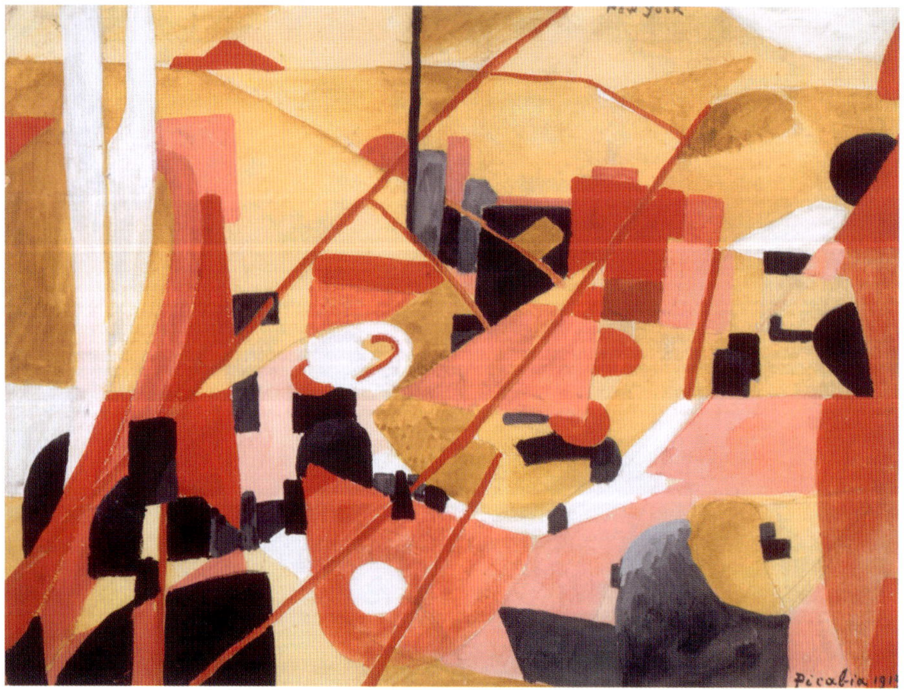

top: Francis Picabia
New York, 1913

bottom: Francis Picabia
New York, 1913

In 1955, I completed a master's thesis on Francis Picabia. I spent almost three years trying to get inside Picabia's mind, but the attitudes of artists in New York and Paris in the years from 1910 to 1925 seemed as far removed from my immediate experience and understanding as those of some ancient civilization. Florence in the year 1420 seemed no more distant than Paris 1920. The effort to try to understand the recent past was so great that, at its conclusion, I asked myself: why need I, as a painter (I had my first one-man show about the time the thesis was completed), feel bound to continue the traditions of "Modern Art"? I needn't, and with that rejection I felt liberated. But had I been imprisoned before? Yes, and so had most of the art world. And one of our jailers was Francis Picabia.

One of my early memories is from a 1930s movie in which someone like Adolphe Menjou dressed in an artist's smock and beret, in a room with elegantly gowned high-society people, sings a song explaining "Modern Art." Appropriate paintings are around to illustrate his song-lecture. The line I remember best was something like: "We don't paint the whistle, but the (sound of a whistle)." He points to a painting composed of spirals. The song made a number of similar comparisons. The message was a basic art education for most Americans and was supported by many more examples from those decades.[1]

How did such foreign ideas invade our pragmatic shores? Picabia helped bring them here at the time of the 1913 Armory Show. He was one of the few European artists to make the trip (he could afford it). He held a series of newspaper interviews at the time of the opening, and again several weeks later for a one-man exhibition, at Alfred Stieglitz' avant-garde gallery, of watercolors made in New York. This series of watercolors is, for me, Picabia's highest accomplishment as a painter, and is central to his subsequent development. His interviews were given prominence in newspapers, were reprinted, and were widely circulated. Picabia, briefly, was Mr. Modern Art, and his statements were crucial, I believe, to the evolution of aesthetic opinion in this country, largely by way of Arthur Jerome Eddy's 1914 textbook *Cubists and Post-Impressionism*. Consider the following:

> You of New York should be quick to understand me and my fellow painters. Your New York is the Cubist, the Futurist city. It expresses in its architecture, its life, its spirit, the modern thought. You have passed through all the old schools, and are Futurists in word and deed and thought. You have been affected by all these schools just as we have been affected by our older schools.
>
> Because of your extreme modernity therefore, you should quickly understand the studies which I have made since my arrival in New York.

1 See also "When the Dada Daddies Got Real; Or, How I Turned Picabia Inside Out" (p.69).

They express the spirit of New York as I feel it, and the crowded streets of your city as I feel them, their surging, their unrest, their commercialism, and their atmospheric charm.

You see no form? No substance? Is it that I go out into your city and see nothing? I see much, much more, perhaps, than you who are used to it see. I see your stupendous skyscrapers, your mammoth buildings and marvelous subways, a thousand evidences of your great wealth on all sides. The tens of thousands of workers and toilers, your alert and shrewd-looking shop girls, all hurrying somewhere. I see your theater crowds at night gleaming, fluttering, smilingly happy, smartly gowned. There you have the spirit of modernity again.

But I do not paint these things which my eye sees. I paint that which my brain, my soul, sees. I walk from the Battery to Central Park. I mingle with your workers, and your Fifth Avenue mondaines. My brain gets the impression of each movement; there is the driving hurry of the former, their breathless haste to reach the place of their work in the morning and their equal haste to reach their homes at night. There is the languid grace of the latter, emanating a subtle perfume, a more subtle sensuousness.

I hear every language in the world spoken, the staccato of the New Yorker, the soft cadences of the Latin people, the heavy rumble of the Teuton, and the ensemble remains in my soul as the ensemble of some great opera.

At night from your harbor I look at your mammoth buildings. I see your city as a city of aerial lights and shadows; the streets are your shadows. Your harbor in the daylight shows the shipping of a world, the flags of all countries add their color to that given by your sky, your waters, and your painted craft of every size.

I absorb these impressions. I am in no hurry to put them on canvas. I let them remain in my brain, and then when the spirit of creation is at flood tide, I improvise my pictures as a musician improvises music. The harmonies of my studies grow and take form under my brush, as the musician's harmonies grow under his fingers. His music is from his brain and his soul just as my studies are from my brain and soul. Is this not clear to you?[2]

It has continuously surprised me that Picabia, who makes many comparisons between painting and music, seems not to have heard of Kandinsky's ideas at this time; *Concerning the Spiritual in Art* appeared in 1912. It is also a point of passing interest that several early historians of modern painting credit Kandinsky with producing the first abstract painting, while others claim that Picabia's watercolor *Caoutchouc, circa* 1909, is really that monumental landmark; however, as "*caoutchouc*" means rubber,

2 In Arthur Jerome Eddy, *Cubists and Post-Impressionism*, 1914.

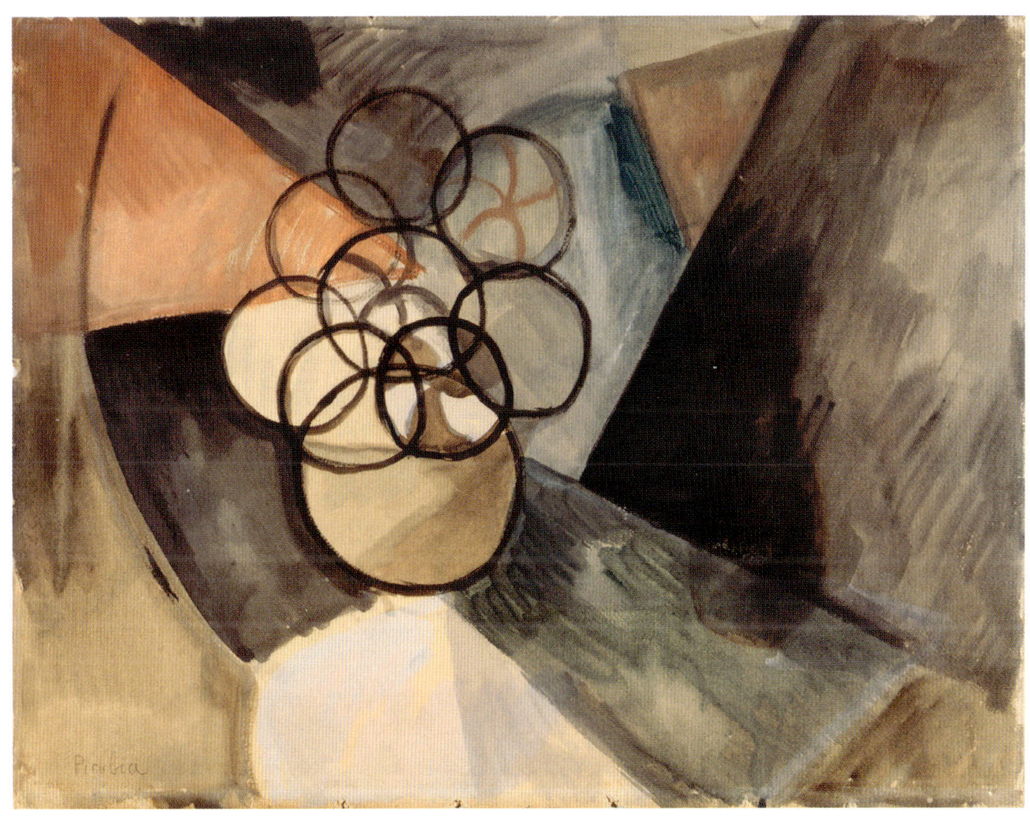

Francis Picabia
Caoutchouc (Rubber), *c.*1909

I read this picture as an attempt to portray a bouncing ball, or balls, and not as Non-Objective.

In another of his 1913 interviews in New York, Picabia seems to speak directly to the painter that I have now become, for I have made it my practice to paint only that which my eye sees:

> Art, art, what is art? Is it copying faithfully a person's face? A landscape? No, that is machinery. Painting nature as she is, is not art, it is mechanical genius. The old masters turned out by hand the most perfect models, the most faithful copies of what they saw. That all their paintings are not alike is due to the fact that no two men see the same things the same way. Those old masters were, and their modern followers are, faithful depicters of the actual, but I do not call that art today, because we have outgrown it. It is old, and only the new should live. Creating a picture without models is art.
>
> They were successful, those old masters; they filled a place in our life that cannot be filled otherwise, but we have outgrown them. It is a most excellent thing to keep their paintings in the art museums as curiosities for us and for those who will come after us. Their paintings are to us what the alphabet is to the child.
>
> We moderns, if so you think of us, express the spirit of the modern time, the twentieth century. And we express it on canvas the way great composers express it in their music.[3]

There it is. The burning spirit of modernity that 57 years later has atrophied into an offensive extreme in our museums that are haunted by the "modern." Today this would be thought provincial – the acceptance of gospel, the word of fashion, from the big center (Paris) by self-conscious country cousins, but 57 years ago these statements were hot news. Fifty-seven years is the life span of some of our senior curators, almost twice the years of some of our notable younger curators (not to mention the ages of our critics).

These statements of Picabia's in 1913 are remarkable from an artist who, as recently as 1909, had been producing run-of-the-mill academic Impressionistic paintings, and who ten years later, as one of the first of the Surrealists (they were pretty much the same group as the last of the Dadas), was incorporating rather lovely studies after Renaissance masters in his work. But then Picabia always turned his back on whatever became "Establishment," even the Dada and Surrealist movements.

The paintings in the Armory Show were themselves a convincing argument for "Modern Art," but Picabia's statements added to the tidal wave

3 In Arthur Jerome Eddy, *Cubists and Post-Impressionism*, 1914.

that washed away the reputations of a number of fine but not experimental or abstract American painters. And their successors have had a rough time of it since (prompting one figurative colleague of mine to suggest recently that representational painters should now demand "reparations" from the museums). Though the American Scene painters of the 1930s managed to gain some community standing, they too were soon drowned by the Museum of Modern Art's aggressive education of the American public, demonstrating a cultural lag of a quarter of a century after Picabia explained what it was all about. That museum's catalogues and exhibitions educated all of us in the kind of art we should look at and the kind we should ignore. It has only been through the sieve of the recent taste for Camp that some nineteenth-century artists not in the direct line of development towards twentieth-century modernism can be studied again with seriousness by younger artists. For many years we have been generally blind to a great deal of very good art that didn't make the approved list. A few strays have been allowed: an occasional Hopper, especially if its coincidental "Cubist" structure could be easily seen. And while the educated were looking another way, Andrew Wyeth took dominion on the hearts of those who "know what they like."

The painting that received the most attention at the Armory Show was Marcel Duchamp's *Nude Descending a Staircase.* It was the title, rather than the image, that made it notorious, the object of wisecracks and cartoons. The *Nude* simply could not be seen by the public's untrained eyes, while the title is as memorable a phrase as any painting has had the luck to get as a label. The image of the painting is taken straight from a diagram in a book that is a later French version of Muybridge's photographic work on the human figure in motion, and thus indicates the path that Duchamp was following, and his relationship to Picabia.

In those years Duchamp and Picabia were close friends, and an artistic team comparable to Picasso and Braque. As a team they must now be acknowledged as the gestators of today's forms of "concept" art. If Picasso and Matisse provide most of our archetypical "painterly" gestures and structures for the continuation of traditional easel painting, with Mondrian teaching the most radical new tricks to the old dog, then Picabia and Duchamp illumine (God help us) the way beyond. Because he was to Duchamp as Picasso was to Braque, that is, the leader, this major exhibition at the Guggenheim Museum now accords to Picabia his place as one of the pivotal artists of our century.[4]

4 The Guggenheim Museum in New York held a large retrospective on Picabia that included 139 paintings, collages, and documents in September 1970, when this article was published.

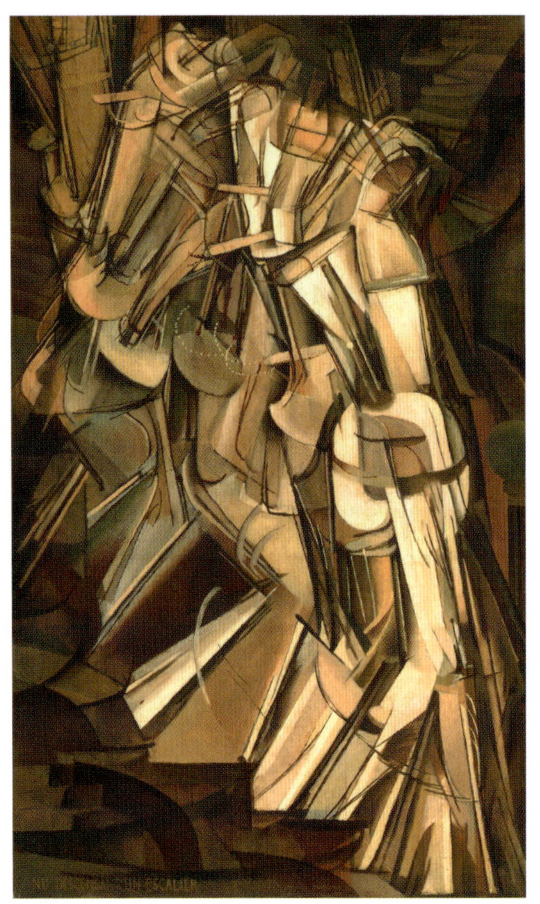

Marcel Duchamp
Nude Descending a Staircase (No. II), 1912

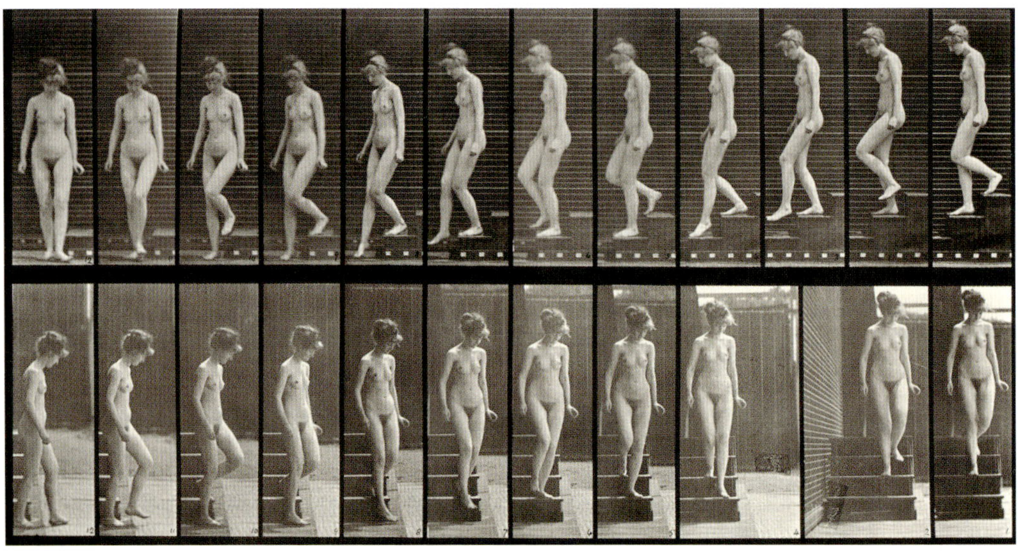

Eadweard Muybridge
'Descending stairs and turning around'
from *Human Figure in Motion*, 1887

I suppose a case could be made to demonstrate that the main influence of Duchamp has been in the area of activity-type art forms more closely allied to dance, theater, music and landscape architecture, while the influence of Picabia has been more limited to what could be called non-traditional easel painting and graphic design, including typography. (John Cage's recent graphic work of fragments of words printed on overlapping transparent plastic panels, titled *Not Wanting to Say Anything about Marcel*, an obvious homage to Duchamp, actually derives from Picabia's typographic style.)

But the germinal field for both men was their serious practice of painting. Duchamp was Picabia's junior by six years, and by the time Duchamp had painted his first Cézannesque portraits in 1910, Picabia had gone through a couple of styles as an exhibiting artist. Starting around 1895 with Pissarro-like landscapes, Picabia developed towards a Seurat-like flat manner with landscapes, then suddenly anticipated the open Analytic-Cubist look, with *Caoutchouc* (Rubber) (p.45). After they discovered each other, the minds of Duchamp and Picabia were in close step for a few years, as they worked their way through a blend of Cubism and Futurism with applied musical analogies, into hieroglyphic puns and games of their Dada style.

The disparity of their fame in the United States for the last 30 years may be accounted for by the strong and imaginative disciples Duchamp attracted during his long residence in this country and the attendant popularization of his lifestyle. Picabia lived the last 30 years of his life in relative obscurity in France. Duchamp's dramatic adherence to the principles of his Gestalt makes a strong journalistic impression. Picabia's remaining decades were spent in producing paintings in several different styles, none so radical as to attract much attention, and he seemingly had lost himself – not a compelling image for journalists. His only disciple had been Marcel Duchamp.

My own interest in the work of Picabia was awakened by a shock of recognition. I had dabbled with American Scene-type painting just before World War II; then for a time, while in the U.S. Infantry, I worked on diagrammatic charts of infantry weapons. After the war, I worked on industrial catalogues, drafting and doing typographic design. My first job in that field was with the man who also was the teacher of my design courses at Carnegie Tech, Robert Lepper. His own paintings and sculptures had long been based on machine elements, and he introduced me to the work of several Americans, notably Schamberg, whose cool, formal compositions employed machine parts as pristine design elements. But my favorite painting then was Paul Klee's *Twittering Machine*, whose elements were not just formal. I liked the possibilities of using machine forms metaphorically, as puns, thematically.

My paintings from about 1947 until 1951, when I started work on the Picabia thesis, were often based on shapes I took from the industrial catalogues I worked on. My masterwork was a painting of a girl (extruded window frame cross-section) being attacked by a shower (diagram of the shower pipes like a stick figure, spigots for hands, and faucet for phallus), but with an Expressionistic use of paint and color.

When I saw the first edition of the Skira books on modern painting, there was a painting by Picabia, *Parade amoureuse* (Amorous Parade), 1917, of two funny machines "relating" to each other. About the same time, I read Gertrude Stein's praise of Picabia as the greatest of modern painters in her *Autobiography of Alice B. Toklas*. This from the close friend of Picasso and Matisse! (Or was it Alice B. Toklas' opinion only?) However, I had seen a Picabia exhibition in 1950, and it hadn't been exactly overwhelming in its impact, nor had I seen anything relating to machines there. That exhibition, at the Rose Fried Gallery, was made up mostly of a number of little canvases painted black, with a few colored dots and circles of different sizes scattered across the surface of each, from the 1940s. And taking up one end of that small gallery was the very large painting *Edtaonisl (ecclésiastique)* (p.56). This large, complicated-looking Cubist abstraction was painted in 1913, 30 years before the black paintings.

In 1950, I considered myself a relatively knowledgeable young American artist, but Marcel Duchamp was to me then only a dim figure written up in magazines as a strange man who had been a Dada artist but had given up art to play chess. Dada was only the funny name of an anarchistic type of movement in which the artists made funny things and acted silly, and about which hardly anything was written until Robert Motherwell edited a book of documents, *The Dada Painters and Poets*, 1951. Picabia was a new name. That exhibition at the Rose Fried Gallery had impressed me as demonstrating a strange kind of reverse progress, from the sophisticated, grandiose painting of 1913 to the simplistic late paintings. Now added to those stylistic extremes were machine diagrams used in paintings in a symbolistic way (where I had thought myself a pioneer), and I knew I was facing an enigma that was capable of being "studied in-depth," with "original research," the requirements of an master's thesis at the Institute of Fine Arts, New York.

To try to understand Picabia's evolution as a painter, I made a thorough investigation of the relationship between the technical devices and the verbalizations of the Cubist painters and their spokesmen, compared to those of the Futurist painters, and contrasted the technical devices and verbalizations of Picabia and Duchamp (for I found it impossible to discuss the work of one without the other) with each of those groups.

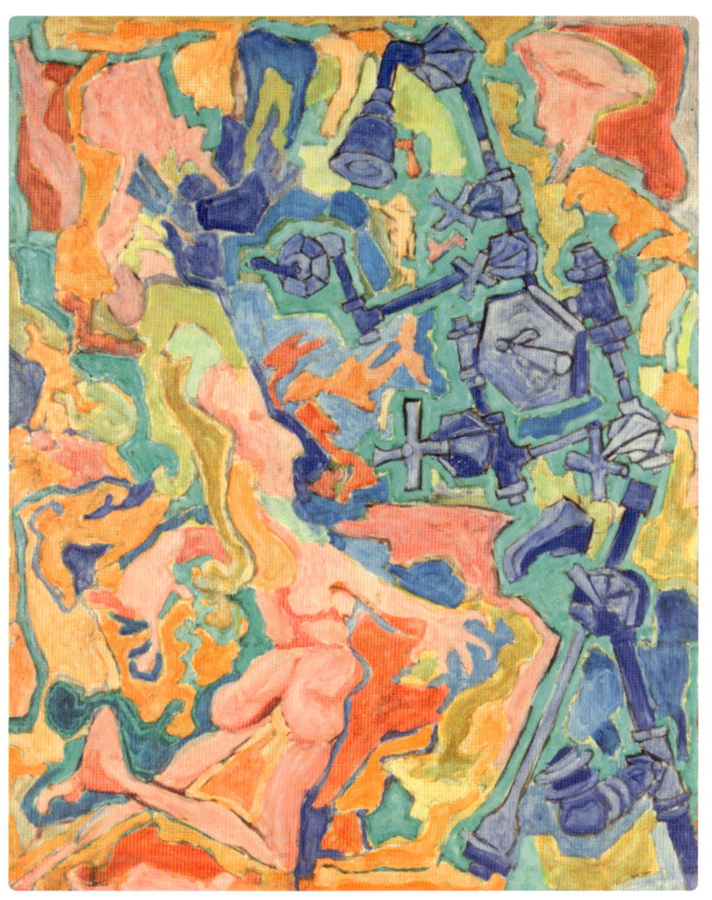

Philip Pearlstein
Death and the Maiden
(Shower Attacking Woman), 1950

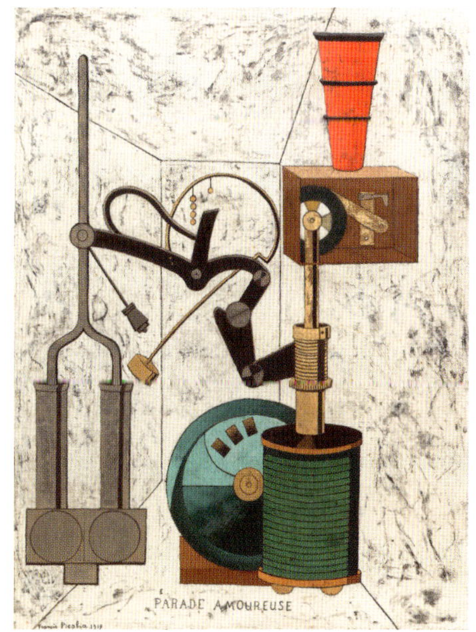

Francis Picabia
Parade amoureuse
(Amorous Parade), 1917

This was a large collating process. The one artist of all those whose ideas I studied to win my genuine admiration was Boccioni. I admired the clarity with which he expressed his complex ideas about painting, and the ideas themselves seemed very intriguing. I also became increasingly enthusiastic about his work and almost decided to switch my subject.

My thesis resolved itself into being a study of how complex literary-type subject matter led Picabia and Duchamp into being extraordinarily inventive with pictorial means. One question was continuously annoying. Which of the two originated the major ideas? I would have liked to discuss this with Duchamp during that time when I could have visited him, but I could not think of a way to phrase the question without offense, nor could I see how at that distance he could be objective in his reply. Also, I was somewhat inhibited by the fact that Mrs. Harriet Janis, who was friendly to me throughout this project, told me that all the answers were recorded on ten hours of taped interviews she and Rudi Blesh had made with Duchamp. Perhaps the answers are still there.

I did spend an afternoon with Walter Arensberg, the patron and friend of Duchamp and Picabia, at his home in Los Angeles. This was just around the time when a number of the pieces from his collection were assembled in his sun parlor for crating and shipping off to the Philadelphia Museum. When I asked about the exchange of influence between the two artists, Arensberg flatly stated that Picabia got the machine subjects and the use of titles on paintings from Duchamp. My collating of external evidence indicated the reverse, but I did not pursue the argument. Arensberg did say that Picabia was a strong egocentric personality, and that his inherited money brought him the friendship of certain personalities and artists, including Duchamp. Arensberg then quoted a French saying to the effect that friends respect, yet take advantage of, the rich ones. This reinforced the impression I had from reading an account by Gabrielle Buffet-Picabia (she was Picabia's wife then and the constant observer of that period of Picabia's life) of the evolution of Apollinaire's book, *The Cubist Painters*, in 1913, and the *Section d'Or* exhibition that it accompanied. Picabia footed the bills for that publication, and Apollinaire allowed himself to expand his categories of kinds of Cubism to include Picabia. Arensberg then went on to speak of Picabia's alcoholism, and said that it was an era (the years of World War I, into the 1920s) of heavy drinking. But early in the 1920s, Picabia was given a life-or-death sentence by his doctors to give up alcohol, which he did, and in Arensberg's opinion Picabia's work thereafter never equalled the early work. He felt that to evaluate Picabia properly it would be best to forget all he did later. The rest of the world seems to have concurred with Arensberg.

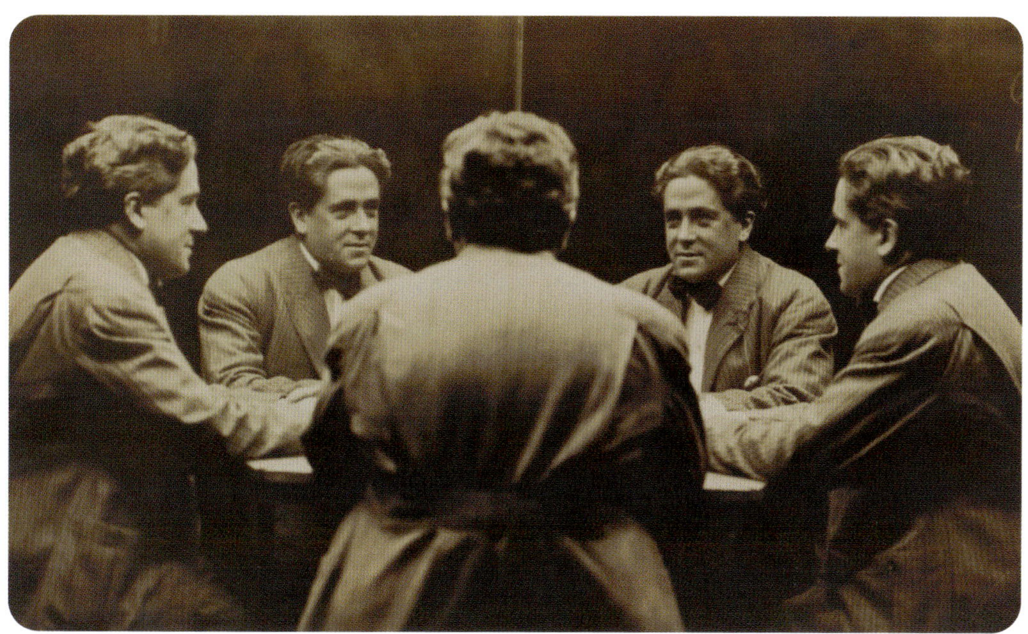

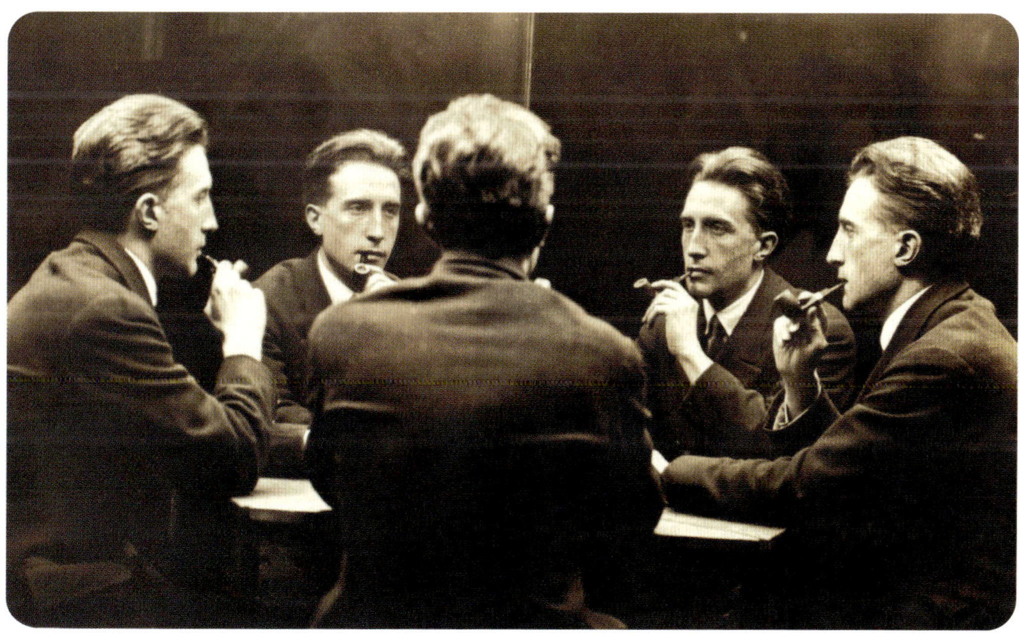

top: Portrait multiple of Francis Picabia
Broadway Photo Shop, New York, 1917

bottom: Portrait multiple of Marcel Duchamp
Broadway Photo Shop, New York, 1917

As I was reaching the end of the initial phase of research, Picabia was briefly in the news; he died in Paris and his estate was tied up in a legal tangle that made interesting newspaper items.

The visit with Arensberg indicated to me that further interviews would be of little help, though the experience might be charming. A letter to Gabrielle Buffet brought the response that she was writing her own book. I decided not to bother Duchamp; I was only working on an master's thesis, and was far more interested in what I was learning from studying the works themselves and the artists' published statements than in reminiscences or opinions.

My study concentrated on the years that saw the development and end of machine symbolism in Picabia's work, from 1908 to 1925. (It is necessary to keep in mind that their symbolism was private and arbitrary; meanings were assigned to pictorial forms at the whim of the moment, and were usually in-jokes for themselves and a small circle of friends. The artist was not concerned with communicating to the world at large.) At first the material I accumulated and Picabia's body of work made no sense to me. Though I knew that everything was satirical, anti-establishment, a kind of Museum of Modern Anti-Art, a key was missing. It was provided by the observation of a friend while we were looking at *Je revois en souvenir ma chère Udnie* (p.33), 1914, at Janis Gallery in New York. My friend pointed out an unmistakable phallic element performing in the painting. I had innocently been reading the shapes simply as automotive. But a consideration of the title, along with the visual sexual activity, showed me what the hero of the statement "I See Again in Memory My Dear Udnie" (which I translated from pig-Latin as "nudie") remembered so fondly, and the iconography of much of the work fell into place. Both Picabia and Duchamp had developed, in hieroglyphic manner, picaresque novellas of the experiences of a couple of ladies. Duchamp's heroine, a virgin, first appears in *Mariée*, 1912. Then, work by work, in the accumulative manner of Rodin's studies for his *Gates of Hell*, Duchamp peopled her ambience. She achieves apotheosis in the large painting on glass, *The Bride Stripped Bare by Her Bachelors, Even*, in which most of the separate works are repeated. Duchamp, in an interview in the 1940s, said that he would paint again if he ever got another idea for a painting.

Picabia did the reverse. He started his epic with a series of large paintings, among which are *Je revois en souvenir ma chère Udnie,* and *Edtaonisl (ecclésiastique)* (which I deciphered as the picture of a clergyman watching a "star dancer" rehearsing with her troupe aboard an ocean liner, in proper art-historical iconographic terms). His heroine is the "*Fille née sans mère*," (p.33) the daughter born without a mother (which I deciphered as "the

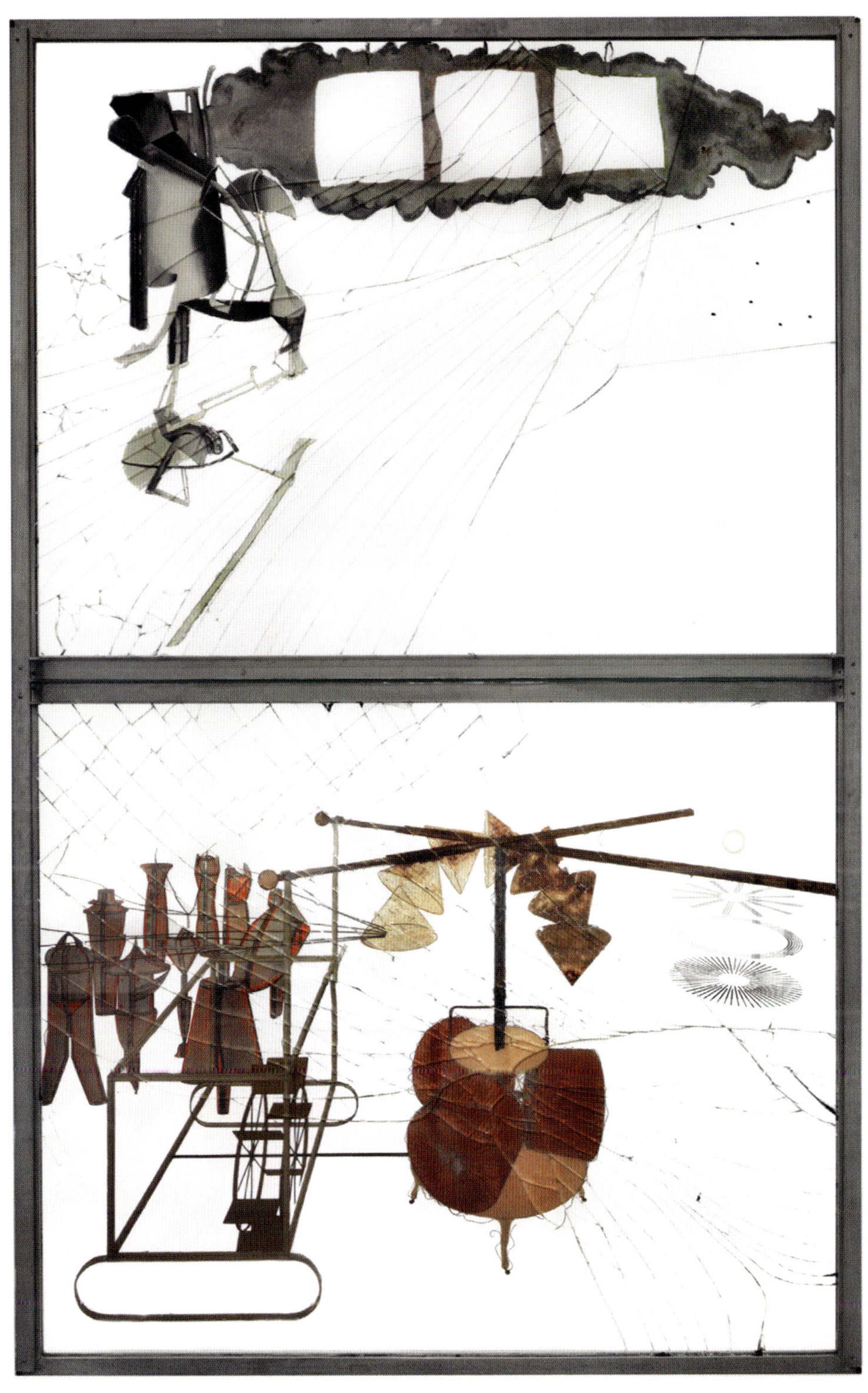

Marcel Duchamp
The Bride Stripped Bare by Her Bachelors, Even (The Large Glass), 1915–23

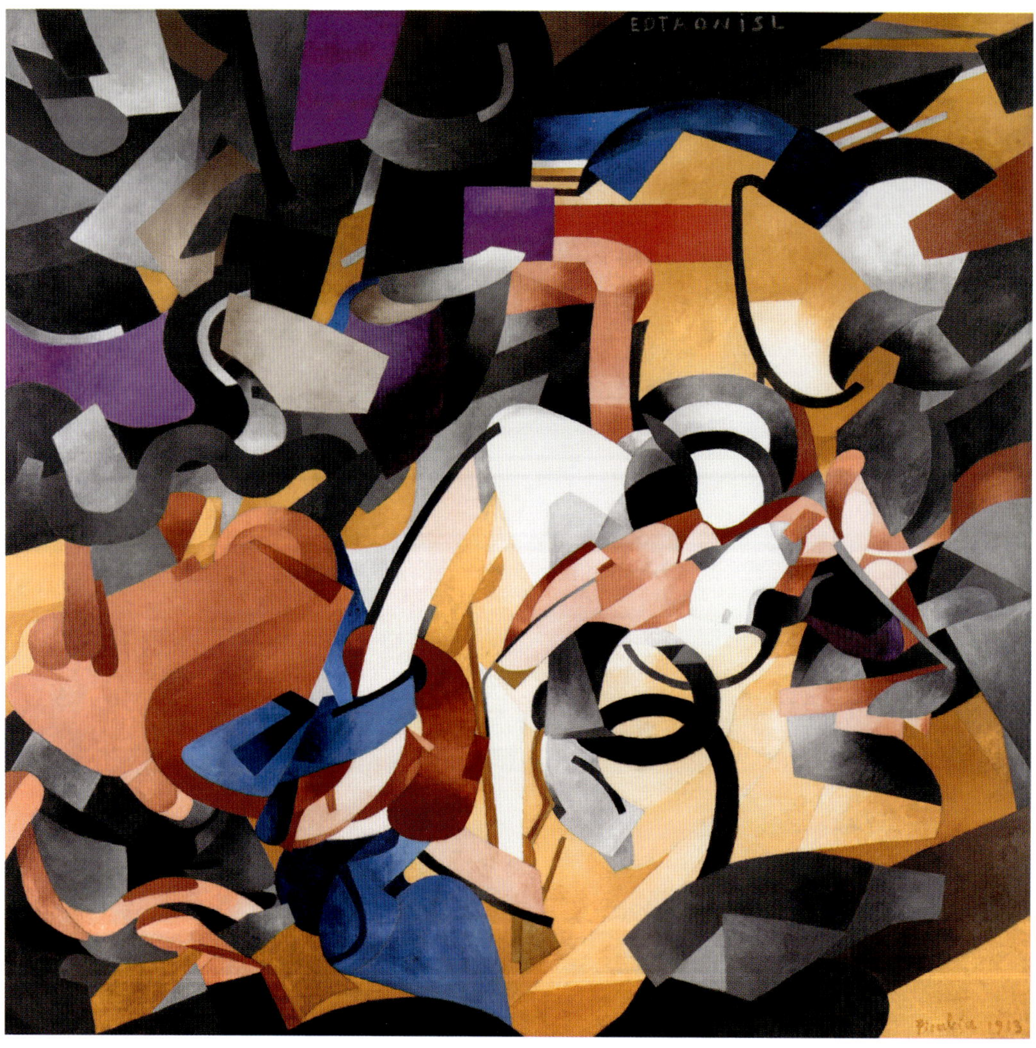

Francis Picabia
Edtaonisl (ecclésiastique)
(Edtaonisl [Ecclesiastical]), 1913

machine"). She travels to America, has her adventures, then several years later writes and publishes a book of poetry which sums up her world view. The poems are even better than her illustrations for the book – I translated every one of them from the French into my own English. But after her first appearances in the large paintings, her many other manifestations are small scale and often no more than line drawings, but each of her appearances further defines her attitudes towards her world. And it seems that when Picabia exhausted his rambling investigation of that world – all through his Dada works – he, too, came to a stop. His work then went off into other directions.

Picabia's parting from that world was nostalgic:

> I have removed myself from certain Dadaists because I was suffocating among them. Each day I become more sad, terribly bored... I don't mean to review the complete history of the Dada movement now, but I want to make a few points: The Dada spirit truly existed for only three or four years. It was expressed by Marcel Duchamp and me at the end of 1912: [Richard] Huelsenbeck, [Tristan] Tzara or [Hugo] Ball found the name Dada in 1916. With the name the movement reached its culminating point, but it continued to evolve, each of us bringing as much life to it as possible... Our success, the pleasures of the game, attracted in 1918 many people who have only the name of Dada: Then everything changed; I saw that Dada, like Cubism, was going to have disciples who *would understand,* and I felt I had to run away from those people... Dada is like a cigarette with an agreeable odor. When the brand name gets consumed, it remains tobacco, and I count on a man of genius to pick it up and give it a new name... I like to walk by myself along unknown streets. One day resembles the next if we do not at least create the illusion of novelty, and Dada is no longer new, for the moment. The bourgeoisie represents the finite, Dada would be the same if it lasted too much longer.

My thesis ended at that point. I had worked my way through modernism and symbolism by writing rather than painting. And I decided I wanted no more of complex symbolism or "modernism" for myself.

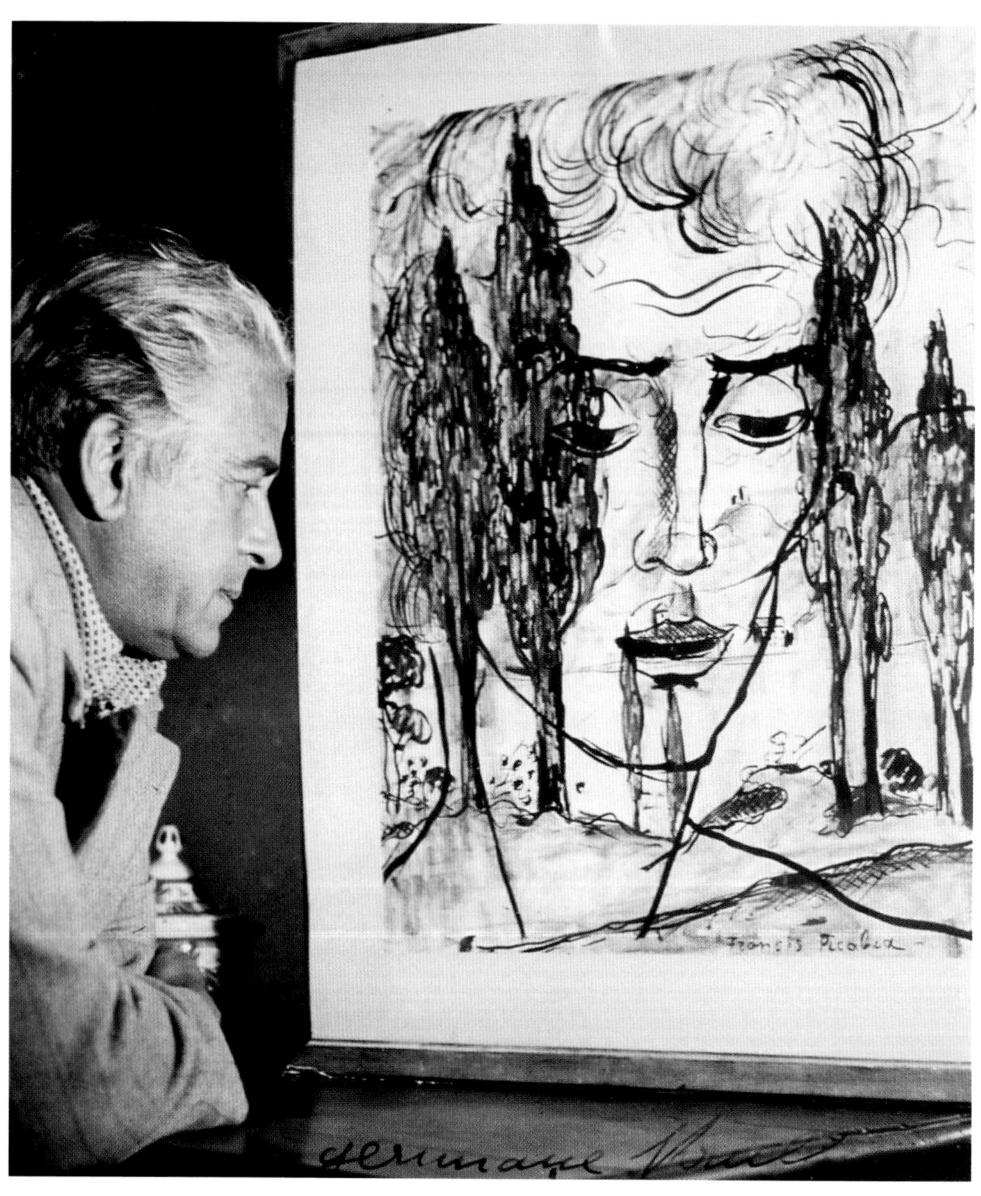

Germaine Krull
Francis Picabia in his studio,
Chateau de Mai, Mougins, c.1935

When the Dada Daddies Got Real; Or, How I Turned Picabia Inside Out*

* First published in *Brooklyn Rail*, February 2017

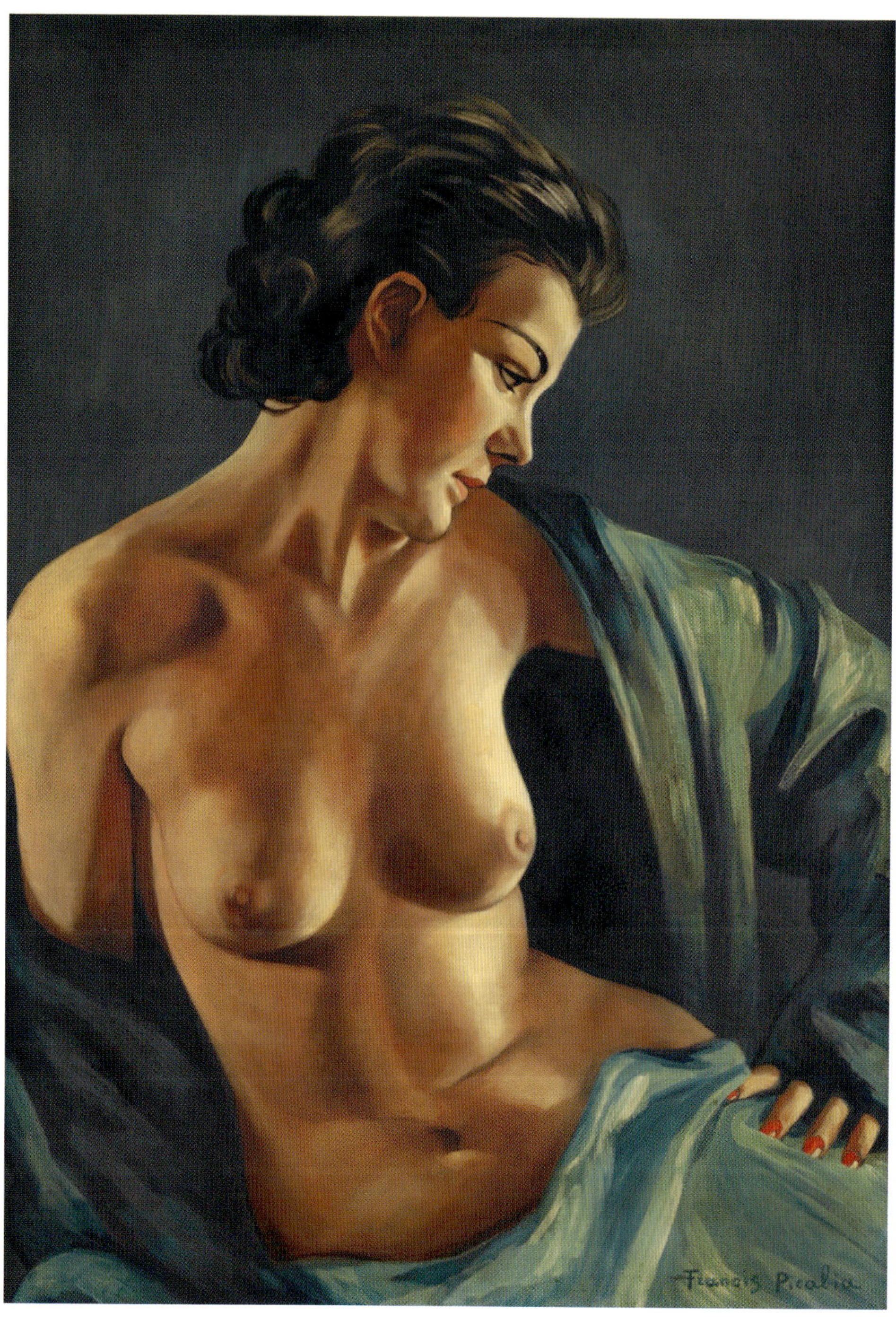

Francis Picabia
Femme au châle vert (Woman with Green Shawl), *c.*1940–1

In 1999, I had an exhibition of recent paintings at a gallery in Paris. At a dinner following the opening, I was seated next to an art collector who spoke minimal English to compliment my minimal French. Still, she managed to tell me of her two recent acquisitions as a collector: an Eric Fischl painting of nudes and one of Francis Picabia's late paintings of nudes. She also managed to tell me that she found my paintings eccentric, and wondered what they meant. Sensing that she was not about to add one of my works to her collection, I blurted out that I had turned Picabia inside out. Then I spent the rest of the dinner trying to explain, in a mix of languages, that Francis Picabia and his friend Marcel Duchamp first determined their subject matter then found the technical means with which to realize it in painting – whereas I start with the technical part and let the subject matter be interpreted however a viewer wants.

I explained that, more than half century earlier, as a student at the New York University Institute of Fine Arts, I had written a master's thesis on Picabia. About halfway through my research, Picabia died. Briefly, I was the leading authority in the English language on Picabia, and published a major article in *ARTS* magazine in 1956 that contained the central idea of my thesis, summed up by the title, "The Symbolic Language of Francis Picabia" (p.22). However, because Picabia and Duchamp were such close intellectual collaborators from 1910 to 1920, the article and the thesis were as much about Duchamp as about Picabia.

In the spring of 1955, almost a year after the article was published, I presented the first draft of my thesis to my acting faculty advisor, Dr. Horst W. Janson. (My faculty advisor of record, Dr. José López-Rey, was away on leave.) After a cursory reading, Dr. Janson asked me to reorganize the material in chronological order, rather than the scheme of grouping ideas that I had worked out. As this was in the Stone-Age time of handwritten first drafts and badly typewritten second drafts, it was about six months until my next meeting with Dr. Janson. The thesis was accepted, and I felt my career in art history had ended. I felt that I now knew all about the history of modernist art, and it seemed to belong to a faraway past. I would now concentrate on my own development as an artist.

My undergraduate career had been interrupted by World War II, when I was drafted into the U.S. Infantry. Before I was shipped off to Italy, I spent several months creating charts of the workings of infantry weapons and paraphernalia for the army. When the war was over and I returned to Carnegie Tech in Pittsburgh, I worked as a low-level graphic designer doing what were called "mechanicals" (trial sketches of page layouts, some drafting of images, preparing the final page designs for the printer) for catalogues of Alcoa aluminum architectural products and American

Standard plumbing units. In college, I did a number of paintings based on shapes I had taken from these catalogues. The experience of drafting all these images led to my interest in the Dada works of Picabia and Duchamp, in which they used the same kind of mechanical shapes.

After graduating college in 1949, I did a group of proto-Pop paintings that included images of the Statue of Liberty, the American Eagle, and Superman (p.13). However, by 1955 the paintings I was producing were based on generalized landscape themes, for which I had adopted the Abstract Expressionist calligraphic use of paint. This was interrupted when I spent the 1958–59 academic year on a Fulbright Fellowship in Italy, where I made a series of drawings of Roman ruins that were realist (though the paintings I developed from them remained Abstract Expressionist in technique).

After my return to New York, the nude human figure replaced landscape as my chief subject, simply because it was easier to find models I could hire to come to my studio than to find the kind of landscapes I would have liked to paint. By 1960 I had abandoned the Abstract Expressionistic calligraphic paint handling, and found myself labeled a "Super-Realist" as I concentrated on painting nude models from direct visual observation in my own studio. Over time, the paintings evolved from simple figure studies to complex compositions. The study I had made of the ideas that motivated Francis Picabia in the first quarter of the twentieth century became a faded memory.

During the early 1950s, the time my thesis was done, the New York University Institute of Fine Arts was home to a group of Europe's leading scholars of art history that the school's director, Dr. Walter W.S. Cook, had appointed during World War II. Dominant among these historians, a committee of whom had to approve the student proposals for their thesis projects, was Dr. Erwin Panofsky, who studied the symbols and signs embodied in a work of art that give it meaning in relation to the society that produced it. Picabia and Duchamp's work from 1910 to 1920 fits that prescription perfectly, and my proposal was accepted. However, as a young artist I was frustrated by that emphasis on societal values. I wanted to know how the work of art was done, so my thesis aimed to demonstrate the manner in which the symbolism embedded in the work of art influences the technology of the artist.

By the early 1950s, Picabia and Duchamp were neglected by the educated art public. (Duchamp, who lived in New York, had a reputation as an eccentric who played chess in Washington Square.) The fact that both would later become cultural icons was not predictable in 1955. Nor was the fact that the last works of both were to be realist. At that point, Picabia's paintings of female nudes copied from erotic magazines were unknown.

Duchamp's three-dimensional installation [*Étant donnés* (Given), 1946–66] of the figure of a naked woman lying on her back with her crotch exposed to the observer (who must look through a knothole in a barn door to see it) was not yet installed in the Philadelphia Museum of Art.

I spent three years analyzing their works, and I realized that their signs and symbols were so esoteric and arbitrary that they would always be open to new interpretations. Along the way, I educated myself in major aspects of the various technologies they borrowed, enhanced or invented out of Cubism, Futurism, and Symbolism.

This aspect of invention in modernist painting continues to fascinate me, but in 1955 I felt saturated with modernism. The big lesson I had learned from writing the thesis was: though the character of a work of art is determined by its subject, its value as a work of art is determined by the elegance of its technology. For the next few years I decided to concentrate on the technology of the style of painting that most excited me then: Action Painting or Abstract Expressionism. I concentrated on the carpentry of putting together the image, and let the meanings of my subjects take their chances with whoever looked at the paintings.

I spent my evening in Paris in 1999 talking my way out of the surprised response I had made to my dinner companion at the mention of Picabia. Because now I was confronted by the fact that my paintings of the nude figure were viewed by this collector as being in direct competition with the nudes by the Dadaist who had been the subject of my thesis half a century earlier.

I believe that the newly aroused taste for Picabia's nudes can be seen as an after-effect of Andy Warhol's Marilyn Monroe multiples. Though created decades before the Warhols, Picabia's nudes were hidden away during a protracted legal battle around the settlement of his estate (there were at least two successive legal wives). If they had been seen at the time of their creation, I believe that they would have been seen as the last twist in a career of many stylistic changes. Like Duchamp's installation in the Philadelphia Museum of the young lady with spread legs, they would have been seen as a nose-thumbing gesture aimed at the art-loving audience. They would have not been seen as Pop art before the historical fact of Pop art.

It is important today to realize that Picabia was important in other ways to the history of modern art. He was the major force in the United States in creating the public awareness of Cubism and Futurism. He seems to have been the prime originator of the second phase of Cubism, usually referred to as "Synthetic Cubism." Alongside André Breton, he was a pioneer in the exploration of ideas foundational to Surrealism. He was just as important in

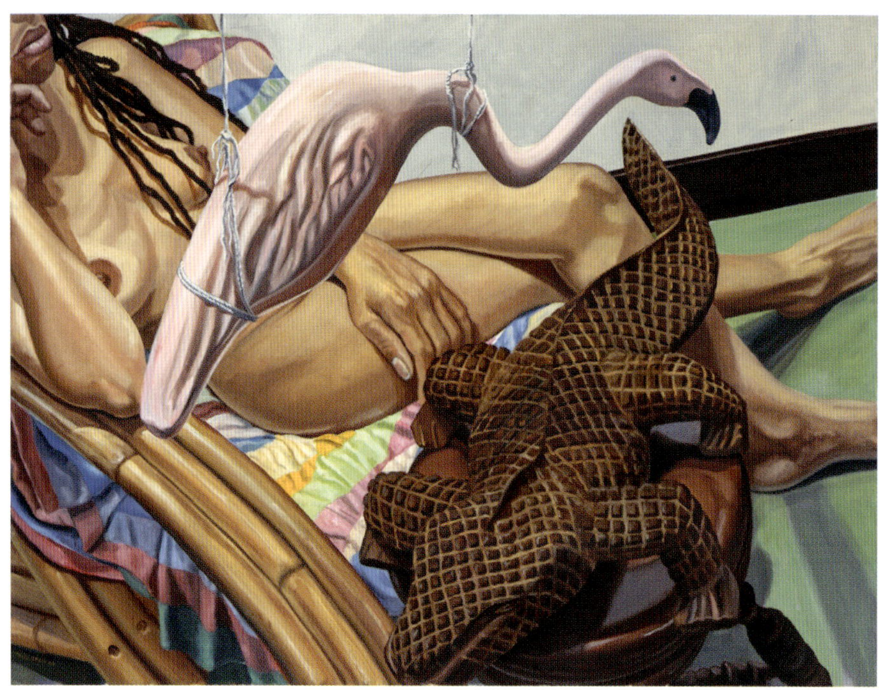

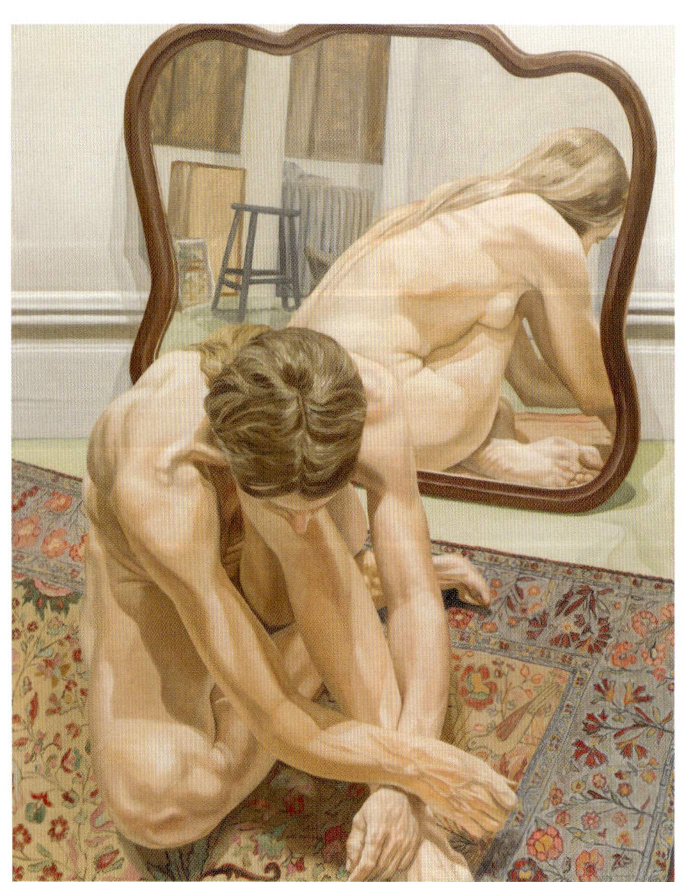

top: Philip Pearlstein
Model with Dreadlocks, Wooden Alligator and Pink Flamingo, 2005

bottom: Philip Pearlstein
Crouching Female Nude with Mirror, 1971

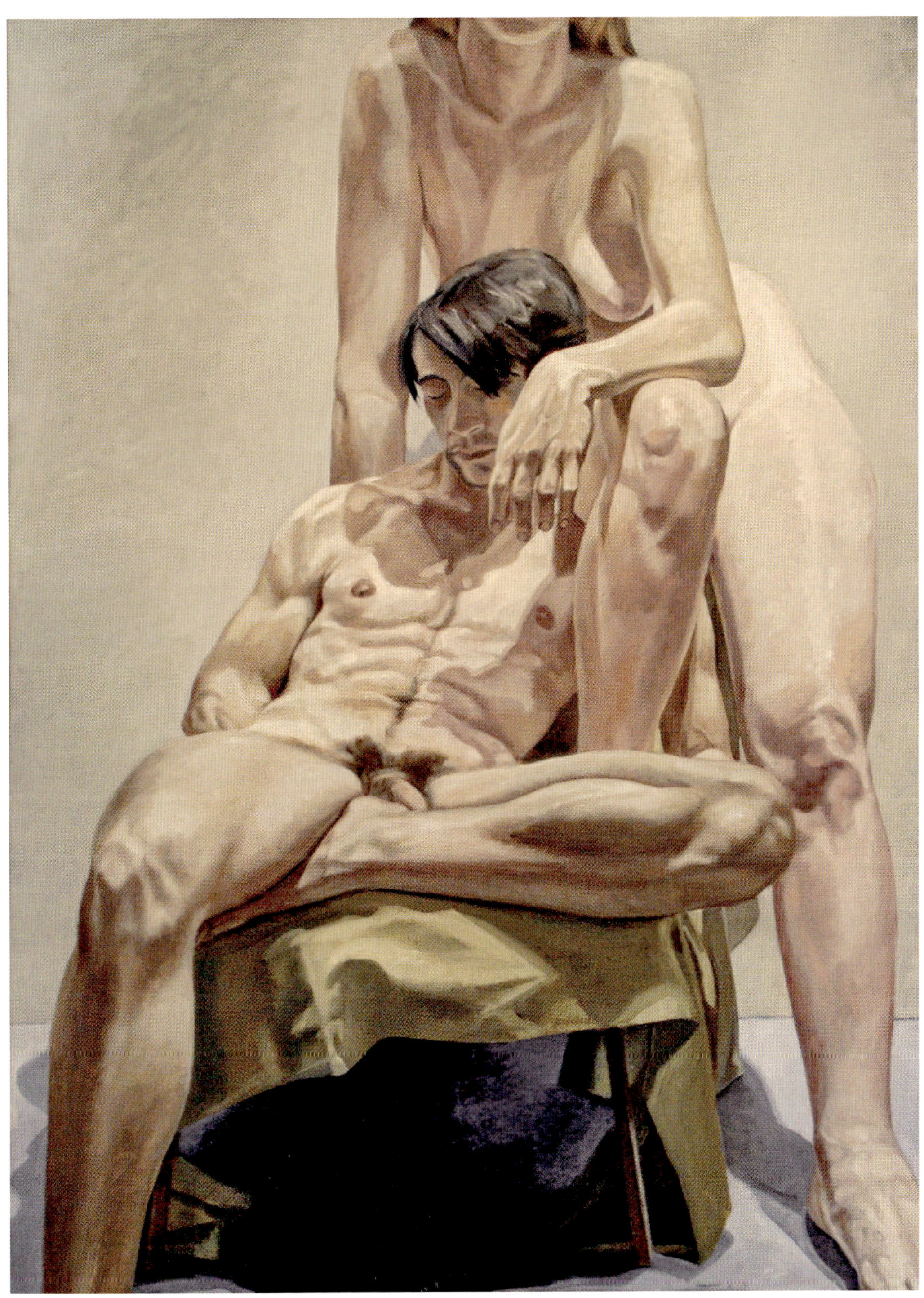

Philip Pearlstein
Models in the Studio, 1965

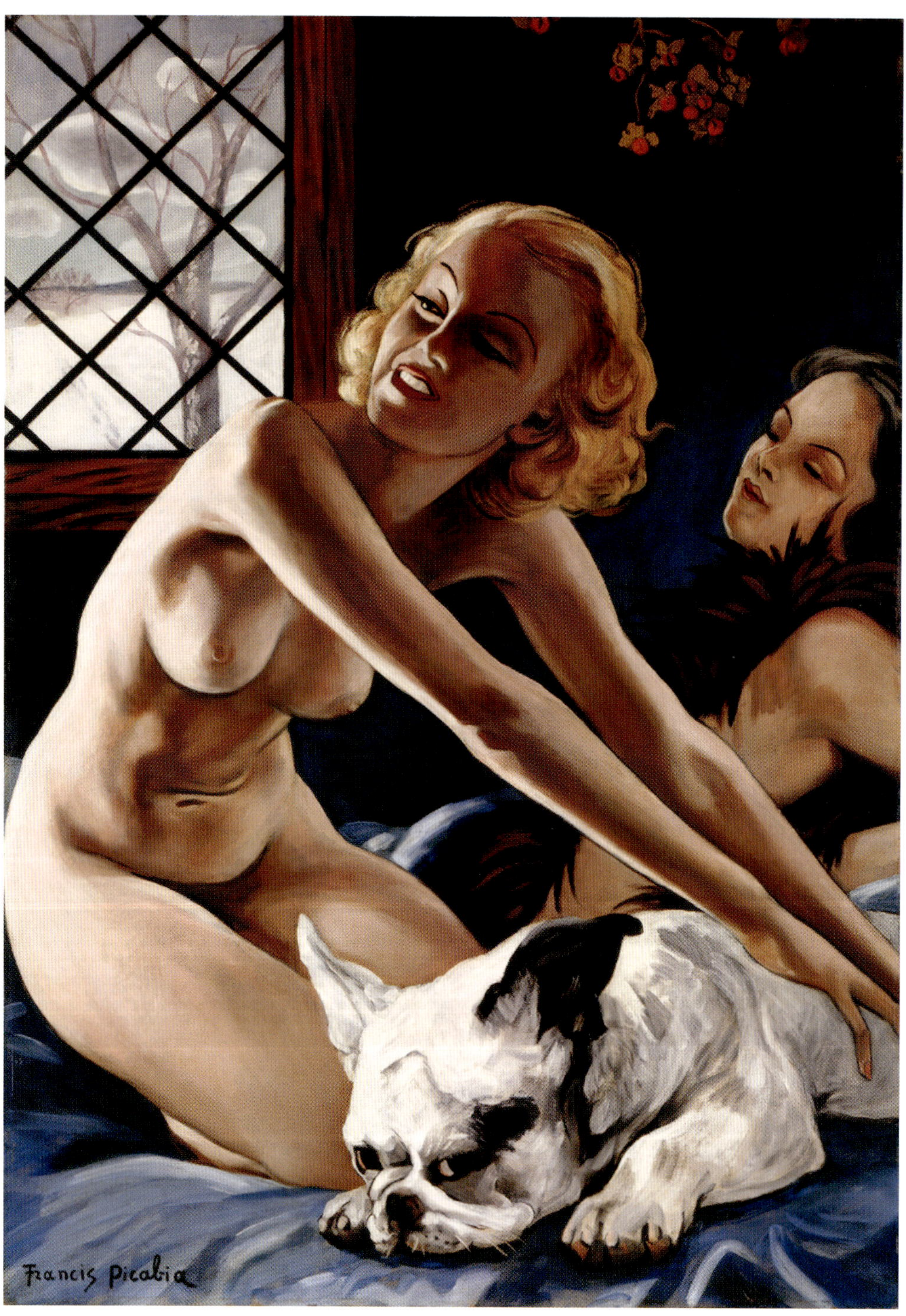

Francis Picabia
Femmes au bull-dog (Women with Bulldog), *c.*1941

the history of early twentieth-century poetry as in painting, co-editing the poetry magazine *The Little Review* with Ezra Pound. In her *Autobiography of Alice B. Toklas*, Gertrude Stein named her friend Picabia the greatest of modern painters.

Picabia was born in Paris in 1879. His father was Spanish, his mother French. His family was wealthy and he lived the life of a playboy until the 1930s. His last years were spent in ill health, comparative seclusion, and poverty. He died in Paris on November 30, 1953. Perhaps because of his wealth, he apparently never felt the need to build a professional career as an artist, indulging in any artistic deviation he dreamed up, as obscure and oblique in symbolism as he wished. Many of his works are private jokes, to be understood only by his circle of friends. He could afford to live, he said, "as a nomad, to traverse ideas as one does countries." He summarized his attitude in the title of his 1949 retrospective show in Paris, *50 ans de plaisirs* (50 Years of Pleasures), and in his statement in the catalogue, explaining that painting for him could be "what opium is to others." Until 1908 his paintings were Impressionistic, followed in 1909 by landscapes that approach abstraction. But then, also in 1909, he made a leap into his future, painting in watercolor *Caoutchouc* (p.45), which has historically been honored as the first abstract painting, but which I demoted when I decided that it has a bouncing rubber ball as its subject. It was his first work to embody characteristics identified with Cubism and Futurism. (I now feel that this painting may have originated as a spoof of early Cubism and Futurism.) And he now became increasingly concerned with abstraction (though the word "abstraction" was not yet in use in 1909). Gabrielle Buffet-Picabia, his wife until their divorce in 1919, wrote that when they first met in 1908, he spoke "of revolutionary trans formations in pictorial vision... a painting endowed with a life of its own, exploiting the visual field solely for the sake of an arbitrary and poetic organization of forms and colors...."

By 1911 Picabia was a member of the Cubist group and had found an intellectual playmate: Marcel Duchamp. As the two artists exchanged ideas and paralleled one another in their paintings, I found it necessary to consider Duchamp's concerns with motion, simultaneity, and machine imagery and symbolism alongside Picabia's.

Picabia arrived first at many of these ideas in the 1909 *Caoutchouc*, which displays movement, transparency, and abstraction. In 1911 Duchamp painted *Moulin à Café* (Coffee Mill), which became the prototype of both his and Picabia's drawings and paintings of machines. I found it odd that Duchamp never spoke of Picabia as an influence, but later named Raymond Roussel, a philosopher, metaphysician, and poet, as among his main influences. Duchamp said that "as a painter it was much better to be influenced by a writer than by another painter and Roussel showed me the way."[1] Duchamp's culminating work of painted glass panels, *The Bride Stripped Bare by Her Bachelors, Even (The Large Glass)* (p.55), was thematically based on a play by Roussel.

In 1912 Picabia became friendly with the poet Guillaume Apollinaire, who, as an art critic, became chief spokesman for the Cubist painters. During the following year, a three-way exchange of ideas about painting and society among Picabia, Duchamp, and Apollinaire led to Picabia's attitudes and subject matter for the next decade.

In 1913, this exchange of ideas led Apollinaire to set up a second main branch of Cubism in his discussions of the Cubist aesthetics. The first main branch, "Scientific Cubism," was concerned primarily with the analysis of real objects. He called the new branch "Orphic Cubism," and defined it as an art of the mind; the forms the artist paints are of his own invention, unrelated to forms in nature. The artist is concerned with the meaning conveyed by the subject matter. As Apollinaire wrote: "Works by Orphic artists must offer simultaneously pure aesthetic pleasure, a clearly perceptible construction, and a meaning, the subject, which is sublime."[2] The idea of publishing a book came about one evening when, according to Gabrielle Buffet-Picabia:

> Picabia, always eager for arguments, action, and planning campaigns, conceived the necessity of a publication in which Apollinaire would analyze in detail the present state of the New Painting... Picabia would pay the cost of publication, and Apollinaire would bring together essays which he had already published, and would add a study of each artist with reproductions.... The project ran into much bickering and opposition.... Apollinaire made a very good best of a bad job.

The book, Apollinaire's *The Cubist Painters*, remains the basic text of the Cubist movement.

In January 1913, Picabia was the only major European artist to come to New York to attend the Armory Show, which introduced the work of so many modern artists to America. In New York, Picabia immediately became part of the circle around Alfred Stieglitz, the photographer, publisher, and gallery owner who pioneered presenting modern art to the American public. During his stay in New York, Picabia gave a series of interviews to the press expressing his aesthetic philosophy. He also made a series of

1 From an interview with James Johnson Sweeney in *The Bulletin of the Museum of Modern Art*, 1946.

2 From Guillaume Apollinaire, *The Cubist Painters*, 1913. Also discussed in "The Symbolic Language of Francis Picabia" (p.26).

abstract watercolor paintings conveying his excitement about New York City that were given an exhibition at the Stieglitz Gallery.[3]

The importance of Picabia's influence on the definition of modern art in the United States is exemplified by my memory of a song from a 1930s movie: "We don't paint the whistle, but the (sound of a whistle)." It was a simplistic presentation of the ideas Picabia expressed in the newspaper interviews given during the exhibition.[4]

Later I became acquainted with some of Picabia's watercolor paintings of New York that Stieglitz exhibited when I spoke to the groundbreaking art dealer Leo Castelli about Picabia shortly after my article appeared in 1956. He offered to show me some of those paintings (the ones that were in his collection), and he gave me black and white photographs of several of them. Of the watercolor paintings exhibited, *Chanson nègre* (p.28) was the one that most successfully demonstrated to the reviewer the capacity of his psychic perception to invent the proper symbols.

Radical as they may have seemed in 1913 to his American audience, Picabia's idea of the direct expressiveness of the aesthetic elements was commonly accepted in nineteenth-century France, and was elaborated in Baudelaire's poem "Correspondances." Though attempts to establish a scientific basis for the theory were never successful, the Symbolist poets and painters accepted it as fact. In "Correspondances," Baudelaire wrote that "scents, colors and sounds answer to one another." Picabia's statement that "We must devote ourselves to setting down on our canvas not things, but emotions produced in our minds by things" has its parallel in Mallarmé's maxim that the artist must "paint not the thing itself but the effect it produces."[5]

In a 1913 interview, Picabia seems to speak directly to the painter that I have become, painting only what my eyes see. He said: "Art, art, what is art? Is it copying faithfully a person's face? A landscape? No, that is machinery. Painting nature as she is, is not art, it is mechanical genius."[6] My paintings of nude figures are painted from the people posing in front of me, and my primary concern is the faithful depiction of the forms in that particular pose and the space and light of my studio. In contrast with my paintings from direct observation, Picabia's late paintings are from reproductions of photographs and paintings that he chose for their subject of naked figures. They are an extension of the readymades of the Dada years, as is Duchamp's figure in the Philadelphia installation

3 For further discussion of Picabia's arrival and influence on modern art in America at the time of the 1913 Armory Show, see "Hello and Goodbye, Francis Picabia" (pp.43–4).

4 Also discussed in "Hello and Goodbye, Francis Picabia" (p.43).

5 See also "The Symbolic Language of Francis Picabia" (p.30).

6 For an extended quotation from Picabia's interview, see also "Hello and Goodbye, Francis Picabia" (p.46).

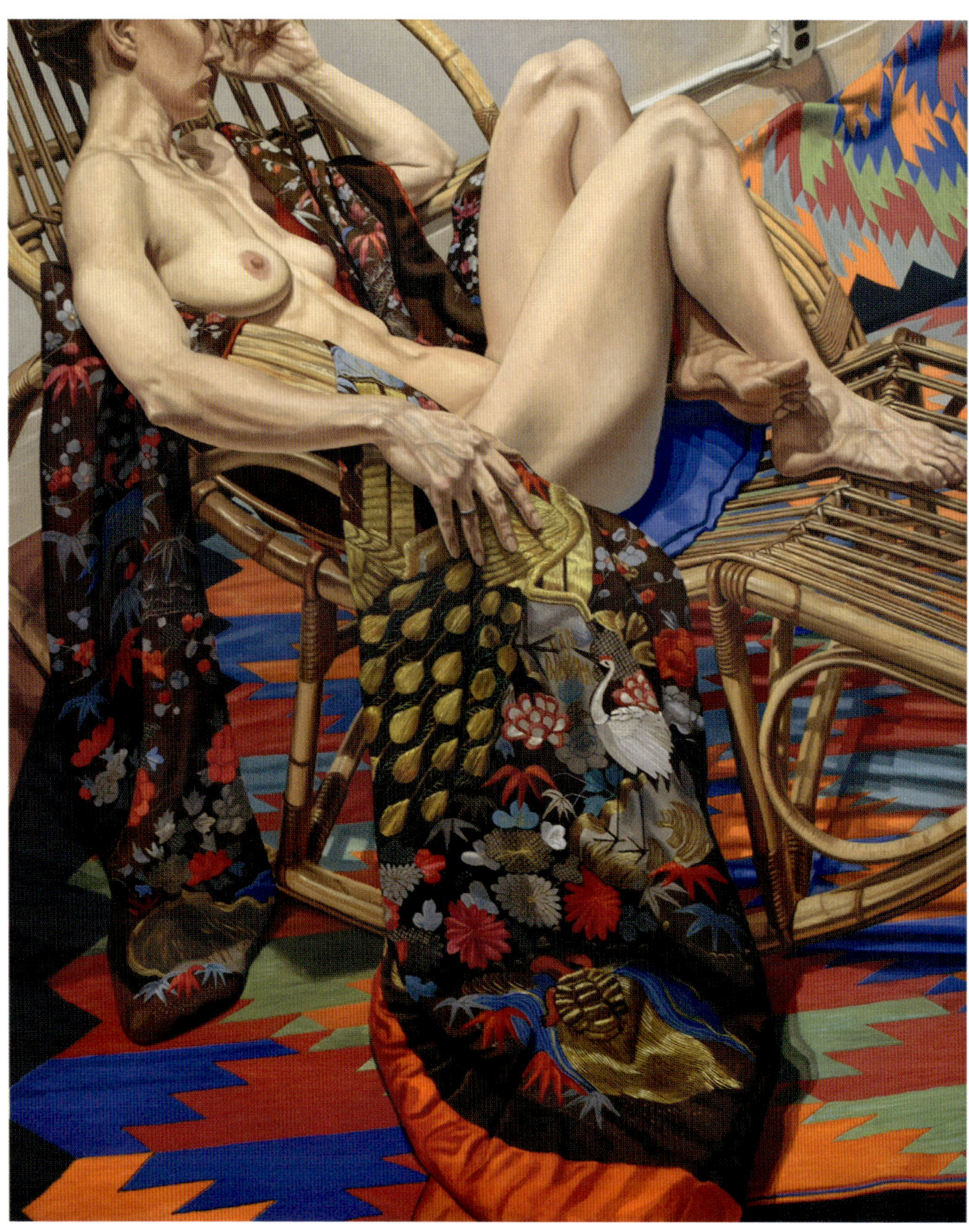

Philip Pearlstein
Nude with Peacock Kimono, 1988

(which was probably assembled from parts cast from life, as is evidenced by his sculptures that are cast impressions of small sections of the model's body, usually of areas where deep creases occur).

The paintings Picabia created in the first half of 1913 are characterized by the sharp contours of the abstract shapes that compose them. These shapes may be seen as his response to the twentieth-century "machine aesthetic." However, he did not actually depict machine forms until after his return to Paris. (As noted, Duchamp did the first painting of a specific machine in 1910, *Moulin à Café*, which diagrams the mechanical workings of a coffee grinder.) It is then, in late 1913, that a shift in Picabia's subject matter also occurred. Until then his subjects had derived from such ordinary experiences as going to a nightclub. For most of the next decade, he drew his subject matter from his attitude towards society at large, developing with Duchamp and Apollinaire what would be defined later by the word Dada: the observation of the futility and contradictions inherent in all aspects of human endeavor resulting from industrialization, along with a condemnation of what were felt to be the false values held by bourgeois society, including the values of "high art" – usually expressed with great wit, but with no political agenda involved.

This exchange of ideas between Picabia, Duchamp and Apollinaire, in which they tried to outdo one another in their blasphemes, was described by Gabrielle Buffet-Picabia as "forays of demoralization, witticism and clowning. Better than by any rational method, they pursued the disintegration of the concept of art, substituting a personal dynamism, individual forces of suggestion and projections, for the codified values of formal beauty.... this climate of invention contained all the germs of what later became Dada."

Picabia and Duchamp saw that machines and machine parts could resemble parts of the human body, as well as serve as a visual symbol of modern society, and created images of machine parts caricaturing human relationships and attitudes. Picabia's drawing *Fille née sans mère* (p.33) was his first depiction of the machine as "woman." Drawn on the back of a New York hotel dining room menu, it became the compositional basis of the large-scale painting *Je revois en souvenir ma chère Udnie* (which I translated as "I See My Dear Udnie Again in Memory"), his earliest work to function this way. In this painting I saw the machine elements as analogous to sexual organs. Duchamp's first painting to depict machine as woman was *La passage de la vierge a la mariée* (The Virgin Becomes the Bride).[7]

Picabia's public participation in Dada activities began during his second trip to New York, after his induction into the French army. According to Gabrielle Buffet-Picabia, Picabia served as a general's chauffeur until

7 See also "The Symbolic Language of Francis Picabia" (pp.32–5).

an influential friend arranged an important mission for him to Cuba. He was to go by way of New York, and sailed with Gabrielle in April 1915. Meeting Marcel Duchamp and a group of old friends in New York, he forgot his mission and stayed. As a soldier in the French army, this long stay should have meant trouble, but he fell seriously ill (due to alcoholism). He got a series of medical leaves of absence that carried him to the end of the war. Gabrielle wrote of their New York years: “No sooner had we arrived than we became part of a motley international band that turned night into day, conscientious objectors of all nationalities and walks of life living in an inconceivable orgy of sexuality, jazz and alcohol.... a group of artists, mostly European, whose leading lights were Duchamp and Picabia, gathered in the gallery of Alfred Stieglitz... or at the home of Walter and Lou Arensberg.”

Sometime in 1952 I visited Walter Arensberg in his home in Hollywood, California. We had tea and cookies, surrounded by the crates that contained his collection, which were soon to leave for the Philadelphia Museum of Art. He told me that early on, Picabia and Duchamp were extreme alcoholics, and that in the early 1920s Picabia's doctor told him that his badly damaged liver was about to kill him. Picabia and Duchamp both stopped drinking, and with that, in Arensberg's opinion, their creative genius left them.[8]

The paintings and drawings Picabia began in 1915 in New York are of mechanical forms executed with objective precision, with words and phrases lettered on their surfaces. He participated in illustrating, writing and editing Stieglitz's newly founded magazine, *291* (the street number on Fifth Avenue of the Stieglitz Gallery), which embodied the Dada spirit, though the word Dada had not yet been coined. It was invented the following year, 1916, by a group of artists and poets in Zurich who shared the spirit and aims of the group in New York, but who were unknown to them.

In January of 1917, Gabrielle and Picabia left New York for Barcelona, where they met another group of artists who were also refugees of the war. In Barcelona, Picabia began to publish *391*, as a sequel to *291*. The cover of the March 1920 issue carried one of the most famous of all Dada works, the reproduction of the *Mona Lisa* on which Duchamp had drawn a moustache (p.31). Duchamp later said of this reproduction that it is a copy by Picabia of his original, which wasn't available, and that the letters of its title, *L.H.O.O.Q.*, make an obscene pun when pronounced in French.[9]

In 1918 Picabia went to Switzerland for medical treatment, and while there he published *Poèmes et dessins de la fille née sans mère* and other books of poetry. These books brought him to the attention of the Zurich Dadaists. This Zurich group had made the Cabaret Voltaire their headquarters. They originally organized to be a focal point of avant-garde art, but

8 Pearlstein discusses his visit to Arensberg in more detail in “Hello and Goodbye, Francis Picabia” (p.52).

9 See also “The Symbolic Language of Francis Picabia” (pp.30–2).

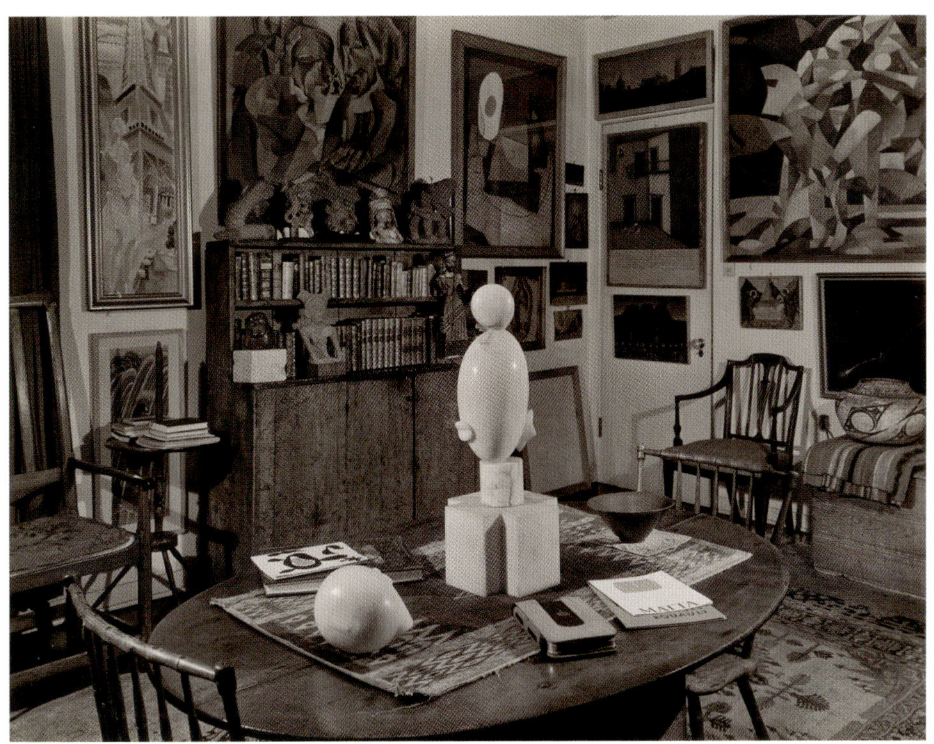

Walter Arensberg's museum house in Hollywood, *c.*1951. Picabia's *Danses à la source* is pictured top right. Photo by Floyd Faxon.

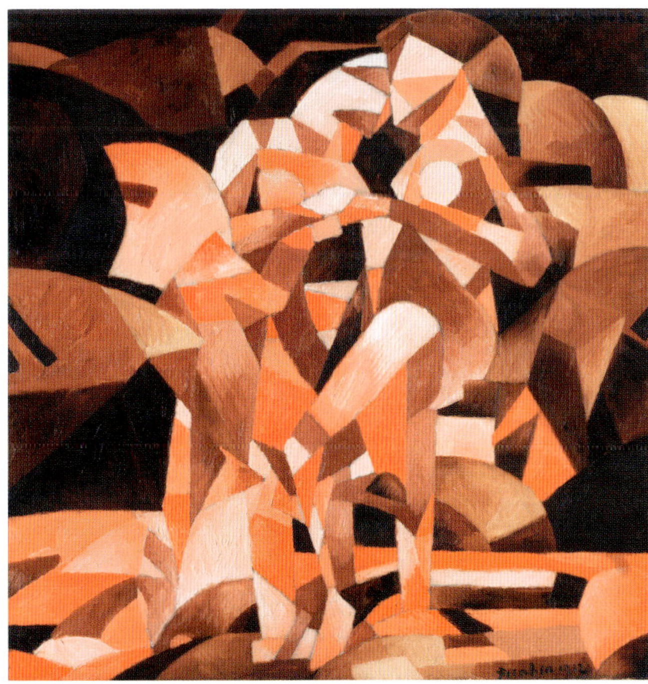

Francis Picabia
Danses à la source
(Dances at the Spring), 1912

soon the expression of the senselessness of the war and their hostility towards and ridicule of society dominated their activity.

Many of the techniques used by the Dadaists had their roots in the work of nineteenth-century writers and poets who experimented with automatism – in which the subconscious dictates the flow of words – and played with the surprise of chance juxtapositions, allowing the sounds of words to dictate their use, inventing words when necessary. The Dadaists transposed these literary principles to their graphic work. As I was working in the field of graphic design at the time, I admired Picabia's inventiveness with typography and page layout in publications. But Picabia had probably found a prototype in Mallarmé's poem *Un coup de dés* (A Roll of the Dice), which was printed with varied typefaces, sizes, and spacings, guiding the reader to place aural emphasis on different words.

It occurred to me, as I translated the poems and calligrams that illustrate *Poémes et dessins de la fille née sans mère*, that Picabia and Duchamp had each created the story of a young woman. Duchamp's story line goes through the 1912 *Bride* and *The Virgin Becomes the Bride*, to the large painting on glass, *The Bride Stripped Bare by Her Bachelors, Even* (p.55) of the 1920s.

Picabia's *fille née sans mère* travelled to America and has her portrait painted in 1913 as *une jeune fille américaine*. Then she is presented again as a graphic in the *Portrait d'une jeune fille américaine dans l'état de nudité* (p.36), in which Picabia peeks at her as a spark plug. Gabrielle Buffet-Picabia wrote that the spark plug is a "kindler of flame." The spark plug is hopefully labeled, "for-ever." I relate the *nudité* in the title of this image to "Udnie" of the earlier paintings, a pig-Latin version of the word "nudie." And in this pig-Latin sense, it is a predecessor to the paintings of nudes that Picabia did in the 1940s. Back in 1917, Udnie finds love in *Parade amoureuse* (p.51), and has a child, *L'Enfant carburateur*. Then in 1918, Picabia published the book *Poèmes et dessins de la fille née sans mère*. Until now, the machine had been viewed by man; this book was her opportunity to view man.[10]

While Duchamp had begun his epic with various studies that led to a culminating monumental work, Picabia started with several monumental paintings, then scaled down to small paintings and graphic illustrations. As seen before, a number of Picabia's paintings and graphic works are similar in nature to Duchamp's readymades. The anti-social implications of the readymades lie chiefly in the joke against traditional artistic means of expression, as well as in the choice of objects which insult bourgeois taste, as in Duchamp's urinal. Picabia's readymades are usually drawings of photographs copied or cut out from catalogues and advertisements.

10 Also discussed in "The Symbolic Language of Francis Picabia" (pp.35–7).

The *Portrait d'une jeune fille américaine dans l'état de nudité* (the spark plug) is an example. A more sensational readymade by Picabia is the 1920 stuffed monkey pulling at his tail, which is sticking out from between his legs. It is titled *Natures Mortes: Portrait de Cézanne, Portrait de Rembrandt, Portrait de Renoir* (p.36). It blasphemes the values of "high art," while an ink blot entitled *La Sainte Vierge* (p.36) blasphemes against religious sentiment.[11] That these works of Picabia and Duchamp were meant to be private jokes – and thus bound to remain "unread" by the multitudes whose values and morals it ridiculed – did not disturb them. I now see a great irony in the fact that Picabia and Duchamp's antisocial gestures led 50 years later to the Pop art movement: the most accessible, democratic, and commercially successful art movement of the twentieth century.

In 1919, after the end of World War I, the Dadaists centered their activities in Paris, where their demonstrations attracted large audiences. At one demonstration Picabia shouted:

> What are you doing here, plunked down like serious oysters – because you are serious, aren't you? The ass, the ass represents life like fried potatoes, and all you serious people smell worse that cow flop. Dada smells of nothing, it is nothing, nothing, nothing. Whistle, shout, bash my face in, and then what? Then what? I'll just go on telling you that you are all fools.

For Picabia, Dada had become a successful art movement, and thus had outlasted its purpose of negation. He then announced his withdrawal from the movement in a series of articles insulting his former friends. For a while he worked with André Breton, who was then formulating Surrealism, on the magazine *Littérature*. But he really did not share Breton's enthusiasm for Surrealism, and after they published the *First Surrealist Manifesto*, he published several issues of *391* attacking Surrealism. He did some paintings, such as *Dresseur d'animaux* (Animal Trainer) and *La Nuit espagnole* (The Spanish Night), that are ambiguous in meaning but probably reflect his take on Surrealism. I think they are among his strongest works.

The paintings Picabia created during the following decades until the outbreak of World War II continue to vary in style, but evoke no concern with social problems. The most interesting works are those he called "Transparencies." In these, separate images are superimposed, reflecting what was a dominant concern among twentieth-century artists: depicting simultaneous events. The symbolism is obscure, but many of the faces and nude figures are copied from Italian Renaissance paintings, offering a field day for future art historians. They also send up a signal, which I did

11 See also "The Symbolic Language of Francis Picabia" (p.37).

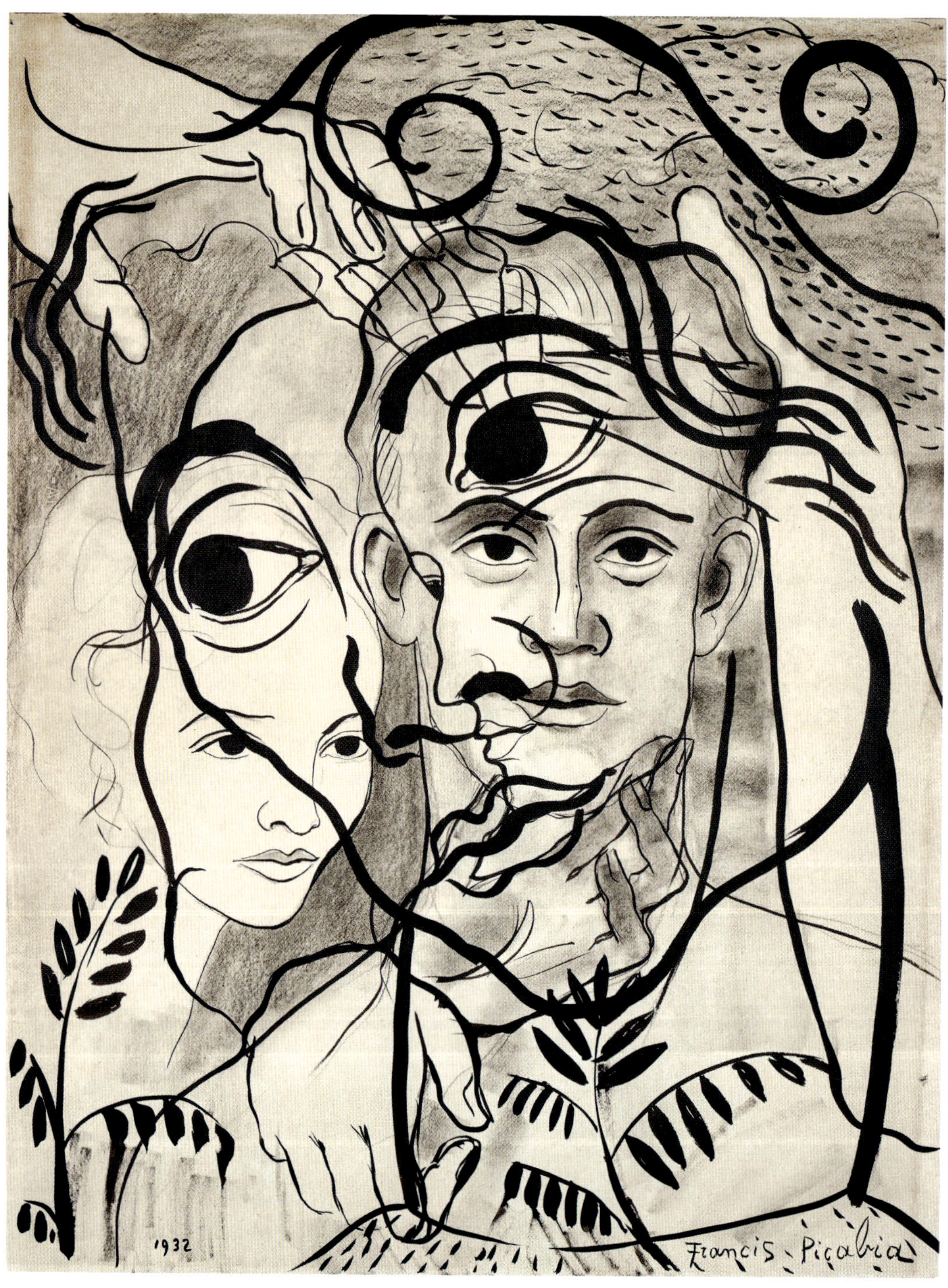

Francis Picabia
Untitled, 1932

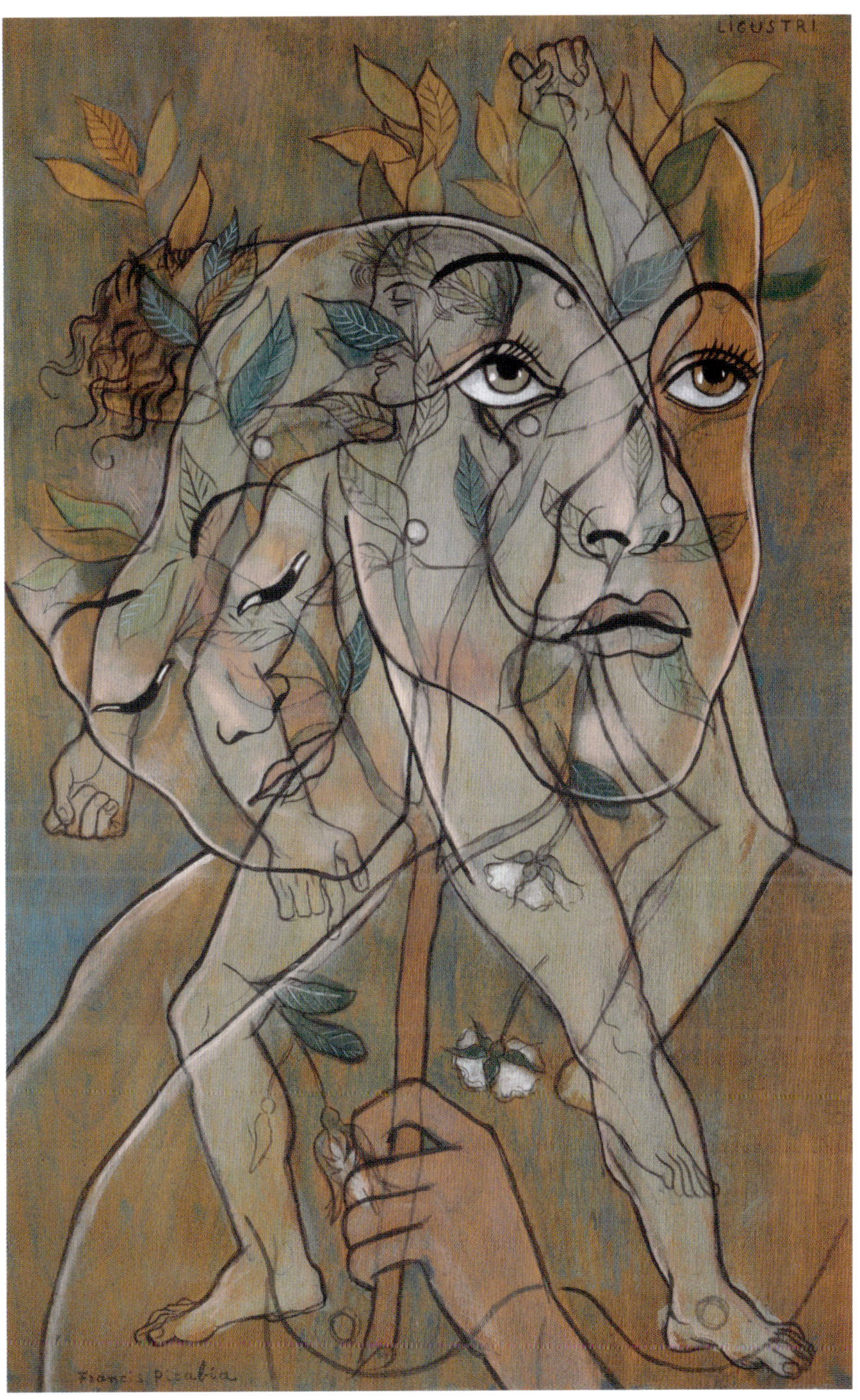

Francis Picabia
Ligustri, *c.*1929

not receive back in 1955, that eventually Picabia would paint images of female nudes.

During the years of World War II, Picabia is reported to have painted realistic, Expressionistic scenes of the horrors of war. These have not yet surfaced, though there is one of a monster's Minotaur-like head (perhaps it is a realist version of Picasso's Minotaur) with the saluting hands of an adoring crowd that may be a reference to that era's destructive dictators.

The first exhibition I saw of Picabia's work was at the Rose Fried Gallery in New York in early 1950. It was mostly made up of small paintings with solid-colored surfaces on which brightly colored dots are scattered, while at one end of the small gallery was the very large painting *Edtaonisl (ecclésiastique)* (p.56), which is now in the Art Institute of Chicago. That painting was too tall for the height of the room and was leaning forward. I remember how puzzled I was by the contrast of the recent small dot paintings with the monumental, complex painting of 40 years earlier. Eventually I decided that the answer lies in Picabia's pronouncement that "our heads are round so our thoughts can change direction."[12]

In 1970, at the time of the Picabia retrospective exhibition at the Guggenheim Museum in New York, I wrote an article for *ARTnews* magazine called "Hello and Goodbye, Francis Picabia" (p.40). Now I must say "hello again," but to a new persona that had been hidden from me. Now I must regard him as my fellow realist painter, and even to wonder whether I had unwittingly anticipated his last stylistic turn, based on my subliminal memories of putting together the ideas of the thesis.

By the way: my dinner companion in Paris did not add one of my paintings to her collection.

12 Also discussed in "The Symbolic Language of Francis Picabia" (p.38).

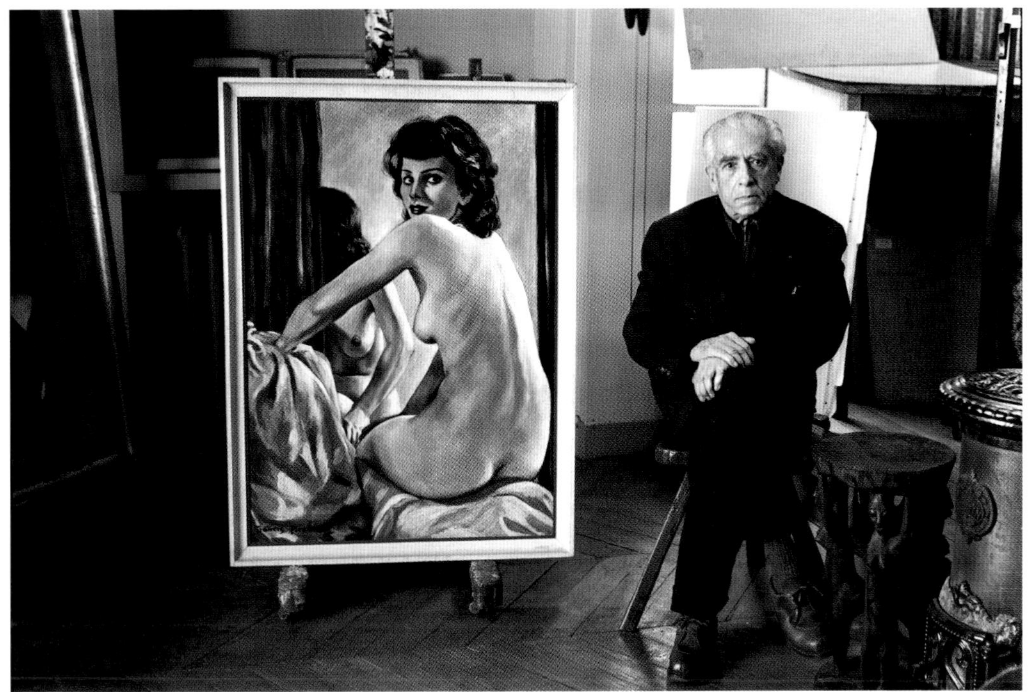

Francis Picabia in his studio, 1950. Photo by Michel Sima

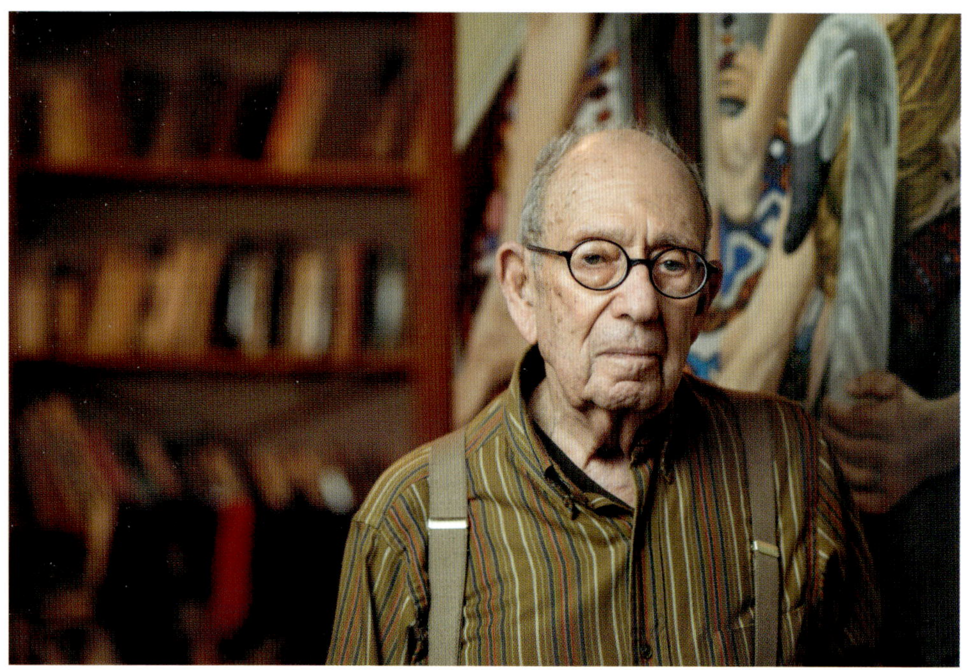

Philip Pearlstein, 2016
Photo by Taylor Dafoe

Biography

Philip Pearlstein (b.1924 in Pittsburgh) was an artist, professor, and art historian. He received his Bachelor of Fine Arts degree from the Carnegie Institute of Technology in 1949, and his Master of Arts degree from New York University's Institute of Fine Arts in 1955, where he completed his thesis on Francis Picabia. His work is included in over 150 public collections and has been recognized in many exhibitions throughout his career.

Pearlstein was a frequent contributor to major art journals and a dedicated teacher. He was an instructor at Pratt Institute, Brooklyn, 1959–63 and Visiting Critic at Yale University, New Haven, 1962–3. Pearlstein joined the faculty at Brooklyn College, New York, in 1963, he was appointed Distinguished Professor in 1977, and retired in 1988. He was elected to the American Academy of Arts and Letters in 1982 and was appointed to serve as its president from 2003–6.

He has received numerous notable awards and honours, including the Fulbright–Hays Fellowship in Italy, 1956–9; National Endowment for the Arts Fellowship, 1968; John Simon Guggenheim Memorial Foundation Fellowship, 1971; Artist of the Year, American Friends of the Tel Aviv Museum of Art, New York, 2010.

Philip Pearlstein died in New York on December 17, 2022.
He continued to paint until the end of his life.

Image Credits

Every effort has been made to contact all copyright holders. The publishers will be pleased to amend in future printings any errors or omissions brought to their attention.

6: © George Grantham Bain Collection. Courtesy Library of Congress, Washington.
8: Philip Pearlstein. *Torso*, 1953. Oil on canvas, 91.4 × 76.2 cm (36 × 30 in.) © Philip Pearlstein.
11: top and bottom: Courtesy Archives of American Art, Smithsonian Institution, Washington.
13: Philip Pearlstein. *Superman*, 1952. Oil on canvas, 102.9 × 91.4 cm (40 ½ × 36 in.) © Philip Pearlstein. Collection of the Museum of Modern Art, New York.
14: Philip Pearlstein. *Two Female Nudes and Mickey Mouse*, 2001. Oil on canvas, 152.4 × 152.4 cm (60 × 60 in.) © Philip Pearlstein. Collection of Artist.
16–17: Photo © Jason Schmidt.
22: © George Grantham Bain Collection. Courtesy Library of Congress, Washington.
24: Courtesy Library of Congress, Washington.
27: top: Francis Picabia. *Bords de la Sédelle*, 1909. Oil on canvas, 69 × 88.3 cm (27 3⁄16 × 34 ¾ in.) © ADAGP, Paris and DACS, London 2023. Centre Pompidou, Paris/RMN-Grand Palais/Photographer: Georges Meguerditchian/Dist. Photo Scala, Florence; bottom: Francis Picabia. *Paysage à Cassis*, *c.*1909–10. Oil on canvas, 50.3 × 61.5 cm (19 13⁄16 × 24 3⁄16 in.) © ADAGP, Paris and DACS, London 2023. Private collection.
28: top: Francis Picabia. *Procession à Séville*, 1912. Oil on canvas, 121.9 × 121.9 cm (48 × 48 in.) © ADAGP, Paris and DACS, London 2023. Courtesy National Gallery of Art, Washington; bottom: Francis Picabia. *Chanson nègre* (I), 1913. Watercolor and pencil on illustration board, 66.3 × 55.9 cm (26 ⅛ × 22 in.) © ADAGP, Paris and DACS, London 2023. Alfred Stieglitz Collection, 1949. The Metropolitan Museum of Art, New York/Dist. Photo Scala, Florence.
31: © ADAGP, Paris and DACS, London 2023. Courtesy Bibliothèque Nationale de France.
33: top: Francis Picabia. *Je revois en souvenir ma chère Udnie*, 1914. Oil on canvas, 250.2 × 198.8 cm (98 ½ × 78 5⁄16 in.) © ADAGP, Paris and DACS, London 2023. Hillman Periodicals Fund. Digital image © 2023, The Museum of Modern Art, New York/Scala, Florence; bottom: Francis Picabia. *Fille née sans mère*, *c.*1914–15. Ink on paper, 26.7 × 21.6 cm (10 ½ × 8 ½ in.) © ADAGP, Paris and DACS, London 2023. Alfred Stieglitz Collection, 1949. The Metropolitan Museum of Art, New York/Dist. Photo Scala, Florence.
34: Francis Picabia. *Udnie (Jeune fille américaine; danse)*, 1913. Oil on canvas, 290 × 300 cm (114 3⁄16 × 118 ⅛ in.) © ADAGP, Paris and DACS, London 2023. Centre Pompidou, Paris/RMN-Grand Palais/Photographer: Georges Meguerditchian/Dist. Photo Scala, Florence.
36: top left: Francis Picabia. *Portrait d'une jeune fille américaine dans l'état de nudité*, 1915 © ADAGP, Paris and DACS, London 2023. Musée d'Orsay, Paris/RMN-Grand Palais/Photographer: Patrice Schmidt/Dist. Photo Scala, Florence; top right: © ADAGP, Paris and DACS, London 2023. Collection unknown; bottom: Francis Picabia. *La Sainte Vierge*, 1920. Lithograph, 55.5 × 37.4 cm (21 ⅞ × 14 ¾ in.) © ADAGP, Paris and DACS, London 2023. Courtesy Yale University Art Gallery. Gift of the Estate of Katherine S. Dreier.
40: Photo © Eliot Elisofon/The LIFE Picture Collection/Shutterstock.
42: top: Francis Picabia. *New York*, 1913. Gouache, watercolor, and pencil on paper, 55.8 × 75.9 cm (22 × 29 ⅞ in.) © ADAGP, Paris and DACS, London 2023. The Joan and Lester Avnet Collection. Digital image © 2023, The Museum of Modern Art, New York/Scala, Florence; bottom: Francis Picabia. *New York*, 1913. Gouache, watercolor, and pencil on paper, 54.5 × 74.7 cm (21 7⁄16 × 29 7⁄16 in.) © ADAGP, Paris and DACS, London 2023. Centre Pompidou, Paris/RMN-Grand Palais/Photographer: Philippe Migeat/Dist. Photo Scala, Florence.
45: Francis Picabia. *Caoutchouc*, 1909. Watercolor, gouache, and India ink on cardboard, 45.7 × 61.5 cm (18 × 24 3⁄16 in.) © ADAGP, Paris and DACS, London 2023. Centre Pompidou, Paris/RMN-Grand Palais/Photographer: Georges Meguerditchian/Dist. Photo Scala, Florence.
48: top: Marcel Duchamp. *Nude Descending a Staircase (No. II)*, 1912. Oil on canvas, 147 × 89.2 cm (57 ⅞ × 35 ⅛ in.) © Association Marcel Duchamp/ADAGP, Paris and DACS, London 2023. The Louise and Walter Arensberg Collection, 1950. Photo The Philadelphia Museum of Art/Art Resource, New York/Scala, Florence; bottom: Courtesy National Gallery of Art, Washington.
51: top: Philip Pearlstein. *Death and the Maiden (Shower Attacking Woman)*, 1950. Casein tempera on Masonite, 76.2 × 61 cm (30 × 24 in.). Collection of Artist; bottom: Francis Picabia. *Parade amoureuse*, 1917. Oil on cardboard, 38 × 29 cm (15 × 11 ⅖ in.) © ADAGP, Paris and DACS, London 2023. Photo: Tom Powel Imaging. Morton Neumann Family Collection.
53: top and bottom: © Centre Pompidou, Paris/RMN-Grand Palais/Photographer: Georges Meguerditchian/Dist. Photo Scala, Florence.
55: Marcel Duchamp. *The Bride Stripped Bare by her Bachelors, Even (The Large Glass)*, 1915–23. Oil, varnish, lead foil, lead wire, and dust on two glass panels, 277.5 × 177.8 × 8.6 cm (109 ¼ × 70 × 3 ⅜ in.) © Association Marcel Duchamp/ADAGP, Paris and DACS, London 2023. Bequest of Katherine S. Dreier, 1952. Photo The Philadelphia Museum of Art/Art Resource, New York/Scala, Florence.
56: Francis Picabia. *Edtaonisl (ecclésiastique)*, 1913. Oil on canvas, 300.4 × 300.7 cm (118 ¾ × 118 ¼ in.) © ADAGP, Paris and DACS, London 2023. Gift of Mr. and Mrs. Armand Bartos. Courtesy The Art Institute of Chicago/Art Resource, New York/Scala, Florence.
58: © Estate Germaine Krull, Museum Folkwang, Essen. Collection unknown.
60: Francis Picabia. *Femme au châle vert*, *c.*1940–1. Oil on cardboard, 105.7 × 75.7 cm (41 ⅝ × 29 ¾ in.) © ADAGP, Paris and DACS, London 2023. Private Collection. Courtesy of Hauser & Wirth Collection Services. Photo credit: Stefan Altenburger Photography Zürich.
64: top: Philip Pearlstein. *Model with Dreadlocks, Wooden Alligator and Pink Flamingo*, 2005. Oil on canvas, 76.2 × 101.6 cm (30 × 40 in.). Private Collection, Ardmore, P.A.; bottom: Philip Pearlstein. *Crouching Female Nude with Mirror*, 1971. Oil on canvas, 152.4 × 121.9 cm (60 × 48 in.). Private Collection, Charlottesville, V.A.
65: Philip Pearlstein. *Models in the Studio*, 1965. Oil on canvas, 182.8 × 134.6 cm (72 × 53 in.). Collection of the Center for Figurative Painting, New York.
66: Francis Picabia. *Femmes au bull-dog*, *c.*1941. Oil on board, 106 × 76 cm (41 ¾ × 29 15⁄16 in.) © ADAGP, Paris and DACS, London 2023. Centre Pompidou, Paris/RMN-Grand Palais/Photographer: Jean-Claude Planchet/Dist. Photo Scala, Florence.
70: Philip Pearlstein. *Nude with Peacock Kimono*, 1988. Oil on canvas, 182.8 × 152.4 cm (72 × 60 in.). Private Collection, Chicago, I.L.
73: top: Photo by Floyd Faxon. Courtesy The Philadelphia Museum of Art, Library and Archives, Arensberg Archives; bottom: Francis Picabia. *Danses à la source*, 1912. Oil on canvas, 120.5 × 120.6 cm (47 7⁄16 × 47 ½ in.) © ADAGP, Paris and DACS, London 2023. The Louise and Walter Arensberg Collection, 1950. Photo The Philadelphia Museum of Art/Art Resource, New York/Scala, Florence.
76: top: Francis Picabia. *Untitled*, 1932. Ink and crayon on paper, 63.5 × 49.2 cm (25 × 19 ⅗ in.) © ADAGP, Paris and DACS, London 2023. Private collection. Photo Alamy.
77: Francis Picabia. *Ligustri*, *c.*1929. Oil, gouache, brush, and black ink over pencil on panel, 151.5 × 96.2 cm (59 ¾ × 37 ⅞ in.) © ADAGP, Paris and DACS, London 2023. Private collection. Photo Alamy.
79: Photo © Michel Sima/Bridgeman Images.
80: Photo © Taylor Dafoe.

THE PAINTINGS OF FRANCIS PICABIA, 1908 - 1930

by Philip Pearlstein

Submitted in partial fulfillment of the requirements for the degree of Master of Arts at New York University, Institute of Fine Arts, February, 1955

CONTENTS

PREFACE

One of the characteristics of much of the painting of the first three decades of the twentieth century is the continual, and often radical change in the superficial stylistic characteristics of successive works by the same artist. In the case of Picabia, though the paintings he produced in 1913 seem to differ from those of 1915, they share the same underlying concepts. The present paper is partly an investigation of these basic concepts in Picabia's work. It is also partly an investigation of the esoteric character of much of the work by Picabia and Marcel Duchamp, a quality their paintings share with many other twentieth century works of art which often confront the spectator with an image of startling uniqueness and strangeness, seemingly the product of a culture whose sole manifestation is this work of art.

The nature of the available material led me to concentrate on Picabia's paintings and aesthetic ideas of the year 1913, and to a consideration of the aims of the Cubist and Futurist painters up to that time. In the course of this investigation there developed the inevitable conflict between the aims of the painters involved, as stated by the artists themselves or by those who acted as their spokesmen, and the visual facts which greet the spectator's eye. I have attempted to circumvent this conflict by first comparing the pictorial aims held by the Cubist painters to those of the Futurists, and comparing Picabia's pictorial aims to both, then going on to consider the paintings themselves in the light of these comparisons.

The Cubist painters, Braque and Picasso, made no direct statements explaining their aims in the early development of Cubism, about 1908 -

1912. They did, however, have spokesmen or interpreters of their aims, among them Guillaume Apollinaire, whose book, The Cubist Painters, was published in 1913. Also in 1913, Albert Gleizes and Jean Metzinger, who were among those painters who adopted the Cubism of Picasso and Braque as a style, published their book, Cubism. I have made use of Christopher Gray's correlation and interpretation of this literature, and discussions of the nineteenth century philosophic, literary, and artistic background of Cubism, presented in his book, The Cubist Aesthetic Theories. In 1913 Picabia made a series of statements defining his own aims as a painter. These are presented in this paper in an organized manner, and placed in the context of the main body of Cubist "thought", for the first time. Picabia's paintings of 1913 clearly embody his stated aims. Daniel-Henry Kahnweiler's, The Rise of Cubism, an intelligent analysis of the aims of Picasso and Braque in the earlier stages of Cubism, was published in 1920. The statements quoted from Marcel Duchamp that relate to his own art of this time were made as late as 1945.

The Futurist painters were their own spokesmen. Their verbalizations of their pictorial aims, however, with few notable exceptions, exceeded their actual pictorial accomplishments. For translation into English of large segments of their most important statements, and for the correlation, clarification of meaning, and philosophical content of that material, I have been dependent on Rosa Trillo Clough's Looking Back on Futurism.

For their valuable guidance and criticisms of this project, I should like to express my gratitude to Dr. Jose Lopez-Rey, who was my advisor, Dr. H. W. Janson, and Dr. Harry Bober, of New York University, Institute of Fine Arts. Mr. Bernard Karpel, Librarian of the Museum of Modern Art, and his assistants were also very helpful, especially in placing at my disposal so many miscellaneous pamphlets, exhibition catalogs, and clippings from newspapers and magazines.

THE PERSONALITY, ATTITUDES AND CAREER OF FRANCIS PICABIA

Francis Picabia was born in Paris in 1879. His father's nationality was Spanish, his mother's French. The family was a very wealthy one, and Francis enjoyed and always loved the luxuries of life. He was gregarious, filled with a zest for living and robustly healthy until the last years of his life which were spent in ill health, comparative seclusion and poverty, though he still resided in the elegant Parisian house of his birth in which he had retained an apartment. He died in Paris in November 30, 1953.

Perhaps because of his wealth, Picabia never felt the need to build a professional career as a painter; thus he could indulge in any artistic deviation his active imagination could invent, without giving thought to the consequences. He never inhibited the expression of his distaste for the contemporary world, his taste for the irrational, his cynicism, or his sense of humor. He could be as obscure and oblique in symbolism as he wished. Many of his works are, in effect, private jokes, meant to be understood only by his circle of friends. He could play with art rather than work at making paintings. He could afford to live "as a nomad, to traverse ideas as one does countries." It was the intellectual activity that excited him rather than the act of painting per se; thus he could be just as happy writing poetry as painting, and just as happy sitting in a night-club as painting or writing. He summed up his attitude towards his art in the title he gave his large retrospective show in Paris in 1949: "50 ans de pleasirs," and in his statement in the catalog that painting for him could be "what opium is to others."

A brief survey of his career shows that Picabia traversed many ideas and styles in painting. Most of Picabia's paintings from 1895 until 1908 were academic Impressionistic works; a few figure studies were painted in a Fauve manner. In 1908 and 1909 Picabia made other landscape drawings and paintings, such as Paysage de Cassis (pl.2, fig.5), that depart in varying degrees from portraying the forms and colors of nature, and also in 1909, the water-color painting Caoutchouc (Rubber), (pl.1, fig.3), which has a bouncing rubber ball as its subject, and was his first work to embody characteristics identified with Cubism and Futurism. These works mark the first stage of his real concern with abstract painting.

Gabrielle Buffet-Picabia (Picabia's wife until their divorce in 1919) states that when she first met Picabia in 1908, he spoke to her "of revolutionary transformations in pictorial vision, and the hypothesis of a painting endowed with a life of its own, exploiting the visual field solely for the sake of an arbitrary and poetic organization of forms and colors, free from the contingent need to represent or transpose the forms of nature as we are accustomed to see them...some of the studies, which Picabia showed to no one, already achieved a total break with pictorial traditions, others were still based upon an objective scheme, which, to be sure, became less and less precise, but in whose structure one could still recognize the impressionistic suggestion of a landscape."[1]

It is curious, in view of this development in Picabia's interests, that he should have held an exhibition of impressionistic landscapes as late as March, 1909, at the Gallery of G. Petit in Paris, and that he should have shown his new studies to no one, for he never again appears so hesitant to be "avant-garde".

By 1911 Picabia was a member of the Cubist group and had become a close friend of Marcel Duchamp; and in considering Picabia's concern with motion and simultaneity, his visual treatment of the machine and his symbolism, it is also necessary to consider Marcel Duchamp's concern with them, for Picabia and Duchamp exchanged ideas and to an extent paralleled one another in their paintings. Picabia arrived first at certain of the ideas they came to share, as seen by Caoutchouc, 1909, in which movement, transparency, and abstraction are already present, while in 1910, the younger Duchamp had only evolved to a Cezanne-like style, as in his Artist's Father. However in 1911 Duchamp painted Moulin à café (Coffee-grinder) (pl.19, fig. 59), which was to become the prototype of both his own and Picabia's drawings and paintings of machines. There is no question of one painter following the other, for both were strong independent personalities, and their paintings are individual creations. Duchamp did, however, allow himself to be influenced by others at this period, and named as those who influence him most, Brisset, author of a philological analysis of language - an analysis worked out by means of a network of puns, and Roussel, a philogist, philosopher, metaphysician, poet and playwright. He admired them most for their "delirium of imagination." "I saw at once I could use Roussel as an influence. I felt that as a painter it was much better to be influenced by a writer than by another painter and Roussel showed me the way."[2]

In June, 1912, Picabia met and became the friend of Guillaume Apollinaire. During the year that followed, apparently influenced to an extent by an exchange of ideas with Duchamp and Apollinaire, the attitudes concerning society and painting that Picabia was to hold for the next decade reached their full development.

By 1912 Picabia had added the concept that abstract shapes and colors were as capable of arousing emotions as were the sounds of music, to the concept of painting which he had held in 1908 - the exploitation of "the visual field solely for the sake of an arbitrary and poetic organization of forms and colors". And by 1913 Picabia transformed these concepts of painting into a language of visual symbols capable not only of arousing generalized emotions but of conveying the subtleties of the artist's thoughts and specific emotions. It may be said he wanted to restore the function of narration to painting, but to achieve this by an exploitation of the potential suggestiveness of abstract art.

Among the paintings which embody Picabia's pictorial concepts of 1912 are _La Procession à Séville_ (pl.2, fig.7), and _Danses à la source_ (pl.3, fig.9). The subject matter of those paintings is relatively simple and in the nature of direct objective observation of human activities. The first is of a religious procession, the second of two figures dancing. The artist expresses neither approval nor condemnation of these activities, nor does he particularly characterize the individuals portrayed. The pictorial relationships and the general mood conveyed were his main concerns.

In 1913 the subject matter of Picabia's paintings, such as that of _Je revois en souvenir ma chere Udnie_,(pl.5,fig.13) and _Edtaonisl Ecclésiastique_,(pl.6,fig.16) became quite complex, and is in the nature of Picabia's comments on aspects of social behavior. In the first painting sentimentality is mocked. The tender feelings of the heart implied in the title is revealed in its true aspect as the memory of sexual intercourse by the visual references to the male and female organs of sex (see p.105). In the second the artist's intention was to depict the beating heart of a clergyman who watches a professional female dancer rehearsing her routine while aboard an ocean liner; perhaps this is a statement of the mistrust of the clergy and church which Picabia expresses verbally elsewhere.[3] From the end of 1913 and throughout the period of his association with the Dadaists, that is, up to 1921, his art became simply a vehicle for the expression of his contempt for society.

The conception of abstract painting as a medium potentially capable of such expressiveness was the subject of debates between Picabia and Apollinaire. (The aesthetic ideas Picabia stated in 1913 are discussed at length on pp.68-85, and are compared to Apollinaire's statements on pp.91-95). This exchange of ideas may have had some bearing on Apollinaire's setting up a second main branch of Cubism in his discussions of the Cubist aesthetics. The first main branch, which he called Scientific Cubism, was that of Braque and Picasso; he felt it to be concerned primarily with the analysis of real objects. The second main branch, which he called Orphic Cubism, he defined as an art of the mind; the forms which the artist paints are of his own invention and not related in any way to objects in nature, and the artist is concerned with the meaning conveyed by the subject matter. "The work of the Orphic artist must simultaneously give a pure aesthetic pleasure, a structure which is self evident, and a sublime meaning, that is, the subject".[4] Apollinaire found it necessary to create a subdivision for each of the main branches. He called the subdivision for the first Physical Cubism, for the second, Instinctive Cubism.

Apollinaire publicly used the term "Orphism", and gave its definition, for the first time in October, 1912, in a lecture given on the occasion of the "Section d'Or" exhibition. This lecture dealt with "the multiple tendencies, from which acknowledgement could no longer be withheld, of abstract art, or...'Cubism drawn and quartered'."[5] This was five months after Apollinaire and Picabia first met.

The "Section d'Or" exhibition, the name of which was contributed by Jacque Villon, had been conceived by Picabia, Apollinaire and Duchamp as a Salon to be held only once. Only works of "an independent nature", by which they meant those by painters who had not - or had not yet - been exhibited at Kahnweiler's gallery, were eligible. (Kahnweiler in his turn denounced those who participated in the exhibition).[6] The immediate stimulus for this show had been Duchamp's withdrawal, after controversy, of his Nu descendant un escalier from the Salon des Independants.[7]

The conception of Apollinaire's book, The Cubist Painters, took place at this same time, or shortly after.[8] Gabrielle Buffet-Picabia relates that during the course of an evening the conversation "lapsed into the subject of painting. Picabia, permanently athirst for polemics, action and plans of campaign, had just conceived the possibility, nay the necessity, of a publication in which Apollinaire would analyze in detail the present state of the New Painting, with special reference to 'Cubism drawn and quartered' (that is, Apollinaire's four divisions of Cubism). The project rapidly took shape... Picabia would advance the cost of publication, Apollinaire would bring together a number of his former essays which had appeared in Les Soirées de Paris and other reviews and would add a study of each artist, complete with reproductions...(The project ran into) much bickering and opposition...Apollinaire made a very good best of a bad job..."[9]

Picabia, in company with his wife Gabrielle, Marcel Duchamp and

Guillaume Apollinaire, nurtured the intellectual viewpoint which in 1916 was given definition by the Dada movement. This was the dispassionate observation of the futility and contradictions inherent in all aspects of life and human endeavor, and they expressed this observation in terms of wit and humor, and in a free anarchic spirit. This attitude also combined a sort of social protest against the degradation of human values that had occurred, with a condemnation of what was felt to be the false values held by bourgeois society. The values of "High Art" were mocked along with the deplorable taste of the multitudes. Nothing remained sacred to them.

This aggressive negative attitude was not in the "Bohemianism" of the 19th century, which was also a revolt against the values held by bourgeois society, the "disavowal of the intellectual and cultural consequences of bourgeois society" by its own intellectual progeny.[10] But the 19th century "bohemians" expressed their revolt chiefly by devoting themselves to the concept of art for art's sake, whereas the Dadaists devoted themselves to direct attacks on society's values (see p. 16).

The Italian Futurists in 1909, had expressed much the same negativity and had also anticipated many of the devices and techniques used to engage in the process of the de-sacrédization later used by the Dadaists,[11] but the Futurists had the very positive political aim of rousing the people of Italy out of a period of lethargy to take their place among the modern industrialized nations. The Dadaists (except the Communists among them) had no positive values to offer in place of those they wished to destroy.

Gabrielle Buffet-Picabia describes the exchange of ideas between Picabia, Duchamp and Apollinaire in which they nourished this negative attitude: Picabia and Duchamp "emulated one another in their extraordinary adherence to paradoxical, destructive principles, in their blasphemies and inhumanities which were directed not only against the old myths of art, but against all the foundations of life in general. Guillaume Apollinaire often took part in these forays of demoralization, which were also forays of witticism and clownery. Better than by any rational method, they thus pursued the disintegration of the concept of art, substituting a personal dynamism, individual forces of suggestion and projection, for the codified values of formal Beauty. These games of exploration in an inaccessible dimension and in unexplored regions of being, this climate of invention which has never since been retrieved, seem to have contained all the germs of what later became Dada, and even of later growths." Gabrielle Buffet-Picabia goes on to name the fruits of this exchange of ideas. "Thus they arrived at certain postulates which soon developed into the arcana of the new plasticity and poetics: such as the calligrammes and conversation poems of Apollinaire, or the 'readymades' of Marcel Duchamp, and above all, the intrusion into the plastic field of the 'machine', this newcomer issued from the mind of man, this veritable 'daughter born without a mother', as Picabia called (it)...[12]

Apollinaire's poems probably influenced the poetry which was Picabia's chief form of expression during the years of World War 1, and Apollinaire's calligrams probably influenced Picabia's Dadaist diagram-like machine drawings on which words and phrases are juxtaposed (see pp.119-121, and footnote 188). The "ready-mades" of Marcel Duchamp are discussed on page 125, and Picabia's equivalent of Duchamp's "ready-mades" are discussed on pages 121-123.

The first stage of Picabia's response to the 20th century "machine aesthetic" is marked by the simplification of forms to flat shapes with sharply defined contours, which had been characteristic of his paintings since 1908. He did not actually depict machine forms until 1913, though the subject of Caoutchouc of 1909 was an object produced by machine. As has been said it is Duchamp who is credited with the first painting of a specific machine. This painting was Moulin à café of 1910; it is an analysis of the mechanical working of that machine. However Duchamp's work of 1911 shows no concern with machines and his Nu descendant un escalier of 1912, as are Picabia's paintings of the same year, such as Procession à Séville, is not of machine forms, but portrays the human figure as made up of sharp-edged rectangular shapes expressive of the "machine aesthetic".

Both Picabia and Duchamp soon perceived new potentials in the use of the machine as a subject for painting. As Gabrielle Buffet-Picabia says: "the discovery and rehabilitation (into the world of the arts from which they had remained ostracized) of these strange personages of iron and steel...was in itself a bold, revolutionary act; but one which, if it had not gone beyond descriptive representation, would have remained very close to the landscape and the still life...(But) the machines soon generated propositions which evaded all tradition...".[13]

Picabia and Duchamp discovered that machines and machine parts could resemble the human physiognomy. This idea, when added to that of the machine as the visual symbol of modern society, provided them with the means of mocking society. They could present their symbol of society as mock personages indulging in a burlesque of human social relationships, attitudes and mores. Picabia's drawing La fille née sans mère, of early

1913, (see p.105, and pl.4,fig.11), which formed the basis of the composition of Je revois en souvenir ma chere Udnie, was his earliest work to function in this way, while the first of Marcel Duchamp's were La passage de la vierge à la mariée (see p.107), and Mariée (see pp.107-108, and pl.5, fig. 14), both of 1912. Picabia's Je revois en souvenir ma chere Udnie and Duchamp's Mariée are discussed on pages 103-108.

In January, 1913, Picabia came to New York City to attend the Armory Show,[14] and stayed for the following six months. In New York he was immediately drawn into the intellectual avant-garde circle around Alfred Stieglitz, the photographer who was also the pioneer in presenting modern art to the American public. These people shared the social attitude held by Picabia, Apollinaire and Duchamp.

During this stay in New York Picabia made the series of statements expressing his aesthetic philosophy which are discussed on pp.68-85. He also made a series of abstract water-color paintings and drawings of New York which attempt to convey the excitement he derived from the spectacle of the highly mechanized dynamic life of New York City. These works were exhibited by Stieglitz. With the exception of the drawing La Fille née sans mère which depicts machine parts, they are like his paintings of 1912 in that they reveal the "machine aesthetic" only in the simplicity and sharp contours of the abstract shapes that compose them. But in the paintings which Picabia made in the second half of 1913, after his return to Paris, the abstract shapes are definitely derived from the world of machinery, as in Edtaonisl Ecclésiastique (pl.6, fig.16), and as in Je revois ensouvenir ma chere Udnie, where the abstract shapes derive from machine elements that resemble parts of the human anatomy. The forms represented in Picabia's works after 1913, as are those of Duchamp's after _Mariée_, are no longer abstract but are specifically representations of machine elements which no longer read as imitations of the human anatomy, but are arbitrarily endowed by the artist with symbolism. Examples of this are Picabia's drawings for his book _Poèmes et dessins de la fille née sans mère_ of 1918 (see pp.120-121, and pl. 13,figs.37 and 39) and Duchamp's _La Mariée mise à nu par ses célibataires, même_, 1915-23, (pp.124-125, and pl.19,fig.61).

The intent of the symbolism of Picabia's paintings, drawings and other graphic experiments from 1913 until he broke with the Dada movement in 1921, remained that of rendering pictorial his attitudes towards contemporary society. In 1921 the poet and critic, Ezra Pound, who had been Picabia's co-editor of "_The Little Review_", paid tribute to Picabia's success in this attempt to render his thoughts pictorially:

"Given the boy genius, Picasso, who apparently couldn't help master-drawing in his etchings of acrobats and who, apart from his pencil and brushes, has so far as one knows, never had an idea in his life...(I) find a means of trying to convey my meaning in the contrast of Picabia, who is regarded or has been generally regarded as a mere eccentric...

"I do not present Picabia as a master painter: nor as a master sculptor in the sense that Brancusi is a sculptor, or Picasso a master draftsman, or Matisse a beautifully gifted manipulator of color; but Picabia does, on the other hand, work in a definite medium to which one may give an interim label of thought...In his beautiful and clear pictures...there is perhaps no sign of visual sensitivity, or at least of that kind of visual receptivity which underlies the nervous outlines of a Picasso, but there is a very clear exteriorization of Picabia's mental activity."[15]

Needless to say, Picabia's and Duchamp's visual language of symbols and the attitudes embodied in them, remain obscure to all but a small audience of initiates. James Thrall Soby even has expressed the opinion that Marcel Duchamp's works were meant to be private family jokes.[16] That their art was bound to remain "unread" by the multitudes whose values and mores it so severely criticized by ridicule, did not disturb Picabia or Duchamp basically, even though Picabia in his 1913 statements performed the social-conscious act of explaining to the public what to look for in his art, as well as what not to look for (see p.71 and footnote 111): he even expressed the hope, as did Apollinaire in his The Cubist Painters and Kahnweiler in his Rise of Cubism, that eventually the public would learn to read the new language of symbols then being invented by the Cubist artists. But Picabia and many of his contemporaries in the field of art firmly retained the "art for art's sake" attitude of their 19th century predecessors. Otherwise he would have clarified, or at least have stabilized, his visual language of symbols, rather than inventing a new language in almost every new work.

The desire to keep art exclusive and for the few sensitive persons capable of appreciating its subtleties found expression in many places in the second decade of this century. For example, in Gleizes' and Metzinger's book Cubism there is this passage: "...let the forms he (the artist) discerns, and the symbols in which he incorporates their qualities be sufficiently remote from the imagination of the vulgar to prevent the truth which they convey from assuming a general character... Decorum demands a certain degree of dimness and decorum is one of the attributes of art".[17] The Futurist Soffici, who, as did his fellow Futurists, in other places expressed concern for the cultural education of the masses, said in an article: "Perhaps the education (of the sensibility of the public) is useless...For me this is axiomatic: whoever is not sensitive to the pictorial savor of a line drawn across a wall with charcoal by a child, to the velvety qualities of its black granulation against the mural whitewash, to the rhythm of its folds and bends, will never be able to enjoy the beauty of plasticity."[18] And one of the circle around Alfred Stieglitz, who himself felt art was the only true expression of the individual in our mechanized society, was quoted as saying "art is by the few and for the few. The more individual a work of art is, the more precious and free it is apt to be; and at the same time as a natural consequence, the more difficult to understand."[19]

Picabia's and Duchamp's audience also shared with them a love for abstract thought, true wit and humor, and a certain affinity and taste for the irrational. This taste for the irrational had been sharpened as the new 20th century saw the fabulous developments of science become commonplace, most pertinent among these being the X-ray to see through solids, the great speeds of travel and communication of the airplane and radio, and the motion picture. Many intellectuals also found the factors that led to the First World War irrational. This heightened sensitivity to the irrational was to flower first in the Dada movement and then in the Surrealist movement.

It was the opinion of Walter Arensberg-the American friend of Picabia and Duchamp, once a member of the Stieglitz circle, whose collection of 20th century painting eventually included the greater part of Duchamp's total pictorial output and Picabia's Danses à la source, Culture Physique (pl.7,fig.19), and Edtaonisl, Catch as catch can (pl.8,fig.20)-that this irrationality is present in some degree in all early 20th century art; that the images in the Cubistic paintings by Picasso and Braque could have been much clearer, but they always left the images they painted somewhat confused, that is, somewhat irrational, perhaps to make the spectator participate, or in a sense recreate the work. Arensberg felt that the central idea in the work of Picabia and Duchamp was "making the irrational rational by irrational means" (a statement that he did not amplify). He pointed out that even in the clarity, that is, the rationality, of the machines of Picabia and Duchamp there is irrationality in the impossibility of these machines to work. Arensberg also observed that the works of these two painters were in the nature of puns which call upon the observer to interpret them.[20]

Of Arensberg's collection, Milton Brown says that it exhibits "the love of cerebration for its own sake...Here is perhaps the most esoteric of contemporary attitudes in which it is not so much the object itself, as its associative overtones which are the touchstones of its significance."[21]

Picabia's public participation in activities that are labelled Dadaistic began during his second trip to New York. This trip came about after he had been inducted into the French army. According to Gabrielle Buffet-Picabia, Picabia had "served as a general's chauffeur up to the day when an influential and understanding friend managed to save him from the barracks by entrusting him with an important mission to Cuba. He was to go by way of New York, and set sail(accompanied by Gabrielle)in April, 1915. Meeting Marcel Duchamp and a group of old time friends in New York, he forgot his mission and pursued his voyage no further. This total incomprehension of the exigencies of war might have turned out very badly for him if, thanks to his dissipated life in New York, he had not fallen gravely ill. He profited by a temporary discharge which, from medical board to medical board, carried him to the end of the war..." No sooner had we arrived (in New York) than we became part of a motley international band which turned night into day, conscientious objectors of all nationalities and walks of life living in an inconceivable orgy of sexuality, jazz and alchohol." "A little group of artists, mostly European, whose uncontested lights were Duchamp and Picabia, gathered in the gallery of Alfred Stieglitz at 291 Fifth Avenue, or at the home of Walter and Lou Arensberg..."[22]

The paintings and drawings Picabia began after his arrival in New York are based upon mechanical forms, and are seemingly executed with a mechanical objectivity; on their surfaces he lettered words and phrases. Dedee d'Amerique (see p.115,and pl.9,fig.22), and Ici, c'est ici Stieglitz (see p.117, and pl.10,fig.26), are examples of these works which Picabia regarded as "anti-painting". He also participated in illustrating, writing and editing Stieglitz' newly founded magazine 291. This strikingly original magazine embodied the spirit that in the following year was given the name of Dada by a group of artists and poets in Zurich, Switzerland, unknown to the group in New York, who had organized and dedicated themselves to the process of the mockery and de-sacridization of all that society held in esteem.

In January, 1917, Gabrielle and Picabia left New York for Barcelona, and there found another group of artists, refugees from the war. Here, Picabia began to publish 391, a sequel to Stieglitz' magazine 291. Most of the material, drawings and text, contained in the numbers of this magazine was the work of Picabia himself. In 1918 Picabia went to Lausanne, Switzerland for medical treatment and while there published

Poèmes et dessins de la fille née sans mère, and other books of poetry. These books brought him to the attention of the Zurich Dadaists whom he met late in 1918 or early in 1919.[23]

The Zurich group of Dadaists was made up primarily of young men who were poets, writers and painters taking refuge from the war. They had originally banded together out of their interest in the arts, and had wanted to make the Cabaret Voltaire, their headquarters, a focal point of the "newest art": Hugo Ball was an intimate friend of Kandinsky, Arp had been in close contact with Picasso and Braque in Paris, and Tzara was a friend of the Futurists.[24] These men were keenly aware, however, of the senselessness of the war the countries of Europe were engaged in, and the expression of this awareness in terms of hostility towards and ridicule of that society soon dominated their activity. Along with the other values held by society the first victims of their revolt were the very arts they practiced. Georges Ribemont-Dessaignes, in his History of Dada says: "...it goes without saying that it was the media that had been most useful to them which they first destroyed... replacing cubism, futurism and simultaneism that had nourished them, they smashed the forms of cubist, futurist and simultaneist thought with means closely resembling the objects destroyed. The real question was the destruction of values...it is not surprising that in the beginning Dada should often have presented a futurist of cubist face, to the extent that Dada itself was often deceived by it."[25]

All the historians of the Dada movement seem to agree that Picabia and Duchamp are the purest exponents of the Dada spirit, and that the moment when Picabia joined the Zurich group was a most decisive one in the history of Dada. Of this meeting Georges Hugnet wrote: "The arrival in Zurich of Picabia, who brought with him the Duchamp-Picabia spirit is a noteworthy date in the history of Dada: on this date the useless begins to drop away and the essential narrows down to that human force, unconscious and willful, destructive and clean, that truly constitutes what Breton was to call 'l'état d'esprit Dada'...(Picabia) contributed enormously to the moral drive of the Dada movement, to its outward manifestation, and likewise to its will and dictatorship. He contributed with his painting and writing..."[26]

The origin of many of the techniques used by the Dadaists to express themselves was in the works of Sade, Baudelaire, Rimbaud, Lautreamont and others of the 19th century who emphasized the importance of the imagination; who experimented with automatism, that is, giving free reign to the subconscience, letting it dictate the flow of words, and who appreciated the surprise element in chance juxtapositions; who allowed the sounds of words to dictate their use rather than their meaning, and who invented words when necessary for their purposes (see footnote 141). The Dadaists who painted as well as wrote - Hans Arp, Max Ernst, Kurt Schwitters, as well as Picabia - transposed these literary principles to their graphic work: for example, Picabia's statements in 1913 of the ability of the subconscience to invent the symbols of a new visual language (see pp.84-85,101); his use of unrelated words and phrases scattered over the surfaces of drawings and paintings; Duchamp's "ready mades" and Picabia's equivalent of them; Duchamp's actual experiments with chance (see p.58), and Arp's compositions "arranged according to the laws of chance"; the abstract "merz" collages of Schwitters and the fantastic representational collages Arp and Ernst produced in collaboration called "Fatagaga". Mallarmé's poem, <u>Un coup</u>

de dés, as published in Cosmopolis in 1897 (see footnote 188), in the printing of which he called for varied sizes of type and type faces and spacings, so that the resulting visual character guides the reader in recreating the aural emphasis to be placed on the different words, provided the prototype for the characteristic typography of the Dada publications and announcements, including Picabia's. The same poem is generally credited as the immediate inspiration for Apollinaire's calligrams.

At the end of 1919 the Dadaists moved their activities to Paris, where their demonstrations soon began to draw large appreciative audiences. To one audience Picabia addressed the following: "What are you doing here, plunked down like serious oysters - because you are serious, aren't you? The ass, the ass represents life like fried potatoes, and all you serious people smell worse than cow flop. Dada smells of nothing, it is nothing, nothing, nothing. Whistle, shout, bash my face in, and then what? Then what? I'll just go on telling you that you are all fools."[27]

Much of Dada took form in what seems superficially to be hilariously funny, but the deeply rooted causes that provoked the mad-caps cannot be forgotten. Real humor and wit is often seen in Dada work, particularly that of Picabia and Duchamp, one of the most famous examples of which is the moustache Duchamp drew on a reproduction of the Mona Lisa, and which Picabia had printed on the cover of 391, March, 1920. Of this cover Duchamp later said it is a copy by Picabia of Duchamp's original which wasn't available, and that the letters of its title, L.H.O.O.Q., make an obscene pun when pronounced in French fashion: "Elle a chaud au cul".[28]

But _391_ is an angry publication, and Picabia printed the picture of the Mona Lisa with a moustache in a spirit of the righteous wrath of genuine iconoclasm, smashing what he felt to be the petrified standards and mentality of his bourgeois contemporaries.

It soon became apparent that in Paris Dada had become a successful art movement and had outlasted its inherent purpose of negation and destruction of all values. Petty personal conflicts arose among various members. Picabia announced his withdrawal from the movement by a series of actions and printed articles insulting those who had been his friends. He formally stated his reasons for withdrawing as follows: "I have separated myself from certain Dadaists because I was smothered amongst them, each day I became more depressed, I was terribly bored...

"I do not wish to recount the full history of the Dada movement here; only to make a point with a few words: the Dada spirit truly existed for only three or four years, it was expressed by Marcel Duchamp and me at the end of 1912; Hulsenbeck, Tzara or Ball found the 'nom-écrin' Dada in 1916. With the word the movement reached its culminating point, but it continued to evolve, each of us bringing to it the most life possible... (With our particular means we had a great success). This success, the pleasure of play, attracted, in 1918, many people who have of Dada only the name; then everything around me changed, I had the impression that, as did Cubism, Dada was going to have disciples who _would understand_ and I soon had only one idea - to run away as far as possible to forget these people. But they amused me for a few hours more...to see them profit easily by their opportunism and their flattery of _serious people_ and the _Nouvelle Review Francaise_. Now Dada has a tribunal, advocates (in reference to the mock trial and demonstration against the writer Maurice

Barres on May 13, 1921)...soon probably gendarmes and a Monsieur Deibler...

"Dada makes me think of a cigarette whose aroma is agreeable. The brand name gets consumed, but the tobacco remains, and I count on the man of genius who smokes it to give it a new name. But let us think no more of the past notwithstanding the aroma of the cigarette; life is only a shadow, let us preserve the illusion that the mind is more...

"I like to walk alone, at chance, names of streets matter little to me, each day resembles the others if we do not subjectively create the illusions of novelty, and Dada is no longer new...for the moment. The bourgeois represents the infinite, Dada would be the same if it lasted too much longer."[29]

However Picabia continued to work in occasional cooperation with Andre Breton who had also broken with most of his former Dada associates, and in whose mind Surrealism was taking on a definite shape. Picabia contributed to Breton's new series of Litterature, beginning with issue no. 4 for which he designed the cover,[30] and Breton wrote a preface for an exhibition of Picabia's work held in Barcelona in November, 1922. However Picabia did not share Breton's enthusiasm for Surrealism, and after the publication of the First Surrealist Manifesto, Picabia brought out several issues of 391 in which he attacked Surrealism.

The paintings Picabia made during the following decades until the outbreak of World War II are varied in style, and share only the general characteristics of not being abstract, and of showing no concern with the social problems of the mechanized 20th century. The most interesting works of this period are those he called "transparencies" (see pp.128-135). In these, two or more separate images are superimposed; they reflect the interest in depicting simultaneous happenings that is one of the dominant concerns of many of this century's artists. Le beau charcutier of 1921 (see p.131, and pl.15,fig.45), which is still a work in the Dada spirit, was one of the first of this type he painted. The symbolism of the later transparencies are obscure and poetic in quality. These paintings were interspersed with and followed by works in other styles: expressionistic, neo-classic, and certain ones of a fantastic-surrealist nature. During the years of World War 11, Picabia is reported to have painted realistic expressionistic scenes of the horrors of war.[31] These were followed by a period of painting "dots" - paintings of richly pigmented surfaces, often black, on which brightly colored dots are carefully placed. Picabia swept aside all charges of inconsistency with: "our heads are round to allow thought to change its direction."[32]

PICABIA'S PAINTING, CAOUTCHOUC, OF 1909

Though Picabia held, from 1913 until 1921, the conception of his art as a vehicle for the expression of thoughts concerning contemporary society, thoughts of such a literary nature that he aimed at making his paintings a visual language of symbols in order to express them, it must be recognized that he was basically a sensitive painter. Thus he, as did Duchamp, chose painting as the chief vehicle to express the thoughts and attitudes he developed as he reached intellectual maturity as a citizen. His subject matter, however complex, exists in terms of the plastic elements of his paintings.

The plastic ideas with which he worked, of which there are four major ones, relate him directly to the plastic concerns of Cubism and Futurism. These four ideas are first found expressed by Picabia in his Caoutchouc of 1909. They are ideas which manifested themselves during the first decades of the 20th century in the work of many European artists who are often unrelated stylistically otherwise. The four ideas were: 1. the attempt to visually simulate the effects of motion, which ranged from the simple desire to show a figure moving through space to the complex desire of expressing the movement of the universe; 2. the concept of simultaneity which tries to express the awareness of many different events occuring at a given moment; simultaneity, rendered as the superimposition of many elements on the surface of a canvas, became one of the chief means used to express motion, and early in the century linear drawing in paint became the primary way to achieve the superimposition of elements; 3. the concept of "pure" or abstract painting which is the painting of forms not borrowed from nature but invented by the artist, and "which is to representative painting as music is to literature"; 4. the portrayal of machinery or of forms derived from machinery, which because of the beauty such forms often have, forms which are themselves invented by man and are not to be found in nature, often attracts artists who do "pure" or abstract painting. The portrayal of machinery is also often bound to the interest in motion - the dynamic, precise, repetitive motions of machines and their ability to reproduce endless identical products, or to hurtle themselves through space. The appreciation of the abstract beauty of machine forms is apparent in many of Picabia's and Duchamp's machine representations, but both artists always contradicted the ability of the machine to move. Their machine representations are always static.

In Picabia's water-color painting Caoutchouc (Rubber) (pl.1,fig.3), an object is represented as being in motion, in a state of continuous change. A number of different views of the object are shown, simultaneously, and in each instance only the contour of the object is shown, as if the object were transparent, so that the superimposed views do not hide one another. The object itself is a manufactured machine product: though the forces of nature are represented in the motion of the ball, picturesque natural details have been banished, and the painting is composed entirely of abstract shapes - the circular shape of the ball itself being abstract. The large areas into which the background of the painting has been subdivided resemble those which are typical of Picasso's and Braque's earlier works of 1907 and 1918, and is suggested even in Picasso's portrait of Gertrude Stein of 1906 in the simplification of the back of the chair and the corner of the room.

Such divisions of pictorial space remain more or less typical of all Picasso's and Braque's later works, and of Picabia's through 1913.[33] In Picabia's work, however, these background areas, because of their usual opposition to the vertical and horizontal axes, aid in creating the sense of dynamic movement Picabia desired, while in the paintings of Picasso and Braque these areas usually follow the vertical and horizontal axes, and so reaffirm the sense of stability their compositions have.

But though Caoutchouc seems much more abstract than either its predecessors or immediate successors in Picabia's work, as it is an obvious attempt to show a bouncing rubber ball, or balls, it cannot claim the distinction Zervos gives it as the earliest example of non-figurative painting.[34]

There was some preparation for the painting of Caoutchouc in Picabia's earlier work, particularly in a series of portrait studies made in Spain in 1902 (pl.1,fig.1). These drawings are in strange contrast to the Impressionistic paintings he continued to do through 1908. They are related to the style of "Art Nouveau", and have two characteristics which became increasingly prominent in Picabia's work after 1908. One is the use of decisively drawn lines, like those with which the contours of the faces are realized; the other is the reduction of forms to simplified, sharp edged shapes, such as those of the hat, necktie, eyes and the areas of light and shade. Those same characteristics are found in Picabia's studies of landscape which are related to Caoutchouc in time, Paysage, 1908 (pl.2,fig.4), and Paysage de Cassis, 1909, (pl.2,fig.5). But in neither of these landscapes is there an attempt to suggest motion.

Both of these characteristics stem from the new appreciation for simplification of form held by the painters of Picabia's generation, an appreciation developed by influences from several sources. One source was the "Art Nouveau" or the "1900 style" whose characteristic hard, sinuous line had originated in the use of new materials by architects who exploited the plasticity and pliability of steel and new techniques of using concrete.[35] This characteristic line, originating in the industrial world, had been grafted onto the work of a number of artists, including the illustrations of Aubrey Beardsley and certain posters by Toulouse Lautrec. In their work this sinuous line, as well as existing independently, often became the contours of flat simple areas of color.

The use of line independently and the flat areas of color also have their stylistic origin partly in the paintings of Gauguin, and in Japanese wood-block prints. More recent sources of influence towards simplification were the simplified pictorial elements of Henri Rousseau's paintings, the simplifications of the art of African Negros and other primitive peoples, as well as the knowledge of that aspect of Cezanne's research which led him to state that all forms in nature can be simplified to the cone, sphere and cylinder.

This new appreciation and practice of the simplification of pictorial elements gave many paintings, those of Picasso and Braque of 1908-12, and Leger's, as well as Picabia's, their "mechanical" look, though they were not of machines or of forms derived from machinery. About this characteristic Brown says: the "simplification of forms down to fundamentals is the stylistic or esthetic equivalent of machine production and machine precision. Although the idea is traceable to the formal research of Cezanne (cone, sphere, cylinder) after Cubism it becomes inextricably involved with the concept of industrial and mechanical functionalism."[36]

Though Picabia had been consistently reducing the forms depicted in his paintings to flat simplified shapes it is not until in his paintings of 1913 that he consciously and purposefully exploited this ability of simplified shapes to suggest the world of machinery without depicting actual machine forms, as in Edtaonisl Ecclésiastique.[37] It must be noted, however, that Picabia depicted actual machine forms for the first time in his drawing La fille née sans mère of 1913, and certain of these elements found their way into the painting based upon this drawing, Je revois en souvenir ma chere Udnie, also of 1913 (see pp.103-104).

The use of line is of great importance in all of Picabia's work, partly because he conceived and composed first in line. This is seen most clearly in his water-color studies painted in New York in 1913 (see pp.66-67), in which the transparent washes of color do not hide the pencil lines that were made first. The surfaces of the pictures were divided up into areas, or shapes, by intersecting pencil lines, and then the areas were filled in with color. It is reasonable to assume that this was his working procedure on all his paintings from 1908 through 1913. It accounts for the sharpness of the contours of all his shapes. His work of the next few years, including the Dadaistic machine-portraits (see pp.117-119) and machine-calligrams (see pp.119-121), are characteristically linear, and the elements of the transparencies of the 1920's exist entirely in line.

Gertrude Stein confusedly described Picabia's concern with line: "Picabia had conceived and is struggling with the problem that a line should have the vibration of a musical sound and that this vibration should be the result of conceiving the human form and the human face in so tenuous a fashion that it would induce such vibration in the line forming it. It was this idea that conceived mathematically influenced Marcel Duchamp and produced his Nude Descending the Staircase."[38] (Stein's statement of Picabia's influence on Duchamp in this matter is to be disregarded). Actually the use of line is significant in Picabia's work primarily because of his long preoccupation with the phenomenon of transparency, and Gertrude Stein's notes of 1930 on Picabia's "transparencies" (see p.129) in which she mentions Picabia's contact with photographic techniques are much more helpful. Picabia's use of transparency was bound up with his concern for the expression of motion and simultaneity. (Other forms with which Picabia and Duchamp expressed their interest in motion are discussed on pp.52-59). The justification for depicting objects as transparent and attempting to project the experience of simultaneity was stated by Gabrielle Buffet-Picabia in 1913, and this may be taken as representative of Picabia's own thoughts: "...out of the ever deepening consciousness of life which we derive from every new scientific discovery there arises new and complex states of mind to which the external world appears more clearly in the abstract form of the qualities and properties of its elements than under the concrete form of our sense perceptions. Or more broadly speaking, we can say that at the same time that we have our perception of the external, we have the consciousness of all that exists above and beyond it."[39] The Futurist Boccioni expressed the same thought: "Why accept bodies as opaque when our new sensibility brings us close to the hitherto unknown objects contemplated by medium and revealed to us by the new discoveries of science?"[40]

The technique of superimposing elements with the elements becoming transparent to allow the overlapped areas to remain visible, allows each one of the succession of images of an object to be seen in the paintings of all phases of Cubism, starting with the "analytic" paintings of Picasso and Braque of 1910 (see pp.38-40), and it allowed the Futurist painters to merge their "bundle of impressions" on one surface (see pp. 48-49). Marcel Duchamp's logical extension of the technique is found in his linear paintings on glass, the first of which was begun in 1913 (see p. 51). Picabia carried the technique to its most obvious and almost banal conclusion in his "transparencies" of the 1920's and early '30's (see pp.128-134).

As this technique exists primarily in terms of line, examples in drawings from all historical periods are common, from the earliest origins of cave art showing overlapping animal representations, through certain linear drawings and oil sketches by Ingres of figures whose limbs are drawn in multiple positions. Transparency is an inconsistency inherent in drawing: convention lets a figure drawn in line without chiaroscuro to be read as solid form, while what actually is seen is like a thin wire construction standing in space - the eye and mind can alternate between these two visions of solid and transparent form. Kahnweiler speaks of this phenomenon inherent to line drawing as having, since Masaccio and Uccello, "always carried within it a germ of revolution", needing only a favourable atmosphere in which this germ could flourish.[41] In Kahnweiler's view, too limited in this instance, the germ did flourish after 1920 in the last works of Juan Gris in which line was divorced from color and "re-established in its original independence".[42] However, as has been shown, the "independent" line in painting always was important in all phases of Cubism, and is basic to all Picabia's work after 1908. And the Futurists used line as their most potent means of visually projecting their ideas of dynamism, simultaneity and interpenetration, experiences that could not possibly be painted in terms of tangible solids.[43] In Marcel Duchamp's work line drawing became increasingly important until in 1913 he adopted the almost exclusive use of precise stereometric drawing, as did Picabia when he began to portray actual machine forms (see pp.42-43).

In Caoutchouc Picabia used transparency as his chief means of describing the motion of the bouncing ball, presenting a number of views of the ball in different positions simultaneously. Because of their transparency, each image of the ball - the linear circles freely drawn with a brush - can be clearly seen. Though all the views of the ball are presented simultaneously, the spectator is to read each image seperately but successively. To describe the ball's bouncing to and away from the spectator, Picabia has made use of the suggestiveness of perspective by making the circles of different sizes. (Note: I do not know the colors of this painting and it is possible, as three of the circles - the center circle of the cluster, the one just below and to the right of the center circle, and the one just above and to the right of the center circle - have indications of designs on their surfaces, that several balls are represented. Even so, the balls are still represented in motion).

There was great originality in Picabia's use of transparency in Caoutchouc at this date, for the cluster of linear circles anticipates by more than a year the surface appearance of Picasso's and Braque's linear scaffoldings of analytical cubism - the "piercing of closed forms" (see p.39). Braque and Picasso, however, used transparency as an aid to analyze form, not to describe motion. But after having used transparency for the first time in Caoutchouc, Picabia immediately abandoned this plastic idea.

PICABIA IN RELATION TO CUBISM AND FUTURISM

Though Caoutchouc is too early a work to embody the full range of intent that Picabia expressed in his statements and in his paintings of 1913, namely that of the ability of abstract art to project the artist's emotions and thoughts, it is none the less a fully realized work in its own terms. In it the artist has clearly stated his interest in projecting the sensation of motion, rendering it as an experience of simultaneity which is lucidly realized by means of transparency. As such, Picabia's pictorial intent and means in this work must be compared with that of the Cubists and Futurists in whose work of the years 1910 through 1912 similar pictorial intent and means are expressed and used. And though in all of Picabia's other paintings from 1909 through 1912 he abandoned simultaneity and transparency, the attempt to project the sensation of motion in them is so dominant that this attempt must also be compared to the Cubists' and Futurists' interest in motion.

It will be seen that Picabia's expression of his interest in motion is closer to, though not identical with, the emotional character of the Futurists' than it is to the Cubists' intellectual one, just as his concern with complex subject matter is closer to the Futurists' concepts than to the Cubists'.[44]

The summaries that follow of the Cubists' and Futurists' concern with motion and simultaneity and use of transparency are drawn largely from Kahnweiler's expositions of the thinking of the Cubist painters,[45] limited primarily to Picasso's and Braque's "analytical cubism" of 1910-12,[46] Christopher Grey's discussion of the Cubist aesthetic theories and their roots in 19th century philosophical concepts,[47] and

Rosa Trillo Clough's investigation of the thinking of the Futurist painters.[48]

Conceding that it is misleading to generalize about styles of painting, for all things pertaining to style are treated uniquely by each painter, it may be said that the intent of the Cubist artists, specifically as seen only in the work of Picasso and Braque done during the years 1910-12, and which is commonly referred to as "analytical Cubism", was - as stated by Kahnweiler - to depict three dimensional form on a two dimensional surface without using the Renaissance system of perspective or chiaroscuro to imitate visual appearances, so as to allow the artist to focus his attention on the structure of the painting, its unity as a work of art, without having to consider the distortion of forms being represented. The intention of the Futurist artists, as stated in the writings of Boccioni, Soffici and Carra, was to experience the movement, the "constant becoming", that for them was the reality of the universe, and to express this so strongly that sensitive spectators of their art would be swept into this experience too. (It should be noted that the Futurists were more successful in expressing their intentions in words than in realising them in their paintings; for the expressive means used by the Futurist painters varied from one work to another and often even within the same work).

From these generalizations a further one may be drawn: the Cubist painters were primarily involved with the problems of painting pictures per se; the Futurist painters were much more concerned with extra-painterly concepts, that is, with the projection of emotional experiences, the sensations of living. If the position of such painters as Picabia, Marcel Duchamp and Robert Delaunay within the Cubist orbit in the years 1911-13 seems equivocal, it is because they chose to partake of extra-painterly concepts not unlike those expressed by the Futurists. Such Cubist painters as these, who corrupted the Cubist purity of Picasso and Braque (of 1910-12), were labeled "Orphists" by Apollinaire; their works, he said, must "simultaneously give a pure aesthetic pleasure, a structure which is self-evident, and a sublime meaning, that is, the subject".[49]

Another factor that often makes it seem as if members of either the Cubist or Futurist groups crossed the boundaries of one another's territory is the interest shared by both groups in motion, and in simultaneity and its expressive means of transparency. However, the Futurists, lacking historical perspective, claimed this interest all for themselves, saw it as their main contribution to painting, and resented that those whose works superficially resembled theirs, such as the Cubist "Orphists", did not acknowledge this resemblance (see p.71). To an extent the Futurists were justified in complaining, for their first pronouncements were dubiously greeted by many who two years later were saying the same things. But the latter were right in not feeling indebted, for they were using expressive means which now reveal themselves as having been "in the air" of Europe at the time, the property of all creative artists: the Futurists had simply made the most noise about it.

It must be immediately noted, however, that though this interest in motion and simultaneity is shared by both groups, it held different implications for each. For the Cubists (Braque and Picasso) this interest, and its expressive means of transparency, was a tool to aid them in the solution of their search for a new way to represent, or more accurately, to measure three dimensional form, while for the Futurists, in keeping with their extra-painterly concepts, it was the expression of the overwhelming emotional impact resulting from complete awareness of all the sensations of life at a given moment, including the experiencing of the very movement of the universe.

The Expression of Motion and Simultaneity in Cubism, 1910-1912

Perhaps somewhat more important than the actual expression of motion to the Cubists was the philosophical concept of reality as something dynamic and constantly changing expressed by, among others, Apollinaire in his book The Cubist Painters, Gleizes and Metzinger in their book Cubism, and by Picabia in his statements of 1913 (see pp.73-76). Christopher Grey discusses the theories of Apollinaire and Gleizes and Metzinger at length, and outlines the main philosophical trends of the 19th century which formed the basis of their thoughts.[50]

Grey states that around 1909 Apollinaire "became enamored of the dynamism of a new age of the machine in which the emphasis was on life, movement, and change rather than the deathlike permanence of any Absolute (the ideal of the Symbolists). To him the new reality must be found in the creative forces which found their expression in the airplane, the automobile, the cinema, the phonograph, and the factories of the new machine age. Progress, rather than fixed perfection, was the keynote, progress as a revelation of the inherent dynamism of the universe...It is Apollinaire, more than anyone else, who turns the search of the artists under the influence of decadent symbolism toward the New Dynamism..."[51]

Grey presents as one of the main philosophic sources of this new dynamic element the development of metaphysics through Nietzsche and Bergson, who rejected the concept of a static, unchanging and perfect reality which had been at the basis of the transcendental idealism of the 19th century and which profoundly influenced the ideas of Baudelaire and the later Symbolist school.

Nietzsche was one of the first to reject the concept of a permanent, perfect reality. He saw life itself as the basic reality and constant change as its essential characteristic; man was to rejoice in living and not search for a death-like permanence. The essential concept Henri Bergson expounded in all his books, and which had an enormous and immediate influence on French intellectual society in the last decade of the 19th century, is that of the ceaseless flow of change: "The universe endures. The more we study the nature of time, the more we shall comprehend that duration means invention, the creation of forms, the continual elaboration of the absolutely new". "The duration of the universe must therefore be one with the latitude of creation which can find place in it."[52]

Grey points out that the Cubists stressed two means of portraying this dynamic reality. One is the idea of "moving around an object to seize several successive appearances, which fused in a single image, reconstitute it in time".[53] Yet a normally constructed picture cannot give the sense of uniform and enduring change in time, the "becoming". It can only show instants in the becoming. Grey presents the following quotation from Bergson which contains the idea stated above, and is at the same time a clear statement of the reasons which lead to its ultimate rejection by the Cubists: "To analyze, therefore, is to express a thing as a function of something other than itself. All analysis is thus a translation, a development into symbols, a representation taken from successive points of view from which we may note as many resemblances as possible between the new object which we are studying and others which we believe we know already. In its eternally unsatisfied desire to embrace the object around which it is compelled to turn, analysis multiplies without end the number of points of view in order to complete its always imperfect translation."[54]

The other method of portraying the dynamic reality stressed by the Cubists was adapted from Cezanne. This was the idea that form and color are so inextricably intertwined that neither can be complete without the careful control of the other. Gleizes and Metzinger say "every inflection of form is accompanied by a modification of color, and every modification of color gives birth to form".[55] And of Cezanne they say: "He teaches us to overcome the universal dynamism. He reveals the reciprocal and mutual modifications caused by supposedly inanimate objects...His work, a homogeneous mass, shifts under the glance, contracts, expands, fades, or illumines itself..."[56]

Though the Cubists, especially Picasso and Braque, were concerned with the expression of motion in their paintings, their compositions are essentially architectonic; that is, the large divisions of the surfaces of their paintings follow dominant vertical and horizontal axes, creating a sense of stability and balance, and when certain shapes or planes depart from these main axes they are still supported, they do not seem to be falling. This remains true throughout all the phases of Cubism. In the "analytical" phase of Cubism with which we are mainly concerned here, the skeleton structures, though weightless and measuring only space, respect and respond to the pull of gravity and are constructed to s tand upright.

In contrast to this stability are many of the "Orphist" works, such as paintings of Delauny which consist primarily of areas of color, often circular in shape, and paintings of Picabia including the water-color paintings he made during his trip to New York City and the oil paintings he made on his return to Paris in 1913, which, as do virtually all the paintings by the Futurists, defy or abandon stability. It is the loss of stability that leads Kahnweiler to denounce such works, even when it occurred briefly in the work of Juan Gris in 1915.[57]

The sense of movement in the paintings of analytical Cubism results largely from the repetition of similar units over the surface. This is the "moving viewpoint" which presents portions of several views of the same object, used to give a more complete description of the objects portrayed as well as to provide a sense of movement. The units actually repeated most often are the lines that form the right angles of the transparent planes that measure the space occupancy of the objects. This measuring of the different views of the object, however, is not clearly stated, only certain single lines or right-angles are picked out and emphasized, for Braque and Picasso are true painters, conscious of making paintings, not engineering charts, and these points of emphasis are their means of creating visual interest and rhythms over the surface. In later phases of Cubism, after 1912, in addition to retaining elements of the above, repetition is found in the placement of colors and textures in varying quantities over the surface.

The repetition of similar units over the surface of a painting was the 19th century's main means of expressing motion, a subject which is discussed at length by Balcomb Greene[58] Greene points out the repetitiveness found in Seurat's work - his pointillist technique itself, as well as the repetition of the dancer's legs in his Chahut, and the "moving viewpoint of the artist" which creates a series of visual units, each viewed head-on, across the canvas as it is found in the Grande Jatte. Greene points out that the idea of the moving viewpoint appears in Cubist doctrine about 1910, and that it is also important in Futurism. The Cubists, however, extended this idea so that an object is viewed from many angles and over a space of time, with the course of movement not made clear, but only loosely arranged on a centripetal plan, while the Futurists Balla and Russolo most closely adopted the regularized movement of Seurat's across the canvas.[59]

The expression of motion in the analytic phase of Cubism was achieved by a complex elaboration of the expressive means of a simultaneity, that is, by the superimposed elements being rendered as transparent.

A brief summary of the climactic development of Picasso's and Braque's Cubism as outlined by Kahnweiler shows that early in 1910 two developments resulted from these painters' "urgent desire to express the third dimension, depth (or, in other words, the volume and density of objects) by other means than the effects of light - that is to say trompe l'oeil and chiaroscuro". One was the introduction of several views of the same object juxtaposed in one picture; the other was the use of independent planes superimposed one over the other as a substitute for relief modelling of a continuous surface, a technique they first used in their sculpture. During the summer of 1910 Picasso forged "a new tool for the achievement of the new purpose"; he pierced the closed form. Closed forms are objects contained by their own surfaces, this "skin" must be painted as the contact point between the body and light, using chiaroscuro, which can provide only an illusion of the form of objects. "Picasso's new method made it possible to 'represent' the form of objects and their position in space instead of attempting to imitate them through illusionistic means." This was "effected by a process of representation that has a certain resemblance to geometric drawing. This is a matter of course since the aim of both is to render the three dimensional object on a two dimensional plane. In addition, the painter no longer has to limit himself to depicting the object as it would appear from one given viewpoint, but wherever necessary for fuller comprehension, can show it from several sides, and from above and below". The painter begins from a definite and clearly defined background and works towards the front by a scheme in which each object's position is clearly indicated, both in relation to the definite background and to other objects, instead of beginning from a foreground and giving an illusion of depth by means of perspective. Each object was depicted from different angles.

"Real details", the color of the objects, even their substance, indicated by imitations of wood, marble, etc., were recorded often on only a part of the surface, the main purpose of which originally was to help the spectator's perception. The "real details", acting as a stimulus of memory images, combine with the scheme of forms to construct the finished object in the spectator's mind.[60]

This entire procedure exists, according to Kahnweiler, as a means to allow the artist to focus his attention on the structure of the painting, its unity as a work of art, without having to consider the distortion of the forms being represented; it is "this conflict between representation and structure", which Kahnweiler believes caused Cezanne so much anguish.[61]

Nowhere in Picabia's work is there to be found this intense preoccupation with describing forms. Picabia never bothered to pierce the closed form. The circles in Caoutchouc cannot be considered as analyzing the form of the ball, they merely describe the ball in its different positions. And in the paintings, Tarentella (pl.3,fig.8), La procession à Séville (pl.2,fig.7), and Danses à la source (pl.3, fig.9), all of 1912 (see pp.63-65), which are close in style to such paintings of Picasso of 1908 as Harlequin and his family and of Braque's Houses at l'Estaque, of 1908, in which the solid forms are literally cubed,[62] Picabia took over the solid cubed form simply as a convention, with which he could construct forms reminiscent of forms in nature. Picabia's cubes did not result from an analysis of the forms of nature as did those of Picasso and Braque. Picabia's cubes differ further from Picasso's and Braque's in that he gave each facet more emphatic separation and definition of edge. Even the more varied shapes in his paintings of 1913, such as those of *Edtaonisl Ecclésiastique*, are derived from this 1908 style of Picasso and Braque, and in those paintings Picabia exploited the tendency of such simplified forms to suggest the world of machinery (see p.25). The same is true for the work of Marcel Duchamp from 1910-12, including *Nu descendant un escalier*, *Jeune homme mélancolique dans un Train*, and *La Roi et la Reine entourés de Nus vites*, all of 1912, though in the earlier *Les Joueurs d'échecs* (pl.18,fig.57) of 1911, the forms are clearly rendered as transparent and are not so markedly faceted or rectangular. In Duchamp's *Mariée* of 1912 (pl.5,fig.14), which followed those already mentioned of that year, there are no faceted cubed forms; the surfaces of the forms are painted instead as continuous surfaces with traditional chiaroscuro, and all the forms are opaque.

However, the expressive means that Picasso and Braque used to pierce the closed form (to render superimposed elements as transparent so thay can be seen simultaneously) reappears later in Picabia's and Duchamp's work. Kahnweiler compared this new technique of representing objects and their position in space to stereometric drawing, which is the same as geometric drawing or "mechanical" drawing: he said it can, "to give a thorough representation of the object's primary characteristics, depict them as stereometric drawing on the plane, or through several representations of the same object can provide an analytical study of that object which the spectator then fuses into one again in his mind...(It) does not have to be in the closed manner of stereometric drawing; colored planes, through their direction and relative position can bring together the formal scheme without uniting in closed forms...".[63] In comparing the new means of analytical Cubism to stereometric drawing, Kahnweiler recognizes the prosaic origin of the technique the Cubists "discovered". It is not the technique itself which is of significance - for it is one of long common usage by draftsmen for all building and manufacturing purposes, and by artists who carefully constructed their pictures according to the rules of perspective formulated by Brunelleschi: Ucello's stereometric drawings of hat frames and fountains, and Piero della Francesca's perspective diagrams are examples - but it is the use of this technique in painting that is significant. It is another example of the influence of the machine age penetrating the fine arts, here in basic expressive means. Yet Picasso's and Braque's version of the technique is deliberately unclear and evocative rather than coldly descriptive, for they wished to preserve the poetic qualities of painting. Marcel Duchamp, beginning in 1913, in his preliminary studies for La mariée mise à nu par ses célibataires, même, and in the final painting itself, used the technique of stereometric drawing with precision, clarity and cold logic to draw the machine elements that form his subject (see pl.19, fig.60). While the same coldness and precision, but usually not the logic, is present in Picabia's stereometric "machine-portraits" such as three printed in 291, no. 5-6, 1915 (see p.117), Ici, c'est ici Stieglitz (pl.10, fig.26), Le Saint des Saints (pl.10, fig.27), and Portrait d'une jeune fille Americain dans l'état de nudité (pl.10, fig.28), and the drawing Tableau peint pour raconter non pour prouver of 1915 or 1916 (pl.9, fig.25). Of those mentioned, however, only the last can rightly be referred to as stereometric drawing, and it is a flat frontal view and not a perspective diagram. The others are more rightly termed "technical illustrations"; but they none the less exist in a form of mechanical draftsmanship taken over from industry. Certain of them, as does the Portrait d'une jeune fille Americain dans l'état de nudité, seem to be actually lifted or copied from industrial catalogs. Many of these drawings, as is the Ici, c'est ici Stieglitz, are deliberately illogical. Picabia's drawings for the book Poémes et Dessins de la fille née sans mère (pl.13, figs.37 and 39) of 1918, are made up of segments of unrelated mechanical diagrams, resulting in an evocative and poetic effect rather than a coldly descriptive one.

The Expression of Motion and Simultaneity in Futurism

The ultimate goal of the Futurists' concern with motion lies in their insistence on the presence of the expression in their paintings of an intensely felt experience. This provides a point of comparison to certain ideas held by Picabia during the years 1910-13 which is discussed on pages 96-99. It also marks one of the essential differences between the Futurists' and the Cubists' ways of thinking, for the Cubists, particularly in the analytical phase of 1910 through 1912, believed that the plastic element in painting was sufficient in itself.[64]

This difference between the Cubist and Futurist views is stated by Carra: "The Cubists, because of their objectivity, are satisfied to look upon things as they appear to someone who moves around them, and to express them pictorially by what is really a geometric transcription. But we Futurists strive, with the power of our intuition, to identify ourselves with the central core of things so that our ego, on beholding them in their uniqueness, becomes one with them...Whereas the Cubists produce the static externals of the plastic world we Futurists, relying on our concept of dynamism, do not give the external and accidental shape of a movement, but rather the synthesis of the plastic rhythms inspired by that movement when we identify ourselves with it."[65]

The Futurists did credit the Cubists with, and adopted for their own ends, the reaffirmation of tangible concreteness, proclaiming the existence of line, studying the measure of the surfaces which it encloses, and thus opposing the Impressionists' flow-of-light concept of the world.[66] But the Futurists rejected the staticism and the cold gravity of the Cubists. And though Boccioni admired Picasso's paintings in which the volumes and lines are not arranged to reproduce or suggest external forms but are arranged to satisfy a purely plastic lyricism, Boccioni felt that the resulting "plastic emotion" was not genuine in them, that it was the "fruit of a cold, scientific mensuration", whereas the "plastic emotion" in the Futurists' paintings had the "dynamic fire, the confounding violence, and the marginal variety of forms (that) transcended the power of the intellect". Picasso cut up his object into sections and laid the pieces on the canvas as though upon a dissecting table. Forms, according to Boccioni, to be endowed with life and motion and capable of arousing emotion in the soul of the spectator must not be drafted by calculating reason, but must be inspired by "rapturous sensation and intuition."[67]

The Futurists, as does Boccioni in the above statement, tended to identify their many extra-painterly aims with their methods of picture making. Clough points out that the movements that the Futurists spoke of were not movements at all in the ordinary sense of the word, but "intrinsic qualities of bodies or reciprocal relationships between these bodies, plastically intuited as movements".[68] But the intuiting of these reciprocal relationships was conceived of as an intense, rather mystic experience by the artist, and ultimately, by the spectator too. In Carra's words, the "absolute motion" of objects is felt by the artist, only when he completely identifies himself with the "central core of things" so that his ego becomes one with them on beholding them in their uniqueness, when his plastic faculty "intuits the organic substance both in its general characteristics of porousness, impenetrability, rigidity and elasticity, as well as in its particular traits of color, temperature, consistency and shape; plane or concave; convex or angular; cubic, conic or spiral; elliptical or spherical".[69] To feel these qualities of an object is, according to Boccioni, to seize "its plastic potentiality which is nothing but its force, its primordial, psychological momentum".[70]

Boccioni did attempt to give at least a sampling of the kind of feeling for motion the Futurist painter intuited from relationships between plastic elements; "two objects of different form influence and characterize each other by the varying potentiality of their absolute motion. The weaker one, whether of static or dynamic temperament, will always yield to the force of the mightier one be it static or dynamic...Place a sphere near a cone and you will experience in the former a sensation of dynamic urge and in the later a feeling of static indifference. The sphere tends to move; the cone to imbed itself. The atmospheric zone which bounds the conic surface facing the sphere is an empty one and generates the sharp profile of the cone. The opposite zone, influenced by the movement of the sphere, produces an atmospheric density traversed by a color spot indicating a disturbance which blurs the profile of the cone in response to the expanding circles and ellipses flowing out from the sphere. Moreover, whereas the sphere engenders horizontal bulges suggestive of a tendency towards diffusion, the cone creates descending penetrations and angular limitations at the apex."[71]

The sum of the above statements by Carra and Boccioni is what the Futurists termed dynamism. They found precedence for this concept of dynamism in the work of the Impressionists, in which they found "the reciprocating chromatism which welds an object to its milieu and is a first attempt at pictorial dynamism...For the first time in the history of art an object was painted, not as an independent body, but as one conditioned and perfected by its milieu, which in turn was modified by the influence of the objects it contained. The human cheek which for centuries had obstinately retained its rosy color, now for the first time began to be tinged with the green hues reflected from the surrounding lawn."[72]

They also found confirmation of their ideas in the writings of Bergson (see pp.35-36), quoting from him: "All movement in passing from one resting position to another is absolutely indivisible".[73] Boccioni echoed Bergson for the most part when he said of dynamism that it is "the lyrical view of forms interpreted in the light of the unending manifestation of the rapport between their relative and their absolute emotions, between the milieu and the object it enfolds. It is the creation of a new form which partakes of gravity and expansion, rotation and revolution. In short, dynamism is life itself in the form which life creates in its infinite, uninterrupted becoming. This infinite becoming is attained through intuitive research for total unique form which makes the object partake of the life of the universal."[74]

Though the Futurists shared Bergson's conceptions with the Cubists as one of the sources of their ideas, there is a vast difference of degree in their response to it. Clough says that Cosmic dynamism controlled the Futurist's imagination: "in his state of poetic furor the artist tore from the object the concealing envelope, the outer form, and sank deep within, until he came into contact with those dynamic waves which constituted the object's inner reality. (In transferring) this dynamic image to the canvas...the inner vibrations, reciprocal emanations became geometrical figures, lines, surfaces and volumes plastically diversified through form and color. The well disposed beholder... was to go through the inverse process and from changes of color and form to reproduce feelings of motion, thus coming into contact with the 'dynamic source of things'...The Futurist painting was the 'spark that kindles the imagination of the spectator' with the dynamic fire which had previously consumed the painter's soul..."[75]

Simultaneity, in the Futurist concept, as stated by Boccioni, "is the condition under which the different elements constituting dynamism (the subject of Futurist paintings) reveal themselves...

It is the lyrical exponent of our present conception of life which is based on the rapidity and contemporaneity of knowledge and communications ...All plastic investigations conducted by the Futurists have their basis in simultaneity."[76] To this Soffici adds: "External velocity, by intensifying our mental action has modified our perception of space and time. As a result we have the sensation of the contiguousness and contemporaneity of things and events, or simultaneity of sight and emotion." Simultaneity is the "principle which bids the artist unite in one picture bundles of images (forms, colors, rhythms)..."[77]

This "bundle of images" can be united in one picture only if space as ordinarily conceived is destroyed. "Space does not exist. Millions of miles separate us from the sun, yet that is no reason why the house before us should not be encased in the solar disk...How often it happens that upon the cheek of the person with whom we are talking we see the horse that passes far away at the end of the street..."[78] "A street pavement wet with rain and illuminated by electric lights sinks down to the center of the earth..."[79]

If the painting, made up of a "bundle of images" is not to be simply a grouping of separate pictures units, then the pictorial elements must not all be conceived as opaque, but as capable of becoming transparent when necessary so that none blocks out views of the others. "In our work we can secure effects similar to those of the X-ray. Opacity does not exist...Our bodies become parts of the seat upon which we rest and the seat becomes part of us. The omnibus merges in the houses that it passes, and the houses mix with the bus and become part of it."[80] Space was conceived to be as solid as the objects it surrounded, yet it remained transparent and took a positive role in the play of interpenetration.

The use of transparent elements was termed by the Futurists "simultaneous interpenetration of surfaces," and was defined as the intersection of planes composed of lines and volumes, the planes differing from one another in thickness, heaviness and degree of transparency. As each plane is of a pure complementary color, they produce a great variety of chromatic tones by their intersections. The result is a "projection of plastic influences and reactions which gives to the painting a simultaneity of aspects and a wealth of movements heretofore unknown."[81]

The most basic elements in this Futuristic painting technique are line and color. In their terminology line became "force-line", and color "color-form". A "force-line" was a "direction of color-form" which in turn was the representation of movements of matter along the trajectory determined by the structure of the object and its action."[82] And these "force-lines" were the paths by which finite things reached infinity: "all objects, as a result of what Boccioni happily calls physical transcendentalism, tend toward infinity by virtue of their force-lines whose continuity is measured by our intuition..."[83] Force-lines were the continuation of the rhythms which the object imprinted on the artist's mind and which would eventually force the spectator's mind into the midst of the action; force-lines were used by the artist to indicate where his construction ended and where the intuition of the spectator began to operate.[84] The most direct examples of the use of force-lines are the wedge shapes used to suggest speed and force, as in Russolo's <u>Revolt</u> of 1911.

Clough presents this summary of part of a lecture by Boccioni: he proclaimed the " 'absolute and complete abolition of the finite and finished line.' The artist was to 'tear open the contour of a thing and push the enveloping milieu into it' ...with the aid of these force-lines...the painter can represent an open window as a 'variable, irregular opening into which the bodies of the external world insert themselves borne in by a conducting vehicle (the atmosphere) which penetrates the room in the form imprinted upon it by the potentialities of the external objects themselves.' The Futurist painter thus saw and depicted 'a stupendous spectacle enacted by the influence of both the force-lines of the external objects and the force-lines of the window and the conducting body (the atmosphere), with the latter gradually creeping in, in a varying density of straight thrusts and foreshortenings."[85]

In Picabia's work of this period, 1909 through 1913, only the overlapping circles of the bouncing ball in <u>Caoutchouc</u> are transparent, and so seem to destroy space. But actually this painting has a strong sense of space, and the cluster of circles are contained within a box-like space, however distorted, which is defined by the planes into which the background is divided. The lines forming the edges of these rectangular planes are furthest apart towards the edge of the picture and converge as they touch the group of circles, creating reference to linear perspective.

The elements of all Picabia's other paintings of the period are opaque, and have density. When he became preoccupied with superimposing transparent elements in certain of his paintings of the 1920's he very literally united in one picture a "bundle of images", but he did so without a hint of the Futurists' pictorial dynamics. Picabia did not tear open contours of things to push the enveloping milieu into them. He merely superimposed one line drawing, composed of finite and finished lines, on another, and the drawings remain indifferent to their effect on one another (see pp.132-133).

Duchamp used transparency in the Moulin à café, 1911, but this painting is essentially conceived without space; it is a flat two-dimensional design. In his painting Les joueurs d'échecs, also of 1911, and in the studies that precede it (pl.18), conventional space and space occupancy of objects have been completely destroyed; all the transparent elements in the painting interpenetrate one another; the figures of the spectators merge with those of the players, and the chess pieces hover between the players' heads.

Duchamp used transparency to a lesser extent in Nu descendant un escalier and Jeune homme mélancolique dans un Train of 1912,[86] and the path of the figures' progression through space is clearly defined. The forms of Le Roi et la Reine entourés de Nus vites,[87] and Mariée, 1912, are opaque, and their full roundness is indicated. In 1913, with the first studies for La Mariée mise à nu par ses célibataires, même, that are painted on glass, among them Glissière Contenant un Moulin à Eau,[88] Duchamp reached a compromise; the forms are rendered for the most part as flat areas of color; they are opaque and their density is suggested by the lines, precisely placed according to the laws of Renaissance perspective, which define them: the glass on which the forms are painted is completely transparent so that the forms are seen as if suspended against the environment of the painting.

Picabia, in his statements of 1913, expresses ideas that parallel the belief held by the Futurists that the artist's experiences could be transcribed as abstract forms and colors which in their turn guide the spectator's senses to a reconstruction of the artist's experiences (see pp.76-77, 79-81). But though Picabia was greatly interested in conveying a sense of motion, he was not interested in the movement of the universe as were the Futurists, and of course he did not share the Futurists' intent to hurl the spectator into the cosmos.

Picabia's interest in motion was more subtle and went through a number of transformations. (The examples of Picabia's work mentioned below are more fully discussed in their proper places further on in the text, while a brief survey of Marcel Duchamp's expression of motion is on page 54). In Caoutchouc Picabia had been interested in the simple motion of a bouncing ball; in La ville de Paris, 1911 (pl.2,fig.6), in the movement of city life; in Tarentella (pl.3,fig.8) and Danses à la source, of 1912, Danseuse étoile sur une transatlantique and Danseuse étoile et son école de danse, of 1913, in the movements of dancers. But in other works, Picabia, as did Duchamp, transformed this simple concept of portraying movement as action into other, more complex concepts which, however, still remain rooted in the philosophic concept of reality as an everchanging, constantly evolving entity. Je revois en souvenir ma chere Udnie, Edtaonisl, Ecclésiastique of 1913, and Le Beau Charcutier of 1921, are among those paintings by Picabia which have the interplay of physical, psychological and social relationships between persons as their subject, which is also the subject of Duchamp's La Mariée mise à nu par ses célibataires, même. To an extent such subject matter parallels the

Futurists' concept of "states of mind" (discussed on page 98); however the Futurists' concept never became so literary or so subtle.

In his paintings _Yvonne et Magdeleine Déchiqutées_, 1911, and _Passage de la vierge à la mariée_, 1912, Duchamp took as his subject the change from one state of being into another; in the former the change is the result of time, in the second it is the result of an act. By painting several works on glass, Duchamp exposed them to the risk of actual physical change in time, knowing that eventually they would break.

The spectator is called upon to act intellectually, to solve the puns or riddles contained in most of Picabia's Dadaist machine-portraits, calligrams and illustrations. Another transformation of the concept of motion by Picabia and Duchamp was that of the "significant gesture", either a gesture of choosing, or a gesture of defiance of popular values or taste. Examples of the former are _Mirroir de l'apparance_ (pl.12,fig.33) for which Picabia chose a commercial photograph of the harp of a grand piano, on which he made a few alterations and then presented as his own work, and _Réveil Matin_ (pl.12,fig.34), made by stamping ink-dipped parts of an alarm clock which Picabia chose. These, and others of their kind, are Picabia's equivalent of Duchamp's "ready-mades", which are objects whose significance, aesthetic or otherwise, Duchamp recognized and to which he made additions or merely signed his name. Examples of gestures of defiance are Picabia's _Portrait de Cezanne_ (pl.14,fig.43) which is a stuffed monkey that pulls its tail between its legs, and Duchamp's _L. H. O. O. Q._, the reproduction of Da Vinci's _Mona Lisa_, on which he drew a moustache. Picabia's "transparencies" of the 1920's embody the idea of motion as change of subject, or of scene.

Survey of Duchamp's Expression of Motion

Duchamp's Moulin à café of 1911, and perhaps both versions of Nu descendant un escalier, the first of 1911,[89] the second of 1912, are his only paintings to be concerned simply with the mechanics of forms in movement. His other experiments with motion are characterized by the seeking out of variations of the concept, and of new technical means for their expression.

The face of the central figure of La Sonate,[90] 1911, a portrait of his mother is divided by a central line that is at once the line of the woman's nose and lips, and the delineation of right and left profiles. None of the elements of the painting are rendered transparent.

In Yvonne et Magdeleine Déchiquetées, Sept., 1911,[91] Duchamp painted a study of change from one state of being into another by the passage of time. It portrays Duchamp's two sisters twice; as young women and again as middle aged. Each representation is in profile, the nose and forehead being the most clearly characterized features. A discordant pictorial movement results from the fact that the profiles, while appearing to move across the canvas in a regularized progression from small to large, at the same time alternate: the end, and smallest profile on the left faces left, while the repetition of that face as the largest one in the center faces right. Only the nose of this largest profile is clearly defined so that the last head on the right whose whole profile is defined, seems largest. This right hand profile faces left while its other likeness faces right. This painting is Duchamp's most romantic, its forms the least rigid and the most organic. Transparency is not used in this work.

Portrait, 1911,[92] shows five images of the same woman, which also optically merge to form one figure (an effect which isn't seen in black and white reproduction).

Duchamp's next major work of 1911, *Les joueurs d'échecs*, presents the psychological interchange between the figures. The intense interest of the chess players and their spectators in the game is clearly stated. In the first preliminary drawing (pl.18,fig.55) the two large profiles of both players, each individually characterized by his nose, seem to kiss in their mutual absorption in the game. The eyes of both profiles are formed of the lines that are the eyebrows and noses of the same player, again characterized by the shape of their nose, now drawn back in individual thought. In the second drawing (pl.18,fig.54), and the first oil sketch (pl.18,fig.56), the small shapes of the chess pieces dance about and across the players, and the spectators are merely indicated in the background. In the final version (pl.18,fig.57) all the elements are rendered as if made of transparent plastic, becoming opaque only toward their emphasized contours. The heads of the players are each shown in more than one position; their slow movement through space is simulated by repetition of similar contours - of noses and foreheads - and the curvilinear lines that suggest the players' arms.

Duchamp's *Nu descendant un escalier*, no. 2, 1912 (pl.19,fig.58), a mechanistic presentation of a figure in motion, makes use of the same pictorial devices as does the final version of *Les joueurs d'échecs*, though its elements are not rendered nearly so transparent, and they are more abstract. *Jeune Homme mélancolique dans un Train*, 1912, also shows a figure in motion, but only from the waist up. The torso vibrates with the motion of the train, while the legs remain stable. The painting uses the same pictorial means, as those of Nu descendant un escalier. Three merging repetitions of the figure are given, each successively smaller and less clearly defined, which suggests the movement of the train across the vision of the observer.

Le Roi et la Reine éntourés de Nus vites, 1912, contrasts two groups of stationary elements with a series of moving ones. In this painting Duchamp again employed the same technical means as in Nu descendant un escalier, but here transparency is hardly suggested. The suggestion of the fast movement of the swift nudes that move diagonally from lower right to upper left, comes chiefly from the repetition of many elements of similar size, shape and color, and their opposition to either vertical or horizontal axes. The elements that form the King and Queen, based on chess pieces, are larger, as well as more varied in size and shape, than those of the earlier paintings and they obey stabilizing vertical axes. The same pictorial devices to suggest motion are used in Passage de la vierge à la mariée, 1912.[93] The concept of motion here is, as its title states, the change from one state of being to another as the result of an act. Mariée, dated August, 1912 (pl.5,fig.14) is an elaboration of the central area of the preceding painting, and portrays the tense state of the virgin as she anticipates the act that will change her from a virgin into a married woman (see p. 107). None of the elements are rendered as transparent. The suggestion of motion results chiefly from the repetition of thin attenuated elements that generally follow one another around a large curve that enters the composition from the lower left and passes up around to the upper left.

The subject of the large painting on glass La Mariée mise à nu par ses célibataires, même, worked on in New York City, 1915 through 1923, is a literary interplay between personages (see pp.124-125). This painting, and several studies for it, also on glass, are a logical, if extreme, use of transparency in painting. The glass is meant to be placed in the middle of the room so that the painted elements are seen against a continuously changing background. In the earlier studies, among which are Glissière contenant un moulin à eau, 1913-15, painted on glass (see footnote 88), and Broyeuse de Chocolat, no. 2, 1914,[94] as well as in the final painting, all the mechanical components are shown in static rest, but the repetition of similar elements on these components create a strong implication of movement. The repeated elements are: the rectangular paddles placed between the rims of the two wheels, and the radiating spokes of the wheels in the mill contained in the Glissière; the lines that radiate from the center of the faces of the rollers and continue along their sides in the Broyeuse de Chocolat, no. 2; and in the final painting itself, in addition to the above, the series of interlocked cones that curve through the upper center of the lower panel, and the radiating lines that form the middle disk of the "splash" or "Témoine oculistes" which was added to the upper right side of the lower panel in 1920. The lines that form the disks of the "splash" are mirrored, so that the spectator not only sees the room behind the glass but himself partially reflected in the mirrors.

In 1913 Duchamp began to experiment with other, non-pictorial forms expressing variations on concepts of motion, of philosophic and sometimes pseudo-scientific nature, often carried out with tongue in cheek.[95]

Among these variations are the "ready-mades" which belong to the realm of "significant gesture". What is important here is the act of choosing, partly for sincere aesthetic reasons, mostly in defiance of popular conceptions of "good taste". The "ready-mades" were a series of manufactured objects which Duchamp elected to elevate to being objects of "art" simply by the act of isolating them, perhaps placing his signature on them, occasionally altering them slightly to heighten their effectiveness. The first was a bottle-rack chosen in 1914. To an extent the "ready-mades" had their basis in the Cubist "collage" (see note 198).

In another group of experiments, some of them related to the final large painting on glass, Duchamp was concerned with the results of movement left to chance. In his first experiment with chance, he let a draft of air blow a piece of gauze against a screen three times, each time recording the accidental variations of the square's contours, which he repeated on the large amorphous shape of the upper panel of the final version of *La Mariée mise à nu...* A similar experiment, called *3 stoppages étalon*, 1913-14, consisted of dropping three separate threads, each one meter long, from a straight, horizontal position one meter above horizontal panels, onto which the threads were attached in the positions they had landed. These lines were traced and arranged into three different groupings, for a total of nine, which were superimposed on the "Nine malic forms", both the individual study on glass,[96] and as they appear on the final painting. An earlier experiment consisted of making nine marks on a glass by shooting matches dipped in paint from a toy cannon; the nine points became the locations for the base of each of the nine "malic forms."

Another of Duchamp's concepts, that of motion as change, change wrought by the forces of nature in destroying the works of man, led him to consider painting on glass in the first place, for he knew that the glass would be broken sooner or later.[97] It also led him to "grow" or "raise" dust: once when the large glass lay under a six-month's accumulation of dust he dropped fixative on the glass where the dust covered the cones - he repeated this act on each of the successive cones, raising seven months dust, eight months dust, etc., to give each of them its tone.

Duchamp also engaged in a long series of experiments of producing actual motion, as well as the optical illusion of motion. In 1916 he mounted a bicycle wheel on a kitchen stool that was meant to be spun by hand. In 1920 he attached a series of glass blades of graduated size, painted with white and black lines, and which were spaced a meter deep on an axle turned by a motor. When set in motion only shimmering circles formed by the painted lines remained visible. Also in 1920 he made a movie of circles and spirals, and in 1926, in collaboration with Man Ray and Marc Allegret, he made another movie, Anemic Cinema, a filming of the "Rotary demisphere" he built in 1925, which consisted of a series of eccentric circles painted upon a hemisphere; when rotated by a motor the circles optically spiralled alternately away from and then toward the observer. A further application of this idea are a series of optical discs called "Rotoreliefs", made in 1935, which when placed upon a revolving phonograph turntable, produce the optical illusion of objects moving in three-dimensional space.

PICABIA'S PAINTINGS AFTER CAOUTCHOUC OF 1909, THROUGH THE FIRST HALF OF 1913

After having achieved the effect of motion in Caoutchouc by means of simultaneity and transparency, Picabia abandoned these plastic ideas. To obtain the effects of motion in all his other paintings of the next decade, he depended upon the sense of movement inherent in diagonals and curves, and the loss of stability that results when the pictorial elements do not obey the vertical and horizontal axes of the canvas, and the staccato pictorial rhythms that are created on the canvas by means of spotting and repeating shapes more or less similar in size, contour, color and value.

Even in Caoutchouc, to help simulate the effect of motion Picabia had used the device of repeating similar shapes, that is, the circles, and of abandoning the use of stabilizing vertical and horizontal axes in the large background areas, the axis of each of which opposes the vertical and horizontal axes, though a vertical axis, along which the overlapping circles cluster, is stated in the composition.

Picabia's use of these pictorial devices reached their climax in the two paintings entitled Edtaonisl, the one subtitled Ecclésiastique (pl.6,fig.16), the other Catch as Catch Can (pl.8,fig.20), of 1913, in which all the pictorial elements whirl about in free defiance of gravity.

Thus Picabia used purely traditional painterly means to suggest motion. In fact the staccato pictorial rhythm of Poussin's Rape of the Sabine Women is achieved in much the same manner as it is in Picabia's Danseuse étoile et son école de danse, 1913 (pl.7,fig.18).

Except for the transparent suggestions inherent in the line drawings of his Dadaistic machine-calligrames, and the occasional device of having these surprinted over a page of printed matter (pl.13,fig.40), Picabia did not use transparency again until 1920.

In Picabia's first works to approach abstraction, such as the painting Paysage de la Creuse of 1908,[98] which is close to the drawing Paysage of the same year (pl.2,fig.4), and the pastel Paysage de Cassis of 1909 (pl.2,fig.5), there is no concern with depicting motion. They are stabilized compositions. Natural space and aerial perspective are suggested in them, though the two dimensional character of the canvas is emphasized.

The painting Paysage de la Creuse closely resembles in style the landscapes painted by Picasso and Braque of the same year, 1908, particularly Picasso's Landscape with Figures,[99] but in its colors it is much further removed from nature than the latter. The trees and patches of sky are bright red, the other elements are painted in greys and blacks; the total color effect is somber and has no relation to the brilliant colors of Fauve landscapes, although Picabia was probably encouraged in his use of unreal color by the daring colors of the Fauves.

The shapes that compose these three landscapes by Picabia are simplified and abstracted from nature, but they nevertheless definitely have their origin in the forms of nature. The shapes that compose his paintings of 1911, 1912 and 1913, described below, are composed of abstract shapes, all of which the artist may use to refer to the forms in nature, but which he did not base on natural forms.

Picabia's Paysage of 1911 (pl.1,fig.2), is full of pictorial movement, though no moving objects are represented. The suggestion of motion results from the predominantly curvilinear character of the shapes of which it is composed, and which do not have definitely stated vertical or horizontal axes, but are left to float about in defiance of space. A pictorial rhythm is set up by the spotting of the different values and colors which at the same time set up the pictorial balance, keeping the painting a self contained unit. There is almost no suggestion of natural space in it; the two dimensions of the canvas are emphasized.

The word "space" as referred to in the above and following descriptions of Picabia's paintings of this period, needs qualification. Both solid form and space are treated as positive matter. Often color distinguishes the two, as in Procession à Séville, in which shapes that compose the figures are grey, black and orange-red, while the shapes that compose the sky against which the figures are silhouetted are of various shades of blue. In black and white reproduction this distinction is lost. In many instances the distinction between form and space is made by the grouping of particular shapes which by their character suggest figures, and buildings, and by logic of their position suggest earth, pavement, or sky; often the contours of certain shapes carry vestiges of perspective.

La Ville de Paris (pl.2,fig.6) of 1911, has as its subject the scurrying inhabitants of the city. It is composed of abstract shapes, whose edges are almost entirely straight. But the abstract shapes build up images of sky, buildings, pavement, people, and in the right hand corner of the painting, a horse drawn carriage. Though the shapes are two dimensional, they suggest forms in natural space; the horses and carriage are foreshortened, the segments of pavement extend into the background. In contrast to the lack of vertical or horizontal axes in the Paysage, strong vertical axes are given by the shapes of the buildings with their stripes of windows, the legs of the horses and the carriage; strong horizontal axes are given by the lines in the sky (clouds), the line where the buildings meet the pavements, the axle of the carriage. But the shapes that form the scurrying people and the divisions of the pavement, oppose these axes, and by their opposition suggest motion. A sharp staccato pictorial rhythm is set up by the spotting of the different colors and values of the smaller shapes. In its pictorial means, this painting resembles Severini's Boulevard,[100] 1910-11.

Port of Naples,[101] 1911, is compositionally similar to Paysage, described above (pl.1,fig.2).

The titles of three paintings of 1912, Tarentella, Procession à Séville, Danses à la source, reveal the kinds of movement of the human body portrayed: the dance, and a religious ritual, in this case self-flagellation. Nothing has been added to his vocabulary of the preceding year. Tarentella (pl.3,fig.8) is close to La ville de Paris in its use of smaller straight-edged shapes which combine to suggest figures, and most of which oppose both the stated vertical axes that are repeated over the surface, and the implied horizontal axis of the plane that the smaller shapes rest on. The opposition of small shapes to vertical and horizontal axes, the large curvilinear movements in the sky, and the staccato rhythm set up by the spotting of colors and values create the sense of motion. The dancing figures that are suggested move in space.

La procession à Séville (pl.2,fig.7), is composed of a mountain of black, grey and red-orange straight-edged shapes, almost all similar in character, which combine to form figures dressed in ceremonial robes who whip themselves as they move along. These figures whose robes are black and whose faces and hands are red-orange, are silhouetted against a blue sky that is also sub-divided into straight-edged shapes. Though a vertical axis is implied in the overall mountain of shapes, with the exception of certain edges following vertical and horizontal axes, all the shapes are placed in opposition to the stabilizing axes, and it is this opposition which simulates motion. The repetition of so many similar shapes, and the spotting of values and colors, particularly the red-orange that is repeated across the surface, sets up what is now Picabia's typical staccato pictorial rhythm. These figures do not move in a natural space; they are piled up in an unreal way on top of one another against the blue sky. This painting, in its piling up of faceted shapes each of which is in opposition to the implied vertical axis of the over-all mass, recalls Picasso's

Harlequin and his family of 1908. But there is a difference of degree between the two paintings. Picasso's has many less faceted shapes, each of which is larger in scale, and each opposes the vertical axis in a regularized way, their contours often paralleling one another. Picabia's is a mass of faceted shapes each of which turns in its own direction; and the edges of each facet has the same degree of sharpness which results from maintaining the original linear drawing. Picasso's edges often melt into one another. The general effect of Picasso's painting remains stabilized and serene. Picabia's writhes.

Danses à la source (pl.3,fig.9), the last painting Picabia completed before his trip to New York, is stabile and architectonic in comparison to the two of 1912 already discussed, though it has dancing figures as its subject. This results from the dominating vertical direction of the figures and the strongly stated horizontal base they stand on. The sharp-edged two-dimensional shapes are fewer in number, larger in scale, and are more varied in contour and size than those of the earlier paintings. Both curvilinear and straight-edged shapes are given prominence. The opposition of most of the shapes to the horizontal and vertical axes, and the spotting of values and colors creates a sense of slow, dignified movement, as compared to the staccato, fast pictorial movement set up in Tarentella. The figures of this painting, which move on a shallow stagelike space, are the most easily read of all those discussed so far; yet the colors of this painting depart furthest from reality. The nude figures are painted in hot oranges and lighter pinks, the background shapes are dark reds, browns and greys. This is essentially the same un-naturalistic color scheme Picabia used in the painting Paysage de la Creuse of 1908.

Two of the water-colors Picabia painted in New York in the first half of 1913 also have dancers as their subject: Danseuse étoile sur un transatlantique (pl.6,fig.15), and Danseuse étoile et son école de danse (pl.7,fig.18). Of the two, the former is most abstract, most difficult to read. The shapes seem to derive from the structual elements of an ocean liner, and they suggest a section of deck with ventilator superstructures; but the "star" dancer is not readily discernable. (Note: I do not know the colors of this painting, and it is possible that the colors more clearly characterize the points of reference made by the shapes, for Picabia at this time was working in a language of visual symbols). The repeated vertical and horizontal directions of important shapes, and the large plane that serves as a base for the structures, stabilize the composition; suggestions of motion come from the large curves of other shapes, and the spotting of the values.

The second of the two water-colors of dancers, Danseuse étoile et son école de danse, is more complex in its interweaving of sharp-edged shapes. Its sense of staccato movement results from the opposition of most of these shapes to vertical and horizontal axes, and the repetition of similar shapes, colors and values. Picabia's working procedure is clearly discernable in this water-color. The contours of the areas were first drawn with pencil lines, then the areas were filled in with clear, unmudied and unmixed colors - burnt sienna, ultramarine blue, and black - used opaquely in the dark areas and thinned with water for the lighter tones. It was painted with decision and only one or two areas reveal re-working. The figures of the dancers are dissolved into the all-over pattern of the painting, lost to the point where picking them out becomes merely conjecture; but it seems that the "star" dancer is right in the center of the composition, with other dancers on either side. A flesh colored area in the lower center seems to be the calf of her leg. Her arms are outstretched on a diagonal line that points up to the upper right corner of the picture: the greatest suggestion of motion in the painting comes from the progression of conical shapes that move along this diagonal. The shapes are flat, two-dimensional, though certain ones seem to bend slightly in space. Each of the areas has a positive value; there are no real background or foreground shapes, only the bright blue that colors certain of the areas creates the suggestion of airy space behind the brown, black or grey ones.

Others of the water-colors made in New York, among them La ville de New York aperçue le corps (pl.7,fig.17), and Moi aussi j'ai vecu en Amerique,[103] suggest the dynamic movements of the city's life as described by Picabia in a statement quoted on pages 74-75. They would be analyzed in essentially the same terms as those above.

However, with Chanson Nègre (see p.104,and pl.4,fig.10), another of the New York series, Picabia was not concerned with the dynamic aspects of city life, but with the sensuous swaying rhythm of a "blues" song. The "nègre" is made up of the cluster of curvilinear shapes in the upper right center of the painting. These shapes form only an ambiguous elemental symbol of a human being that seems to be all head with huge lips. The sensuous quality is enhanced by the colors, which are burnt amber, black, the white of the paper in untouched areas, and one long line of alizarin crimson, that of the linear element that curves up on the left side of the "nègre". Although the shapes are flat the floor plane does recede. The singer seems to stand in a darkened room, illuminated by a theatrical spot-light.

PICABIA'S AESTHETIC IDEAS IN 1913

During his visit to New York in the first six months of 1913 Picabia made a series of statements in the form of interviews with the art critics of the New York press who regarded him as the spokesman for the Cubist painters. Most of these statements were reprinted in Stieglitz' publication Camera Work, along with other special interviews, reports, and Picabia's own preface to the catalog of his one-man show at Stieglitz' gallery 291. All of these statements were intended to explain his aesthetic ideas to the American public which had just been confronted for the first time with the work of the modern European artists in the huge exhibition now referred to as the Armory Show of 1913. Picabia's statements apply particularly to his paintings of 1912, and to the water-color paintings he was currently producing in New York. Thus he was primarily concerned with explaining abstract painting, often called "pure" painting.

An excellent definition of abstract, or "pure" painting, one true for Picabia and the Cubists as well as for the Futurists, was made by the Futurist painter Soffici. He said: "...pure painting is that art which is neither descriptive nor anecdotal, psychological nor moral, sentimental nor educational." "Pure painting is a reinterpretation of forms devoid of any ulterior or extraneous purpose, forms which are not intended to express or to evoke anything over and above themselves. They are...pictorial realities having in themselves and only in themselves, their raison d'être. Their harmony, resulting from the combination of lines and surfaces, and colors, from the play of their shadows and light, from the design and chiaroscuro, is their only law..."[104]

All the Cubists were concerned with pure painting. As Apollinaire said in 1912: "The secret aim of the young painters of the extremist schools is to produce pure painting. Theirs is an entirely new plastic art. It is still in its beginnings, and is not yet as abstract as it would like to be. Most of the new painters depend a good deal on mathematics, without knowing it; but they have not yet abandoned nature, which they still question patiently hoping to learn the right answers to the questions raised by life." "Real resemblance no longer has any importance, since everything is sacrificed by the artist to truth, to the necessities of a higher nature whose existence he assumes but does not lay bare." "Thus we are moving towards an entirely new art which will stand, with respect to paintings as envisaged heretofore, as music stands to literature."[105]

Picabia's statements reveal that he was never interested in abstract forms and colors for their own sake in formal relationships, but that he, as did the Futurists, attempted to use abstract forms as vehicles for projecting onto the canvas the "emotional, temperamental, subjective states" of his mind resulting from his experiences in life. In his water-color paintings of New York City, Picabia abandoned painting the forms of nature, and moved close to pure, or abstract painting. At the same time his subject matter, the ideas he wished to express, assumed great importance. His paintings became a sign language, of which the shapes and colors are the syntax. With this language he wished to state ideas rather than to describe scenes or objects; for he felt that "pure art cannot reproduce a material fact. It can only make real the immaterial or emotional fact...art and the camera are opposites (the camera cannot reproduce a mental fact..." Picabia wanted to restore what may be called the function of narration to painting, and he wanted to accomplish this by an exploitation of the potential suggestiveness of abstract art.

Picabia's statements reveal that almost all of his aesthetic ideas in 1913 are those found also in Apollinaire's The Cubist Painters of 1912, in which they appear partly as Apollinaire's explanation of Orphic Cubism, in which branch of Cubism he placed Picabia, and of Picabia's aims, but also because Picabia, though evolving individualistically, did draw from the same fund of current thought. In his book Cubist Aesthetics, Grey discusses the basic similarity in the ideas expressed in Apollinaire's book and those Gleizes and Metzinger express in their Cubism of 1913, similarities which verify the existence of a common basic fund of ideas.

Picabia's paintings of 1912, and his work of 1913, including the water-colors made in New York, and the oils made upon his return to Paris, such as Edtaonisl, Ecclésiastique, because of the impossibility of relating the shapes of which they are composed to any specific natural forms, are examples of Orphic Cubism, the second of Apollinaire's major divisions of pure painting, which he defined as "the art of painting new structures out of elements which have not been borrowed from the visual sphere, but have been created entirely by the artist himself, and been endowed by him with fullness of reality. The works of the orphic artist must simultaneously give a pure aesthetic pleasure, a structure which is self-evident, and a sublime meaning, that is, the subject. This is pure art. The light in Picasso's paintings is based on this conception, to which Robert Delaunay's inventions have contributed much, and towards which Fernand Leger, Francis Picabia, and Marcel Duchamp are also addressing themselves."[107]

About Orphism Apollinaire also said: "The last and most glorious phase of Cubism is the art of dynamism obtained by the use of complementary colors and simultaneous contrasts."[108] And he said that Cubism in its Orphic reincarnation would show that "this simultaneity alone is creation, the rest is only enumeration," and that "Orphism is simultaneity. Suggestive, not only objective painting."[109] When the Italian Futurists saw Apollinaire and others write of Orphism in this way they claimed these same arguments proved the derivation of Orphism from the Futurists. The Italian painters remarked they were first derided by everybody including the French critics for their insistence on dynamism and simultaneity, and that later, when their ideas and methods had gained acceptance, the French appropriated them and claimed it new though the Futurists had proclaimed it in their 1910 Manifesto.[110] But as has already been pointed out the Futurists and Cubists and others were sharing ideas that manifested themselves generally in the work of artists throughout Europe; the Italian Futurists could actually lay claim only to the terminology.

In his statements of 1913 Picabia addressed himself to the American public to tell them what to look for in his paintings.[111] He explained why the artist can no longer paint realistically and that the artist instead now tries to paint his feelings about his experiences; he described the kind of experiences that he was trying to paint, and he explained how these experiences became transmuted into the shapes and colors of his paintings. He said, "We must devote ourselves to setting down on our canvases not things, but emotions produced in our minds by things. We must be subjective. It is our own expression about what we feel or see that will have vitality if it be worthy...Now that representation by paint or by the camera has progressed so far, the way in which we artists can best express what we feel is by the purely subjective, by the abstract. That is what some of us are trying to do."[112] The presence of the camera leads "the artist to see that he must have a field to himself. The camera cannot reproduce a mental fact. Logically, pure art cannot reproduce a material fact. It can only make real the immaterial or emotional fact...art and the camera are opposites ...absolutely consistent art would make no attempt to reproduce objects at all." "The attempt made by most artists to reproduce the third-dimension of space is a mistake, as it is only a trick. The canvas has only two-dimensions and this natural limitation should be observed..."[113]

Picabia expressed the thought that not only was it unnecessary to depict scenes and objects as the camera does, but that to do so would be to actually distort "reality" - for in today's world we know much more about the world than merely what meets the eye. Gabrielle Buffet-Picabia, in a statement that may also be taken as that of Picabia said: "Out of the ever deepening consciousness of life which arises from every new scientific discovery there arises a new and complex state of mind to which the external world appears more clearly in the abstract form of the qualities and properties of its elements than under the concrete form of our sense perceptions. Or more broadly speaking, we can say that at the same time that we have our perception of the external, we have the consciousness of all that exists above and beyond it...The old language of the artist is no longer appropriate for the last new needs of our being."[114]

To this Picabia added, in the preface to the catalog of his exhibition: "The objective representation of nature through which the painter used to express the mysterious feeling of his ego in front of his subject 'motive' no longer suffices for the fullness of his new consciousness of nature. This representation bears no longer a relationship to his new conception of life, and has become not only a limitation but a deformation. 'The objective representation of nature is a deformation of our present conception of nature.'

"Reality imposes itself upon us not only under a special form but even under a qualitative form.

"For example: when we look at a tree we are conscious not only of its outside appearance but also of some of its properties, its qualities and its evolution. Our feelings before this tree are the result of the knowledge acquired by experience through analysis; hence the complexity of this feeling cannot be expressed simply by objective and mechanical representation.

"The qualitative conception of reality can no longer be expressed in a purely visual or optical manner; and in consequence pictorial expression has had to eliminate more objective formulae from its convention in order to relate itself to the qualitative conception."[115]

Picabia elaborated on the theme that the reproduction of external appearances is unnecessary, and that that which is important is the projection onto the canvas of the emotional, temperamental and subjective states of the artist's mind resulting from his experiences in life. He said: "...Aristotle said that art is a copy of life. But that is exactly what art is not. Art is a successful attempt to render external an internal state of mind or feeling, to project onto the canvas emotional, temperamental, subjective states. All great art in the past has done that (even when it had elements of the objective... (It) has partly reproduced external objects, but it has done so in such a way that the emphasis has been laid on what was going on in the imagination and feeling of the artist). Great art has always been crystallized feeling which in itself is unseen...Art can express the fourth-dimension of the soul, but not the third-dimension of actuality. And if it cannot legitimately render the third-dimension, it cannot legitimately portray objects which exist in space, and so involve the third dimension. There should be no perspective in painting.

"Art deals with deep, brooding fundamental, simple soul states. How do these states arise? They are the result of the artist's experience in life. Suppose the artist has felt the quality of our skyscrapers, of our city and our life, and tries to reproduce it. This experience has affected his mood. He renders plastic that mood on canvas. But the resulting picture has no skyscrapers in it and no city ...only the results of the skyscrapers and the city on his temperament." 116

Picabia gave the public a concrete illustration of his experience of New York City and of how it became transmuted into his water-color paintings. "You of New York should be quick to understand me and my fellow painters. Your New York is the cubist, the futuristic city...you should quickly understand the studies I have made since my arrival in New York.

They express the spirit of New York as I feel it, and the crowded streets of your city as I feel them, their surging, their unrest, their commercialism, and their atmospheric charm.

"You see no form? No substance? Is it that I go out into your city and see nothing? I see much, much more, perhaps, than you who are used to it see. I see your stupendous skyscrapers, your mammoth buildings and marvellous subways, a thousand evidences of your great wealth on all sides. The tens of thousands of workers and toilers, your alert and shrewd-looking shop girls, all hurrying somewhere. I see your theater crowds at night gleaming, fluttering, smiling, happy, smartly gowned. There you have the spirit of modernity again.

"But I do not paint these things which my eye sees. I paint that which my brain, my soul sees. I walk from the Battery to Central Park, I mingle with your workers, and your Fifth Avenue mondaines. My brain gets the impression of each movement; there is the driving hurry of the former, their breathless haste to reach their homes at night. There is the languid grace of the latter, emanating a subtle perfume, a more subtle sensuousness.

"I hear every language in the world spoken, the staccato of the New Yorker, the soft cadences of the Latin People, the heavy rumble of the Teutonic, and the ensemble remains in my soul as the ensemble of some great opera...

"I absorb these impressions in my brain, I am in no hurry to put them on canvas. I let them remain in my brain, and then when the spirit of creation is at flood tide, I improvise my pictures as a musician improvises music. The harmonies grow under his fingers. His music is from his brain and his soul just as my studies are from my brain and my soul. Is this not clear to you?"[117]

Picabia reiterated his creative procedure in other words. He spoke of having left the plane of the five senses which he called "matière pensée" (material thought), and of being concerned solely with psychic perception which he called "pensée pure" (pure thought). To illustrate the difference between them Picabia said if he had painted <u>Procession à Séville</u> through "<u>matière pensée</u>" he would have produced a more or less photographic interpretation of it; but he had evoluted to the interpretation of the idea or concept of a religious procession, deriving out of it religious and other emotions from his aesthetic nature, and these he materialized in a harmony produced through the arrangement of color and form - "the language which the evolutive art itself imposes on itself." "...it is the realité of conception that the new movement tries to produce and not the realité of vision, the painting of yesterday...look at a canvas 'd' origine matière pensée' and you have a 'fixité'; so there is limitation. Look at one of mine. Naturally you could not find any 'fixité', because it is infinite, just as my emotions are. It expresses a 'pensée pure', which evidently blends with the infinite."[118]

The technical means by which the "new consciousness of life and nature" and the artists "soul states" are rendered plastic are those of abstract, or pure painting. "The resulting manifestations of this state of mind which is more and more approaching abstraction, can themselves not be anything but abstraction. They separate themselves from the sensorial pleasure which man may derive from man or nature (Impressionism) to enter the domain of the pure joy of the idea and consciousness."

Picabia went on to say that he attempted to give the purified results of experience by means of establishing an equilibrium, and that other artists have other means. Those means are what he called "style". It is through his style that an artist expresses his soul."[119]

Gabrielle Buffet-Picabia echoed the same idea: "works of this movement seem to us a combination of different volumes of form and color, one balanced by another, in which it is impossible to find any vestige of representation either concrete or symbolic...(These works) form a unity, a wholeness, in themselves and awaken an emotion of the same kind as that which music evokes." And "...the essential thing (for the spectator of these paintings) is to have an impression of the volumes of color which form the equilibrium in the picture and to take an abstract and impersonal pleasure in this equilibrium...(as in giving) ourselves up to the emotional impression which we feel when we listen to music. For the expressive value of line and color is as logical as that of sound; to deny one is to deny the other."[120]

Both Gabrielle and Picabia made the analogy between painting and music to support the argument that abstract shapes and colors in painting can convey the emotion and mood of the artist. Picabia said: "The rules of musical composition are sufficiently hampering in themselves to the composer's mood, or call it inspiration. Words, as of songs, still further confine his vision of melody, even though they give in the beginning the impression that evokes his mood. Songs without words, the expression of the impression made on him by a great poem without the necessity of following in musical form the literary form of the poet, leaves him far freer, give his subjectivity far wider scope...

May a composer be inspired by a walk in the country...and produce a reproduction of the landscape scene, of its details of form and color? No; he expresses it in sound waves, he translates it into an expression of the mood. And as there are absolute sound waves, so there are absolute waves of color and form...."[121]

According to Gabrielle Buffet-Picabia the analogy between painting and music appeared in the discussions between Apollinaire and Picabia on the subject of abstract painting that took place in the summer of 1912. She reconstructs the general line of their discussions thus: "We may suppose that Apollinaire extolled Picasso and Cubism and that he appeared uneasy and reticent on the subject of Picabia's development. 'It is an inhuman art, unintelligible to feeling and which runs the risk of remaining purely decorative.' 'Are blue and red unintelligible?' replied Picabia. 'Are not circles and triangles, volumes and colors, just as intelligible as this table or this cup?' And he doubtless added a few digs on the subject of Apollinaire's devotion to the Cubists." Gabrielle Buffet-Picabia claims that it was she who as a professional musician first contributed to the discussions the references and comparisons to music: "And I not to be out done: 'May not one conceive of a use of color and pure form corresponding, in the visual domain, to what music is in the domain of sound?' "She feels that her arguments "to which they as non-musicians had not given a thought did not remain without effect...one day Apollinaire announced solemnly he found a name for the new development in painting. Henceforward, side by side with <u>Cubism</u> and <u>Futurism</u> there would be <u>Orphism</u>, represented by Delaunay, Leger, Picabia, Duchamp and others."[122]

Apollinaire's book, <u>The Cubist Painters</u>, contains not just one "Orphic" comparison of painting to music, but several such comparisons, among which are the following: "It will be an entirely new art which will stand, with respect to painting as envisaged heretofore, as music stands to literature." "It will be pure painting, just as music is pure literature." "The music lover experiences, in listening to a concert, a joy of a different order from the joy given by natural sounds, such as the murmur of the brook, the uproar of a torrent, the whistling of the wind in a forest, of the harmonies of human speech based on reason rather than on aesthetics." "In the same way the new painters will provide their admirers with artistic sensations by concentrating exclusively on the problem of creating harmony with unequal lights."[123] And about Picabia's painting Apollinaire says: "This art is as close to music as the opposite of music can be. One might well say that the art of Picabia would like to stand, with respect to past painting, as music stands to literature, but one cannot say that it is musical itself. The truth is, music proceeds by suggestion; here, on the other hand we are presented with colors which are not supposed to affect us as symbols, but as concrete forms..."[124] (But as Picabia used color to help convey the emotion and mood of the artist, Apollinaire is in error in saying that Picabia's colors are not supposed to be symbols - see pages 91-92).

Perhaps Gabrielle Buffet-Picabia's suggestions did call Apollinaire's immediate attention to the analogy of painting to music, but it is also true that there is a tradition for this analogy in 19th century French art, as well as a tradition for the concept that abstract shapes and colors can convey the emotions and moods of the artist. Christopher Grey, in his Cubist Aesthetics, discusses the concept of correspondences held by Mallarme and others, and its influence on the work of the Cubists.[125] Grey points out that the concept of correspondences is based on "the assumption of a direct relationship between the quality of a sensation and the type of emotional response aroused by it. Beyond this, there is the assumption that the sensations received by any sense can produce a specific emotional response if the sensations have the requisite quality..."[126] "It is on the basis of the concept of correspondences that the abstract artist believes that he may eliminate all 'literary' elements from his painting yet remain master of the full range of human feeling. It lends authority to the idea that the artist need not be dependent on the forms of nature in the creation of concrete forms expressing the human spirit."[127] Grey says that the origin of the idea was far older than its development in the work of the Symbolists, that the attribution of direct emotional expressiveness to music is found in Plato, and that the acceptance of these ideas was not limited to any one artistic group in the 19th century. "The academician, Charles Blanc, who formulated many of the ideas widespread in the 19th century...dealing essentially in terms of correspondences...says: 'Straight or curved, horizontal or vertical, parallel or divergent, all lines have a secret relation to emotion.' Again, in speaking of color: 'Above all, let the colorist choose among the harmonies of color those which seem, as the poet says, to be in conformity with his thought,' for 'if there is a great affinity between light and dark and emotion, there is even more between emotion and color.'"[128]

"But one does not have to look for a single source of the idea of the direct expressiveness of the aesthetic elements, for the sources are to be found everywhere in contemporary thought. Briveau made it a part of his lectures on aesthetics at the Sorbonne in the eighteen-nineties. Charles Henry, the Director of the Laboratory of the Psychology of Perception at the Sorbonne, had tried to give the idea a solid scientific basis. It is partly on the basis of Henry's works that such writers as Maurice Denis accepted the theory of correspondences as a proven fact."[129]

All the Cubist painters shared this concept of correspondences, as did the Futurist painters (see pp 97-98). Grey says that the real significance of the Cubist painter's acceptance of the concept was that they took it over as one of the laws of nature "rather than as a product of tradition and association...Tradition, belonging to the realm of conventional reality, was unacceptable to the Cubists. Association, inevitably bringing in its wake material that was not purely visual, had a suspiciously anecdotal quality to the Cubists. But if expression could be attributed to the purely sensory elements on the basis of the innate laws of nature, then the Cubist could feel it possible to portray the whole gamut of 'the manifestations of physical and mental life' without compromising with either conventional reality or with subject matter. He could devote himself to the problem of form alone and feel that his art was as humanly rich as any other art, while being far purer through the exclusion of 'anecdote'."[130]

Picabia's statement, "We must devote ourselves to setting down on our canvases not things, but emotions produced in our minds by things" (see p. 72), has its 19th century parallel in these words of Mallarme quoted by Grey: the artist is "to paint not the thing itself, but the effect it produces."[131]

The analogy of painting and music probably has its origin in the high regard the Symbolists held for music. About this Grey says that the Symbolists, with their concept of an Absolute as the ultimate truth, believed that the "unique role of the artist was to penetrate through the outer encrustation of dross (the world of matter) to the pure essence which was the reflection of idea itself." Poetry was a great step towards the pure essence, but "beyond poetry on a still higher plane lay music as a perfect revelation of the Absolute completely divorced from contaminating materiality. Music had no element of the particular object, but was a pure expression of the ideal essence of reality itself. But as all arts had essentially the same goal...Each must strive for that purity of form that is found in its highest embodiment in music."[132] And even beyond music, on the highest plane, was pure poetry which was silent music, thus surpassing audible music.[133]

Though Grey made no mention of the attempts of the Orphic painters, including Delaunay or Picabia, to produce painting that would be to the eye as music is to the ear, he does point out that all "the Cubist writers from the very beginning had stressed that the fundamental desire of the Cubist was to create a form of painting that would approach in purity that of music. With this fundamental attitude in mind, it is not surprising to find that many attempts were made to incorporate the formal elements of music into painting. The concepts of harmony and rhythm of course, had long been in use in both the fields of music and painting, but encouraged by these basic correspondences between the two arts, the Cubists began to explore further." "As early as his portrait of Picasso in 1911, Juan Gris began experimenting with a visual form analogous to that of polyphony in music..." 134

In his statements of 1913 Picabia expressed the hope that the public would learn to "read" his paintings (see p. 12). He felt that this would occur as soon as the conventions of the new painting would come to be understood.

He said, "Art is one of the means by which men communicate with each other and objectivise the deepest contact of their personality with nature. This expression is necessarily related to the needs of the civilization of the time. It has its conventions as has any means of expression. Its conventions are the limitations of the personality of the artist, a limitation which man tends to extend, as he tends to remove all limitations to his perception. Just as the simple and direct perception of the outside world does not satisfy us any longer, and we try to go deeper into the essence and quality of this simple perception, so have our feelings towards nature become more complicated, and similarly the expression of these feelings." And the artist has made his work express the subjectivity of these feelings. "But expression means objectivity. Otherwise contact between beings would become impossible, language would lose all meaning. This new expression in painting is 'the objectivity of a subjectivity'. We can make ourselves better understood by comparing it to music.

"If we grasp without difficulty the meaning and the logic of a musical work it is because this work is based on the laws of harmony and composition of which we have either the acquired knowledge or the inherited knowledge. These laws are the objectivity of painting up to the present time. The new form of painting puzzles the public only because it does not yet grasp the new objectivity. The laws of this new convention have as yet been hardly formulated but they will become gradually more defined just as musical laws have become more defined and they will very rapidly become as understandable as were the objective representations of nature. Therefore, in my paintings the public is not to look for a 'photographic' recollection of a visual impression or a sensation, but to look at them as but an attempt to express the purest part of the abstract reality of form and color in itself."[135]

Picabia felt that the "new objectivity" could actually become a new language of symbols. The symbols of this language would be invented somehow by the mind while it was in the subjective state. On the occasion of the exhibition of Picabia's water-color paintings at Steiglitz' gallery, he evidently stressed this concept for in one of the reviews of the exhibition the writer says: "Picabia's water-color paintings which purport to be the graphic reaction of the French Cubist to the sights and sounds of New York and of his recent voyage hither...(are) made up of the symbols of a new language for the eye...", and the writer goes on to speak about the search for this new language of symbols by Picabia and others.[136] The painting that most successfully demonstrated to the reviewer the ability of Picabia's psychic perception - his "pensée pure" - to invent symbols was _Chanson Nègre_. The reviewer reports that purple was the inevitable and dominating color that sprang to Picabia's consciousness when he heard the songs of the Negroes, and that Picabia was delighted when he was later told by Stieglitz that "purple was the favorite color of most negroes."[137]

The new language of visual symbols Picabia aimed at could, of course, exist in painting only as analogy, in the chance resemblance, either of the individual invented abstract shapes and colors to others in the known visual sphere, or in the suggestiveness of the over-all grouping and character of all the shapes in the picture. An example of the first are the shapes of his painting Je revois en souvenir ma chere Udnie, made on his return to France, which may be read as completely abstract or as shapes that resemble parts of machinery, or as phallic symbols. An example of the second are the swirling shapes in Edtaonisl, Catch as Catch can, which can be read as the excitement of a wrestling match. These analogies are an application of the concept of correspondences. It is the title given to the painting that gives the spectator the clue to "reading" the composition. In 1916 Picabia said: "In my work the subjective expression is the title, the painting the object. But this object is nevertheless somewhat subjective, because it is the pantomime - the appearance of the title...."[138]

Marcel Duchamp also became interested in the possibilities of a symbolic sign language. He later said that about the time he had been working on Nu descendant un escalier, his "aim was turning inward rather than towards externals. And later, following this view, I came to feel an artist might use anything - a dot, a line, the most conventional or unconventional symbol - to say what he wanted to say.

The nude in this way was a direct step to the large glass (<u>La mariée mise à nu par ses célibrataires, même</u>).[139]"

One of the notes Duchamp made during the course of painting <u>La mariée mise à nu...</u> indicates his ambition in devising a new symbolic language. He says that to increase his repertory of forms he "must take a Larousse encyclopaedia and copy out all the abstract words, those which have no concrete reference, and compose a schematic sign which will designate each of these words...make use of colors to differentiate what corresponds in literature to substantive, verb, declension, conjugation." Further on he notes: "This writing is suitable only for this picture probably.[140]"

The goal of a language of symbols was achieved, to a limited degree, when Picabia and Duchamp abandoned the forms of conventional painting and concentrated on drawing and painting machines, either parts of real ones or ones they invented. The machine element became the constant symbol; whatever else was added to it in every new drawing or painting qualified it, gave it a new inflection, another nuance. Their vocabulary was restricted, but infinitely varied. With it Duchamp was able to create a painting, <u>La Mariée mise à nu par ses célibataires, même</u>, that had the complexity of a play, with a cast of individual characters - the various machine elements, and a series of dramatic events - the grouping of the elements (see pp.124-125). And with this vocabulary Picabia made his machine-calligrams virtually as articulate as are his poems, which, though the individual phrases are often incomprehensible, have an overall effect of suggestiveness.

This search by Picabia and Duchamp for a new language of visual symbols paralleled a major developement in European literature which was characterized in general by the search for new means of expressing ideas. Picabia's poetry and Duchamp's published notes for <u>La mariée mise à nu...</u> are products of this search.[141]

Picabia's Aesthetic Ideas Compared to the Cubists', 1912

To a great extent, of course, every painting is symbolic, made up of signs invented by the artist, whose meanings are usually established by long tradition, and are easily "read" by any spectator accustomed to them. But the sign language, made up of the pictorial elements, was invented anew by Picabia and Duchamp for each of their paintings. And the difficulty of reading their paintings was further increased as, in addition to the use of visual puns (analogies) whose interpretation is dependent upon the observor's relating the resemblance of the pictorial elements to other forms in the visual world, with the title or other words and phrases placed on the surface of the work serving as keys, they often arbitrarily assigned meanings to pictorial elements which the unaided spectator could not possibly guess. That the audience capable of "reading" such works is necessarily limited to an initiated few does not matter here, for the intellectual concept behind each particular work led the artist to give it its unique visual qualities, and these confront the spectator whether or not he can "read" them. In attempting to analyze the visual characteristics of these works it is necessary to grant the validity of the total concept.

It was outside the realm of the Cubist painters, Picasso, Braque, and Gris to become concerned with a language of symbols. Though they searched for new plastic means they kept their researches limited only to that which pertained to painting.

Kahnweiler, though fascinated by the relationship between writing and painting, and devoting pages 41 - 53 of his book on Juan Gris to categorizing the types, and discussing at length, the signs and symbols invented by man to convey thought, still limited the ideas that may be signified by a painting to the objects of a still-life set-up.

Kahnweiler believes, in complete agreement here with Picabia (see p.83), that a work of art is completed only when its "message" is "read". He writes: "This entity (a painting) has a two-fold existence: It exists autonomously in itself, by itself as an object; but outside itself it has a further existence - it signifies something. Its lines and forms are there to compose certain signs, and by virtue of this the painting is a representation of thought by means of graphic signs - writing...if the spectator 'reads' the picture... (he) will then 'see' what the painter intended to represent: he will have identified the sign with the object signified."[142] Kahnweiler felt that because of their preoccupation with the problems inherent in painting per se, the Cubist painters deliberately dealt with simple objects: box-like houses, trees, glasses, bowls, musical instruments, etc.. The simplicity of the symbolic contents of these paintings, and the fact that the painter included "real details" - indications of local colors, textures, etc., to help stimulate the perception, made these works easy to "read". That the public found these works obscure was due to the fact that "the artists had invented new signs which at first no-one was able to read. Moreover, these signs melted into the architecture of the picture in such a way that the simple-minded beholder was frequently unable to isolate them individually and thereby read the picture more easily..."[143]

When Kahnweiler uses the terms "conceptual painting" and "painting of ideas" he definitely does not refer to such elaborate intellectual conceptions as that of Duchamp's La mariée mise à nu...[144] "True conceptual painting" for Kahnweiler was what Gris invented when he "finally gave up presenting the beholder with a great variety of information (acquired by empirical observation) about the objects which he displayed. He now offered a synthesis: that is to say, he packed his knowledge into one significant form, a single emblem...the justification for calling this conceptual painting is the fact that the picture contains not the forms which have been collected in the visual memory of the painter, but new forms..."[145] And a "true painting of ideas" was what Gris envisaged when he "explained, for example, that the eyes which one always thinks of in full face can equally be represented full face in a profile head."[146]

Picabia, in 1913, could have stated in complete agreement with Duchamp that he wanted "to put painting once again at the service of the mind." Both he and Duchamp would have used the word "idea" to mean mental, intellectual activity in the broadest sense, beyond ideas that had reference only to the physical acts of painting. In 1946, referring back to 1911 - 1912, Duchamp said; "I wanted to get away from the physical aspect of painting. I was much more interested in recreating ideas in painting. For me the title was very important... I was interested in making painting serve my purposes and in getting away from the physicality of painting (which he feels was introduced by Courbet)...I was interested in ideas - not merely in visual products ...to put painting once again at the service of the mind..." "There was no thought of anything beyond the physical side of painting (at that time). No notion of freedom was taught. No philosophical outlook was introduced. The cubists of course were inventing a lot at the time. They had enough on their hands at the time not to be worried about a philosophical outlook, and Cubism gave me many ideas for decomposing forms. But I thought of art on a broader scale."[147]

Apollinaire, in The Cubist Painters also refers to "an art of conception," by which he means one that is the opposite of "an art of imitation." And by virtue of his definition of Orphic Cubism he admits the possibility of subject matter beyond the mere portrayal of objects, though he does feel that there must be an "inner frame of the picture...(which) marks the limits of its profundity, just as the actual frame marks its external limits."[148] He felt that this kind of inner frame was provided by Picabia in the titles he gave his paintings. Of this, he says that for Picabia, "the formulation of the title is...not separable, intellectually, from the work to which it refers. The title should play the part of an inner frame, as actual objects, and inscriptions exactly copied, do in the pictures of Picasso. It should ward off decadent intellectualism, and conjure away the danger artists run of becoming literary. Analogous to Picabia's written titles, to the real objects, letters, and moulded ciphers in the paintings of Picasso and Braque, are the pictorial arabesques in the backgrounds of Laurencin's pictures. With Albert Gleize this function is taken by the right angles which retain light, with Fernand Leger by bubbles, with Metzinger by vertical lines parallel to the sides of the frame cut by infrequent echelons. The equivalent will be found, in some form or other, in the works of all the great painters..."[149]

Surprisingly Apollinaire reveals a number of contradictions in his thoughts on Picabia's art in the essay he devotes to it in his The Cubist Painters.[150] He first describes the intellectual concepts and the importance of the subject matter in Picabia's work, and then denies their presence. He says that for Picabia "the formulation of the title is...not separable, intellectually from the work to which it refers." "Each picture of Picabia has a definite existence, the limits of which are set by the title. These pictures are so far from a priori abstractions that the painter can tell you the history of each one of them: Dance at the Spring is simply the expression of a plastic emotion experienced spontaneously near Naples." Elsewhere Apollinaire says: "Picabia...tried to give himself entirely to color, without even daring, when approaching his subject, to grant it a personal existence. I must remark here that a title does not mean the artist has approached a subject." And, "an artist like Picabia here foregoes one of the principle elements of all painting: conception." Apollinaire ends his essay by urging Picabia "as a painter of pictures, to address himself to the subject (poetry), which is the essence of plastic art." Apollinaire contradicts himself again in this essay when he says that Picabia's "color is no longer merely coloring....it is itself the form and light of whatever is represented," and going on to say that "with Picabia the form is still symbolic, while the color is formal;" he failed to recognize that he has already said color is the form, and thus both color and form are symbolic in Picabia's paintings.

A year later, in a review of the Salon d'automne of 1913,[151] Apollinaire again revealed his lack of real understanding of Picabia's paintings. Of Edtaonisl,[152] and Udnie he said: "in these ardent and unbridled works we are shown the astonishing conflict of pictorial content and imagination." He did not grasp that Picabia's "pictorial content" (the forms, shapes and colors) was the visual equivalent of what went on in his imagination. Of Picabia's "pictorial content" itself Apollinaire had said in The Cubist Painters: "this art... could take as its motto the remark of Poussin: 'Painting has no other end than the delection and joy of the eyes'."[153]

By these contradictions it can be seen that Apollinaire never fully grasped Picabia's objectives in painting at this period. Yet it would seem that the aim of an artist to paint the visual equivalents for his emotional experiences, and to invent new vocabularies of meanings for shapes and colors would be an aim to which a poet might readily respond; especially as this idea seems to be rooted in the same concept of the social function of the artist Apollinaire held, that is, the creation of the "reality" that man sees.

In The Cubist Painters, Apollinaire expressed this idea in such phrases as: "The order which we find in nature...is only an effect of art." "Poets and artists plot the characteristics of their epoch." "Without poets, without artists, men would soon weary of nature's monotony." "It is the social function of great poets and artists to continually renew the appearance nature has for the eyes of men." "To create the illusion of the typical is the social and peculiar end of art." In discussing this aspect of Apollinaire's ideas, Grey notes that in it is epitomized "many such ideas as Baudelaire's dislike of nature and preference for artificiality, Hegel's rejection of nature as formless, which is echoed by Oscar Wilde and Whistler. Even the idea, though carried to new extremes, that man has created the 'reality' which he sees, is not original, for it appears in Oscar Wildes's contention that nature imitates art..."[154]

Picabia's statement quoted on pages 83-84 parallels this idea of Apollinaire. In it he states that men use art to express their view of nature which changes as civilization changes, and that the current view of nature is too complex and subjective for direct perception or expression. In the rest of the statement he demonstrated that he was attempting to create the artistic form that will enable "the public" also to see the world in this new way.

In the following statement, though made in 1916, Picabia reiterates the same thoughts, and he ends with a call to the public to make its symbols of the world those of the painter's, for when this will be accomplished, a "sublime and superior language" will result.

"We live in a world in which appearances seem to us absolute realities on account of the conventions that we create for ourselves. Nature and painting can be the expression of the same entity if the expression of painting resembles the ideas we have before concrete objects. "All desires, needs of projecting oneself, all subjective impulses can be expressed through hundreds of possible methods, but to express those desires, one must find an absolutely pure medium of form, and it is impossible for that form, from the point of view of painting, to have any resemblance to the abstract idea; it remains in a cosmic state with the secret significance that exists in us.

"We create first an objectivity to put in it, afterward our subjective will; our work then becomes the mental and metaphysical expression of the outer world, that is to say, it becomes an object living by itself and with its own expression.

"In my work the subjective expression is the title, the painting the object. But this object is nevertheless somewhat subjective, because it is the pantomime - the appearance of the title; it furnishes to a certain point the means of comprehending the potentiality - the very heart of man.

"Our ideas are universal; painting must be an individual reality.

"We immediately understand a painting if we know its conventions, but it is necessary to let our imagination give a form to the metaphysical and invisible world; we must endeavor to make our symbol analogous to the invisible symbol of the painter. Thus the object and the idea become a sublime and superior language..."[155]

Though Apollinaire never completely understood what it was that Picabia was trying to do, he did, however, recognize the validity of the works, and therefore admitted that there was more than one way (Picasso's and Braque's) of being "Cubistic." And only four months after the meeting of the two men, on the occasion of the "Section d'Or" exhibition in October, 1912, Apollinaire lectured "on the multiple tendencies from which acknowledgement could no longer be withheld, of abstract art, or...'Cubism drawn and quartered'", and during which he used the term "Orphism" for the first time in public, and gave its definition.[156]

It is impossible to determine how much of the expansion of Apollinaire's awareness of the developement of abstract art in the work of many painters is due to the direct influence of Picabia.[157] By the time the two men first became acquainted in July, 1912, Picabia, in company with Marcel Duchamp, had already progressed in his thinking and painting far along a path quite different from the analytical Cubism of Picasso and Braque. Spiritually too, he had already withdrawn from the Cubist group, as can be seen in a statement he made six months later in New York: "Cubism is a misnomer...After Impressionism, neo-impressionism, then cubism, which sought geometric third-dimension in painting, the expression of things seen in geometrical figures. But a purely subjective art cannot of course, be bound by any form of expression the moment that expression becomes a convention, an established body of laws with accepted values." "Therefore (the rest of the statement was paraphrased) he has cut loose from cubism, and... (depicts) with entirely unfettered, spontaneous, ever varying means of expression in form and color waves, according to the commands, the needs, the inspiration of the impression, the mood received. Objective expression is strictly barred. He even ignores form as far as possible, seeking 'color harmonies'. Harmony and equilibrium are his device."[158]

Picabia's Aesthetics Compared to the Futurists'

The Futurist painters, like Picabia, were interested in the use of abstract forms and colors primarily as a means of depicting their sensations in plastic terms. For though the idea of cosmic dynamism may have controlled the Futurists' imagination, their first concern was the attempt to project to the spectator the artist's experiences of life, to place the spectator at the "center of the picture" in order to make him relive the intense experience of the artist. The spectator was to be caught up first by the plastic movement generated by familiar objects and then to be whirled into the movement of the universe.

The phrase, "we are going to put the spectator at the center of the picture", in the Technical Manifesto of April 11, 1910, was contributed by Carra (though Boccioni also claims credit for this idea) who drew the idea from an experience he had in 1904, described in his autobiography: while watching the funeral of the assassinated radical Galli a riot broke out against the squadron of mounted police protecting the procession. "Without wishing to, I found myself in the center of the struggle. I saw the bier covered with the red flag careening on the shoulders of the pallbearers. I saw the horses rear skittishly, canes and lances clashing, so that it seemed to me that the coffin would fall at any moment and be trampled by the horses."[159] It was this experience which he painted in the _Funeral of the Anarchist Galli_, finished in 1911.[160]

Thus the actual subject matter of the Futurists' paintings was always of this world. In their statements too, they continually interchanged ideas of the cosmos and descriptions of everyday experiences. The movement of a bus becomes part of the movement of the universe; "The sixteen people around you in a moving tram are one, ten, four, three: they are still and they move...they are devoured by a patch of sunlight, they sit down again - persistent symbols of universal vibration."[161]

The Futurist painters believed, as did Picabia, that they could invent the proper abstract visual symbols, or signals, to which the spectator's senses would respond. They too were relying on the concept of correspondences (see pp. 80-81). In their writings they, particularly Boccioni, went so far as to attempt setting up a rationalized vocabulary of the qualities of motion, and of the emotional and psychological values inherent in various visual forms. (Though in their paintings they attempted to achieve the simulation of motion by any means they could seize on.) Boccioni states: "Every rapidly moving object - a train, car, bicycle, generates in pure sensation an emotional milieu which takes the form of horizontal penetrational at an acute angle. Whereas a standing human figure produces in us the entirely different emotional milieu of the cylinder. Each of these in turn is entirely distinct from the longitudinal, billowy heaviness which is the milieu created by a reclining figure; this again is different from the plastic emotion of a spiral lightness engendered by a flower pot...A slowly shifting crowd awakens in us the inert emotional milieu of perpindicular direction, whereas the same crowd starting off at a run appears in our dynamic consciousness as a maze of acute angles, oblique lines and aggressive zigzags."[162]

In their paintings the Futurists, by their reliance on the concept of correspondences, could evoke a rapidly moving object by painting only the "horizontal penetration at an acute angle", or evoke a running crowd with "a maze of acute angles, oblique lines and aggressive zig-zags." Boccioni used such correspondences literally in the three paintings he called States of Mind, described in the catalog of the First Futurist exposition in Paris as: Those who remain, constructed on a chromatic rhythm of "perpendicular, undulating and weary lines;" Farewell, an "arabesque of confused, jerky, straight and curved lines;" the dynamic emotion of Those who depart is expressed by "horizontal, fleeting, swiftly moving, and convulsed lines," and by "jerky, rapidly receding lines which brutally cut across lonely countenances and stretches of onrushing landscape."[163]

In these paintings of States of mind, "pure", or invented abstract forms are mingled with others that specifically state realistic details; the "pure" forms are used by the artist as a means to project the sensations, the emotions he intends to convey to the spectator, while realistic details reveal the subject the artist is concerned with. However the ideal painting for the Futurist would probably have been one in which the realistic details were entirely missing. For, as Clough summarizes under the heading of Physical Transcendentalism, "The Futurists maintained that the object of the artist's vision is a transcendental 'world beyond all unity of time and place, and beyond the distinction of things.' The creative motion of the universe reveals itself to the artist's mind as pure color and pure form by means of the artist's 'plastic consciousness,' which the

Futurists also termed 'plastic states of mind'; a plastic state of mind is defined as 'the lyrical appraisal of the motion of matter expressed through the correlated forms of consciousness.' These states of mind become 'states of form' and 'states of color' when considered pictorially, and every sensory emotion has a corresponding color and form, or 'color-form'."[164] As succinctly stated by Carra: "Objects fused with their milieu by motion transform themselves in our dynamically responsive consciousness into a rhythm of lines, volumes, abstract and concrete gammas chromatically generated, which, when exteriorized, become to the eye what the sonorous is to the ear."[165]

That Picabia's adaptation of the concept of correspondences is close to the Futurists' can be seen by comparing the following statement of his which has already been quoted on page 74, to the above paragraphs: "Art is a successful attempt to render external an internal state of mind or feeling." "Art deals with deep, brooding, fundamental, simple soul states. How do those states arise? They are the result of the artist's experience in life. Suppose the artist has felt the quality of our skyscrapers, or our city and our life, and tries to reproduce it. This experience has affected his mood. He renders plastic that mood on canvas. But the resulting picture has no skyscrapers in it and no city... only the results of the skyscrapers and the city on his termperament." The technical means by which the soul state is rendered plastic are "the arrangements of line and color in such a way as to suggest the equilibrium of static and dynamic qualities, of rest and motion, of mass and balance."[166]

The Futurists too, as did Picabia, made the analogy between pure painting and music. Carra in the statement quoted on page 99 speaks of "a rhythm of lines, volumes, abstract and concrete gammas chromatically generated, which, when exteriorized, become to the eye what the sonorous is to the ear." And Soffici said that what he had been striving for in his Futurist days was a kind of lyrico-pictorial transposition very similar to that of the musician who suggests the symbolic essence which inspired him in accordance with the laws of his art.[167] Clough quotes another of the Futurists (not named) as saying: "the analogy of music fascinated us. We believed in the possibility of color symphonies devoid of logical meaning and any correlation with nature. Nevertheless, the thought that some one might go even further and produce odor melodies and tactile symphonies frightened us. We saw that by relying on the above analogy we were destroying painting without creating music."[168]

The Futurists, though they relied upon the concept of correspondences, never became expressly concerned with inventing a language of visual symbols as did Picabia. They were, however, concerned with the making of analogies, and of the role of the intuition in inventing analogies. But the Futurists spoke of analogies in relation to poetry, not to painting, and they did not think of it as the means of a symbolic language. In Picabia's paintings analogy formed the new language of symbols he sought; the symbols are read when the spectator is aware of the analogies between the resemblance of invented abstract shapes and colors to others in the known visual sphere. Analogy to the Futurists meant to disclose the communion of all things. Marinetti said: "Analogy is but another name for that immense love which brings distant things into close relationships." And the wilder the analogy the better, for the value of analogy to them was its power to startle.[169]

Picabia and the Futurists were in closer agreement on the role of the intuition (Picabia's "psychic sense" or "pensée pure") in inventing analogies. Picabia believed that the mind, while it was in the subjective state, operating intuitively, would somehow invent the symbols, that is the analogies, of his new language. Marinetti said: "It is impossible to determine exactly when unconscious inspiration ends and lucid volition begins...after hours of relentless toil, the creative spirit seems suddenly to shake off its shackles and become prey to an incomprehensible spontaneity of conception and excitation. The hand that writes seems to break away from the body and move off into the distance far from the brain that like-wise has freed itself and looks down from its lofty station with awe-inspiring lucidity on the images that unwittingly flow from the pen."[170]

Once again Picabia and the Futurists were sharing in an idea that was "in the air" at the time. The idea of the creative role of the artist's intuition and subconscience, often labelled "automatism," was soon to be exploited by the Dadaists and further explored by the Surrealists.

PICABIA'S PAINTINGS OF THE SECOND HALF OF 1913

The abstract shapes that compose Picabia's New York water-color paintings have only the simplification of form that characterizes the "machine aesthetic". But in the oil paintings based partly on these water-colors made after his return to Paris, the forms, while remaining abstract in the sense of having been invented by the artist, and abstract in their color, are forms that refer specifically to the world of machinery. They are, in effect, pictured machine elements, some of which resemble parts of the human body and which the artist has caused to masquerade as personages - either whole or in segments, engaging in specific human social situations. This same transformation had already occurred in Duchamp's work, as seen in Mariée of 1912. With this development the goal of a language of visual symbols was achieved to an extent. The machine became the constant element, qualified anew in each successive drawing or painting. The machine, as the symbol of 20th century society, was made to indulge in mocking charades of that society.

There are, in general, two aspects to Picabia's and Duchamp's machine symbolism: the first emphasizes their attitudes towards human sex and mores, the second their attitudes towards the structure of contemporary society. These two aspects are linked to the two basic ways in which they represented the machine. The first, and with the exception of Duchamp's Moulin à café of 1911 which was a simple analysis of mechanics, the earliest, depends upon their exploitation of the visual ambiguity of chance resemblànces of machine-like, or actual machine forms to the human physiognomy. Examples of this are Picabia's Je revois en souvenir ma chere Udnie, and Duchamp's Mariée. The second aspect coincides with the use of explicit machine forms which allow no visual ambiguity to which both artists next evolved, Duchamp in certain works of 1913, such as the drawing Cimetière de uniforms et livrées (pl.19, fig.60), in which he used explicit machine forms for the first time since *Moulin à café*, Picabia in 1915, when he used explicit machine elements as in *Ici, c'est ici Stieglitz* (pl.10,fig.26), for the first time since the drawing *La fille née sans mère* of 1913. Duchamp's final version of *La Mariée mise à nu par ses célibataires, même* combines both aspects of symbolism and both manners of representation - the first, the sexual, appears in the upper panel, and the second, the social attitude, is contained in the lower panel.

The first aspect, which exploits the chance resemblance of machine elements to parts of the human body, is most fully developed in Picabia's painting *Je revois en souvenir ma chere Udnie*, 1913 (pl.5, fig.13), and Duchamp's *Mariée*, 1912 (pl.5,fig.14).

These two paintings share certain similarities. Both are concerned with sexual intercourse. In both the machine elements are analogous, not to the external details of the human body and its extremities, but to the inner organs of the body. In this way both paintings are like cross-sectional, or cut-away, views of anatomy charts. The color schemes of both are dominated by the use of warm yellow ochers and greys; the main pictorial elements are given an ivory-like glow. Each is carefully painted, with nothing left in a sketchy or indeterminate state, and the areas of chiaroscuro, which are much more elaborate in *Mariée*, are carefully worked out. The same quiet mood is generated by each - though Duchamp's is more austere. Finally it can be said that each painting represents the high peak of each artist's achievement within traditional painting means.

Picabia's *Je revois en souvenir ma chere Udnie* is related to his New York water-color *Chanson Nègre* (see p. 67 and pl.4,fig.10).

<u>Chanson Nègre</u> itself seems to have its compositional origin in the drawing <u>Fille née sans mère</u> (pl.4,fig.11), also made in New York. (This drawing is dated 1912 by the Metropolitan Museum, but as it is drawn on the reverse side of a sheet of paper that bears the letterhead of a New York hotel, it seems certain that it was made after Picabia's arrival in New York, January, 1913). The three works have a number of elements in common. When the originals are seen the compositional resemblance is more striking than in the black and white photos of the two paintings. The "nègre", who is all head, is composed of the grouping of curvilinear elements in the center of the water-color, which is a basic repetition of the curvilinear elements of the embryo-like "fille". Also repeated in the water-color are the strong lower left to upper right diagonal movement of the large curved lines, the shape that is the terminus of the embryonic "fille" which now becomes the "nègre's" feet, the linear element that seems to be the knotted umbilical cord on the left side of the "fille", now larger, as the long linear element that bends to the left of the "nègre". "Udnie" retains the curvilinear elements of the embryonic "fille" in the two large curves which run along the right edge of the painting and contains "Udnie's" inner organs. The spring-like forms at the center of the "fille" are repeated in "Udnie", now attached to a repetition of the terminus shape of the "fille"; the knotted umbilical cord of the "fille" is quite prominent in "Udnie", rising up to nearly the top of the composition, and retaining the purple color it has in the "nègre".

The abstract though symbolic shapes that compose "Udnie" are sharp-edged, flat planes that bend in space, and move in front of, or behind, one another. They are more interesting because of their greater variation in contour and size than those of the other oil paintings of 1913. The composition as a whole is stabilized by the dominantly horizontal character of the background divisions and the rectangles that form a strong, horizontal base. A slow movement is suggested by the large curves, the repetition of the scalloped border-like shapes, the segments of the spring forms, and the spotting of values.

To "read" these paintings by Picabia and Duchamp, the puns, either visual or verbal, must first be found and then interpreted.[171] The pun contained in each of the two paintings was reinterpreted, or otherwise related to earlier or later works done over an extended period of time.

As _Je revois en souvenir ma chere Udnie_ had its compositional origin in the drawing _Fille née sans mère_, it may also be assumed, though it is nowhere stated, that the "fille" of the drawing is implicit in the painting. Picabia's idea of the daughter born without a mother is that the machine was conceived in the mind of man, and she was born into the world through the efforts of his body. That this child of man's intellect should be feminine is due partly to the fact that in the French language the noun "machine" is of the feminine gender, and that reference to a machine as "she" is common usage throughout the modern world. Having created this female being, man provides for her needs and uses her body: in short, she becomes his mistress.[172] And it is in this role that Picabia has painted her here. The rather bourgeois sentiment of the title conjours up the vision of perhaps a middle-aged business man recalling a former love named Udnie. The actual subject of the painting is his mental memory of sexual intercourse with her, and this is presented in ideographic terms; both the male and female principles are represented.

Picabia painted another picture of "Udnie" in 1913, titled Udnie, Jeune fille Américaine (pl.4,fig.12); he had obviously been impressed by a particular type of American girl which he portrayed in this painting as hard, brash, sexy, and all a-flutter. This painting, perhaps the most widely known of Picabia's works, is the least complex composition of the 1913 series. Though all of its curvy shapes defy vertical or horizontal axes, there is a piling up of shapes along a vertical axis in the center of the painting that almost creates a sense of balanced symmetry. In this instance it can be recognized that Udnie is fully clothed. It is almost possible to pick out the details of hat, hair-do, and dress. In a later drawing, Portrait d'une jeune fille américaine dans l'état de nudité (pl.10,fig.28), published in 291, no. 5-6, 1915, Picabia peeked at her again in the nude. This is a drawing of a spark plug, which as Gabrielle Buffet-Picabia suggests, shows her as a "kindler of flame".[173] The spark plug, after the manner of much American advertising, is hopefully labelled "forever". The use of "nudité" here suggests the possibility that "Udnie" of the earlier paintings is a French pig-latin version of the word.

After having given his Fille née sans mère a taste of human sexual life, Picabia let her enjoy love with another machine in the painting of 1917, Parade Amoureuse (pl.11,fig.30). The child which she subsequently bore in 1918 is pictured in L'Enfant Carburateur (pl.11,fig.31).

Now, also in 1918, Picabia endowed her with an intellect, and published the book she wrote, titled Poèmes et Dessins de la Fille née sans mère, 18 drawings and 51 poems (see pp. 119-121).

Duchamp's Mariée is composed of elements taken from the center section of the earlier painting Passage de la vierge à la mariée, the subject of which was the philosophic speculation of the transformation from one state of being, physical and mental, to another, as the result of an act - in this case the sexual act. The subject of Mariée, like the simplification of the title itself down to the noun, is concerned only with the virgin waiting for the act to begin.

The forms of Mariée suggests that only the female principle is represented, and that the bride is a rather wan person who awaits the entrance of the male principle in an almost hysterical state of tension. Every attenuated element of her being shares this tension. In reference to this painting Katherine Kuh states that Duchamp "became more and more concerned with the symbolism of celibacy. For him the celibate life of today's machine-bred man and woman was conceived as a constantly recurring frustration or boomerang...(This is seen in) his own description of the basic idea behind his painting, The Bride. First there is a tank filled with love essence, an essence of only timid power which is distributed by a motor to weak cylinders in direct contact with sparks from the bride's life. The result is 'magnetic desire' which explodes and evaporates. The virgin, who was just arriving at the fulfillment of her desires, faints. This condensed scenario embodies the poetic eroticism in much of Duchamp's late work."[174] This is a portrayal of an attitude towards sex that is far removed from the hedonism of Picabia's.

The visual appearance of the rounded forms of Mariée, with their carefully observed chiaroscuro, was anticipated by the rounded forms of Nu descendant un escalier, no. 1,[175] which had been abandoned in favour of the flat rectangular shapes of the final version.

Mariée makes a third and final appearance, simplified even further, in the upper panel of La Mariée mise à nu par ses célibataires, même (pl.19,fig.61). Celebacy and sterility, of society in general as well as of the individual, are the themes of this painting on glass (see pp. 123-125).

The sexual motif is imbeded too, in Edtaonisl, Ecclésiastique (pl.6,fig.16), another of Picabia's oils of 1913. However the subject of this painting is most difficult to decipher from the shapes and colors alone. The meaning is almost entirely contained in the title, and only half of that, the word "Edtaonisl", appears on the painting. The sharp-edged shapes of the painting are all abstract, invented by the artist, and contain no reference to shapes in nature. Curvilinear shapes predominate, and there is no sense of stability; the shapes float, twist, and interweave in a shallow space. A staccato rhythm is set up by the repetition of similar shapes, colors and values. These repetitions also maintain the pictorial balance of this most elaborate and complex of Picabia's paintings. (There are strong points of visual resemblance between this painting and Severini's Dyanamic Hieroglyphic of the Bal Tabarin, 1912,[176] particularly in the sharp-edged shapes and the staccato rhythms.)

If one takes the liberty of turning the New York water-color painting, Danseuse étoile sur un transatlantique (pl.6,fig.15), upside-down, and Picabia himself set a precedent by turning upside-down another water-color of this series, La ville de New York aperçue à travers le corps (pl.7,fig.17) when he added his title and signature,[177] the composition loses much of its sense of stability - as does the precedent-setting painting just mentioned. The large curves become dominant, and a sense of swinging movement results. And it can be seen that this water-color formed the starting point for the composition of the large (9 ft. square) oil painting. The position of the area of greatest complexity which is now located in the lower right-hand quarter of the water-color composition is retained in the oil painting, as are, in general, its large curving lines, and certain other of its elements. Much has been changed and added to this area of complexity, and it forms only the core of the composition of Edtaonisl Ecclésiastique, which has been considerably expanded on all sides.

Danseuse Étoile et son école de danse, another of the New York water-colors, must be considered as related to this painting, because of the subject matter, that of the "star dancer", and because its over-all staccato pictorial rhythms seem to contain the spirit of those of the final painting.

From the knowledge that "Danseuse Étoile" is in the title of both water-colors, it is simple to demonstrate that by taking away every other letter of the word "Edtaonisl", and forming a new word with them, two words are created E T O I L and D A N S - Étoile Danse. By merging the titles of the three works the subject of the final painting presents itself as that of a clergyman who watches a theatrical "star-dancer" and her troupe rehearsing on the deck of an ocean liner.

Georges Levasque speaks of the beating heart of the clergyman,[178] which may perhaps be represented by the area of greatest complexity in the composition.

Picabia's Catch as Catch Can (pl.8,fig.20), is also subtitled Edtaonisl. This oil painting is the representation of a wrestling match. It also echoes many of the elements of the water-color series. There are almost no stabilizing elements; the staccato rhythm is even more emphatic than in the preceding paintings, and in the case of this painting is actually a descriptive element. Gabrielle Buffet-Picabia relates the following anecdote about the origin of this painting: "One evening (in 1913, after returning from the United States) while dining at the Chinese Restaurant, Picabia, Apollinaire and I, sat next to a Chinese wrestler due to perform that evening in a match of catch as catch can...(He was) a colossus...the face of an implacable idol and kept staring at us with his squinty wide-slit eyes. At the same time he was occupied in emptying a bottle of fiery Chinese alcohol, gulping it down out of a beer glass. Fascinated we followed him to the match. His slow inhuman gestures, the terrifying quality of his attitudes even before the fight began...he literally felled his opponents...Apollinaire...followed all the vicissitudes of the fight with a passionate and horrified interest...This evening inspired Picabia with a Catch as Catch Can, one of the most complete works realized by him at this period..."[179]

The word "Edtaonisl" on this painting suggests that it may now have become Picabia's generalized designation of a star performer. The painting, Culture Physique (pl.7,fig.19), seems to express much of the same spirit and idea as the one above; but it is harder, colder, and more polished; its forms look as if they were literally made of steel.

The Machine as a Subject in Painting

Duchamp's <u>Moulin à café</u>, 1911, was one of the first, if not the first, painting done by any twentieth century artist to take a machine as its sole subject, though, of course, certain artists before 1911 had painted pictures in which machines appear, or had been stylistically influenced by the characteristics of machines, and others, including writers, had been philosophically concerned with the implications of machines.

In the 19th century, Turner and Monet, among others, had painted steamships and locomotives, but always with the mechanical details obscured in favor of the atmospheric effects of smoke and steam. Of more significance was the stylistic influence of the characteristics of machinery in the work of many artists,[180] by virtue of which it may be said that Picabia, because of the portrait drawings of 1902 which show this influence (see pp.25-26), worked in terms of a machine aesthetic long before he turned his attention to the forms of machinery. The same may be said of other painters who are now historically identified with machine subjects in painting. Leger's work, for example, from 1908 on has a highly mechanized look due to his particular way of simplifying form; though his figures often seem analogous to mechanical robots, as do those in his <u>Nus dans un Paysage</u>, 1910, he did not actually portray machine or machine elements. The Futurist painters, too, though they made an idol of the machine, actually portrayed automobiles, or trains in relatively few instances, and those only as early as 1912, and even then with greater concern for what may be called atmospheric effects than for the machinery. Most often they painted men and horses.

The philosophic implications of the machine were seen in different ways in the 19th century. Huysmans, Tennyson, Thoreau, Whitman and Emerson all expressed admiration for the locomotive in their writing.[181] Others, less enthusiastic about the machine as a symbol of human progress, used it as a measuring rod of negative value against human values. Midway in the century Eugene Delacroix cried out against replacing the labor of man with machines. Commenting in his Journal on the possibilities of mechanical ploughing on a vast scale he wrote: "...Will the steam-engine stop at the doors of churches and cemeteries? ...O shameful philanthropists! O philosophers, without heart or imagination! Do you think that man is a machine like the rest of your machines? You deprive him of his most sacred rights on the pretext of saving him from work which you pretend to consider beneath his dignity, but which is, in fact, the very law of his existence..."[182] Mark Twain, conceiving of man as a machine without will or meaning, frequently referred to man as a "mere coffee mill", or a "sewing machine", and said that "man originates nothing, not even a thought...Shakespeare could not create. He was a machine and machines do not create."[183] Others, such as Hans Richer in his Physio-logic artistique, simply and objectively compared man's body to the machine in functional terms. "Compared to the machines of industry the muscle is a most perfect machine, and is considerably more economic, that is to say, given an equal quantity of potential energy it produces more work and less heat. It is also distinguished in that frequent exercise makes it stronger and capable of producing a greater amount of work..."[184]

In the early twentieth century artists viewed the machine in essentially three ways.[185] The first is the romantic way. It places emphasis on the impersonal force of the machine, and was the way of the Futurists. In the original manifesto the Futurists claimed speed as the new "absolute" which "kills time and space and creates the universe", and is to be the principle and criterion of all things, the goal and measure of poetry: the masses of working people alone can interest new poets, masses swarming in factories, deafened by the roar of machines, themselves mechanized and motorized by the contact with metal and the exigencies of speed - in the course of time even these throngs will lose their prestige and be replaced by the "solemn solidarity of attentive, zealous, orderly motors" when "the animal kingdom comes to its end and the Mechanical Realm begins."[186] Clough points out that this original manifesto reveals the enthusiasm of the neophyte; that it is a cry of repressed admiration for a spectacle that elsewhere, in New York for instance, was taken for granted by millions of persons.

The second way early twentieth century artists viewed the machine was with aesthetic appreciation for the machine's abstract design. This was the view held by the majority of artists influenced by the machine. To an extent, artists holding this view also shared some of the Futurists' emotion and acceptance of the machine as a symbol of modernity. The third way of viewing the machine was that of the Dadaists, who saw the machine as the characteristic symbol of contemporary life, which in their view was worthy only of their contempt and mockery; therefore they constructed irrational, foolish images of machines. They imbodied in their attitude some of the protest against the mechanization of life of the 19th century as represented by Delacroix, and much of the negativity of Mark Twain's view of the value of human accomplishments. The machine types characteristic of Dada were those of Picabia and Duchamp.

PICABIA'S PAINTINGS AND DRAWINGS OF 1915 - 1920

The second aspect of Picabia's machine symbolism, embodying his attitudes towards the structure of contemporary society, is the generalized subject of all his paintings and drawings of 1915 - 1921, that is, of all his work which is Dadaist.

Due mainly to the dislocation in his life brought about by World War I, Picabia painted very few works from the end of 1913 to 1920. Most of his creative efforts during this time went into literary activity; he emerged as a poet, and published several small books of poetry, and he became involved in the writing and publishing of several periodicals expressing the Dada attitude which he liberally illustrated with drawings of machine elements, on many of which are placed words and phrases that are of the same character as his poetry.

It is characteristic of the wit and irony of these Dada works of Picabia that the pictured machine elements, which by implication are the very symbols of regularized movement, are rendered incapable of movement.

The paintings of these years are static, with a strong tendency towards symmetry; the subtle departures from symmetry or static repose that do occur become all the more significant, and set in motion subtle pictorial rhythms. In almost all the paintings there are no suggestions of space; the pictorial elements lie flat on the surface, as if in a shallow box.

Dedes d'Amerique, oil, 1915 (pl.9,fig.22), is a square canvas containing a large circle that almost touches the four edges. The circle is painted with gold metallic paint, and the surrounding area with silver. The symmetry is offset only by the long bar that swings obliquely from lower right to upper left, and has its pivot at the very center of the composition. The symmetry of the painting *Tableau peint pour raconter non pour prouver*, oil, 1915 or '16, as in the preliminary line drawing (pl.9,fig.25), is offset only by the placement of the minor elements, particularly the long linear element that comes down the right side. In *C'est clair comme le jour*, oil, 1915 or '16 (pl.9,fig.24), four disks are placed absolutely symmetrically, but variation is brought into the design by the linear elements. *Very rare picture on the earth*, 1915 (pl.8,fig.21), too, is symmetrical except for the subtle play of minor pictorial elements. Quite different is Portrait de Marie Laurencin ~~*Four in Hand*~~, water-color, 1916 (pl.9,fig.21). In it the tilt of the blades of the propeller begins to recall the violent movement of the 1913 paintings; but stability is implied because the propeller and the two wheels connected by a chain stuck out from a vertical wall which, covering the entire surface of the painting, the spectator faces.

Parade Amoureuse, oil, 1917 (pl.11,fig.30), is the only one of the paintings of this period in which the main pictorial elements exist in a definitely indicated space - a sort of narrow room - and even this is suggested only by lines that converge from the sides of the painting to meet the corners of a vertical rectangle drawn in line in the center of the composition. These lines are drawn over the background which is otherwise given the same color and texture over its entire area (and in this, Picabia anticipates the technique of his "transparencies"). This painting is also the only one of Picabia's machine works to portray what seems to be a complete machine unit. The machine parts are at static rest; however, a pictorial rhythm is set up by the harsh curves of the elements that form the bridge between the two larger machine forms, and an implication of movement about to begin is given by the two thin rods that spring out into the space between the two large forms and which end in two objects that look as though they might hit each other, but never can.

L'Enfant Carburateur, oil on wood, 1918 (pl.11,fig.31), is perhaps the most consistent in its style of Picabia's paintings of these years. It is composed of unrelated machine elements that are pictorially well adjusted to each other in size, color and contour. The areas of shading on the metal parts is reduced to a flat pattern, and the two dimensional shapes lie flat on the surface. Though the machine elements are incapable of movement, there is a suspension of motion implied in the hovering of the heavy, squat, sharp pointed cylindrical shape on the left over the spring arrangement below it, and a staccato pictorial rhythm is set up by the play of linear elements across the surface.

Picabia's graphic works of this period, almost all of which seem to have been made to illustrate publications, are varied and rich in invention. His series of machine-portraits, which he published in 291 and 391, were visual puns that seem to mock his friends and himself more than society at large. Issue no. 5 - 6, of 291, dated July - August, 1915, contained a gallery of "portraits". Stieglitz was represented as a camera in Ici, c'est ici Stieglitz (pl.10,fig.26), a drawing in black and red of a camera that will never work because of the dislocation of its elements. Though the drawing is static, with strong vertical and horizontal axes, a sense of potential movement is created by the repetition of the folds of the accordion bellows and the lines of the extension hinge. Picabia portrayed himself as an automobile horn, because he was so fond of automobiles, and called it Sainte des Saintes (pl.10,fig.27). The Portrait d'jeune fille Américaine (pl.10, fig.28) shows the young girl as a spark plug because she is a "kindler of flame" (see p.106). Voila Haviland, is the portrait of Paul B. Haviland, another contributor to 291 (see footnote 172), depicted as a modest little electric table lamp. De Zayas! De Zayas! is the drawing of a mechanistic structure surmounted by a buxom woman's heavy corset. De Zayas, a member of the Stieglitz circle, was a caricaturist whose work was strongly influenced by the Cubists. De Zayas did the typographic calligram that shares half of the page on which Picabia's drawing Voila Elle (pl.10,fig.29) appears in 291, no.9, November, 1915. The typography cleverly mimics the directions of the main lines of the drawing, and this may be significant to the basis of the relationship between the work of De Zayas and Picabia, a relationship that might be investigated in a more complete study, but one that would not reveal anything new on Picabia's development.

In the water-color painting ~~Four-in-Hand~~ Portrait de Marie Laurencin, (see p.116) Marie Laurencin is shown as a four-bladed motor fan, for no particular reason, and another drawing, labelled Marie (pl.12,fig.36), in 391 no.3, March 1917, shows the front view of a motor, again equipped with a four-bladed fan; on the facing page in this issue of 391 is a tiny drawing of a side view of a complete motor which is labelled voila Guillaume Apollinaire, Gloire au Poète. A drawing of an electric light bulb in 391 no.6,

July, 1917, has the words "flirt" and "divorice" lettered in it on either side of the filament, and is titled Américaine.

Another group of Picabia's drawings can only be called machine-calligrams, for while words play an important role in the works already discussed, in these words and lines are of almost equal importance, though the lines do dominate and the words and phrases follow their contours. The lines indicate either the contours of individual machine elements, or electric wires. No shading is used. Each of the indicated elements is related to the others only because of juxtaposition in space - in the manner of the unrelated elements of Cubist collages. The composition of each drawing is not related to the four sides of the page that contains it, but each is a self contained unit, and was considered by Picabia as re-usable. The three drawings made for Tzara's Sept Manifestes Dada are each printed several times, in different directions, on separated pages; and other drawings, including those from Poèmes et dessins de la fille née sans mère, were printed over again in different publications and in different relationships to the pages on which they appear (pl.13,fig.40).

As these machine-calligrams do not necessarily observe vertical or horizontal axes, and occasional elements move in strong oblique directions, all the pictorial elements float freely in space in the same manner as the pictorial elements of the oil paintings of 1913. The occasional use of gears, with the teeth repeated around their edges, heightens the effect of motion in those drawings where they appear. The scattered words and phrases take part in creating a pictorial rhythm by causing the eye to jump from phrase to phrase. The element of transparency and simultaneity enters in the occasional surprinting of certain of these drawings on pages of printed material (see above), causing the eye to play between the two elements, drawing and print.

The proto-type of these machine-calligrams in Picabia's own work was the drawing Fille née sans mère of 1913, later used in 291, no. 4, June, 1915, in which, for the deluxe edition, it was colored with gold, copper, and silver-blue metallic paints painted on each copy by hand. This drawing is more substantial in its appearance than the later ones, because of the more logical relationship of its elements to each other, and the relationship of the whole to the page on which it appears, and the use of shading. Among the best of the machine-calligrams are the eighteen with which Picabia illustrated Poèmes et dessins de la fille née sans mère, two of which are Hermaphrodisme and Égoiste (pl.13, figs.37 and 39).

Actually Picabia meant these drawings to be considered not as his work but that of La Fille née sans mère, who until now had been viewed by man. This book was her opportunity to view man in turn. And she did this with deep feeling, expressing her thoughts, most of the time quite as incoherently as Picabia's own poems but suggestively none the less, on what she saw of man's anguish, and doubts about such subjects as war, religion, love and the senselessness of life.[187] Her drawings of machine elements are more delicate and tentative than those Picabia had drawn earlier, such as Ici, c'est ici Stieglitz, and approach quite close to being the equivalent of Apollinaire's calligrams,[188] for the words and phrases that hug and follow around the directions of the lines are as visually important as the lines, to the extent that the lines often seem to be a short cut to creating the pattern that Apollinaire, with a few exceptions, made entirely with words (pl.13, fig.38).

Certain other of Picabia's machine-calligrams, such as the Portrait de Tristan Tzara, 1918 (pl.14,fig.41), and Dada Movement, 1919, and Les yeux chauds (pl.14,fig.42), exist entirely for the sake of the words. They are less lyrical and less interesting pictorially. The portrait of Tzara, with its use of words that add up to a disparagment of the man, predicts Picabia's split with the Dadaists in 1921.

Another group of Picabia's illustrations are in the nature of the "ready-mades" of Duchamp. They are drawings either copied, or actually cut from catalogs and advertisements, and used by Picabia for his own purposes. Among his efforts in this direction is Miroir de l'apparance (pl.12,fig.33), used as the cover of 391 no. 2, February 10, 1917, and which is a photograph probably taken from a manufacturer's advertisement of the string arrangement of a grand-piano, on which Picabia has thickened certain of the lines making them blacker, more emphatic, to give a more interesting pictorial structure to the work; the pictorial rhythms set up by the patterns of the different groups of strings is exciting and its use quite original.

Ballet mecanique (pl.12,fig.32), is an un-touched photograph of an actual machine form, printed on the cover of 391, no. 7, August 1917. Its elements suggest a revolving, circular formation of a chorus of dancers.

For the drawing Réveil Matin (pl.12,fig.34), used as the title page of Dada 4-5, May 15, 1919, Picabia dissasembled an alarm clock, dipped some of its parts in ink and stamped them on paper, and added lines that suggest a metal framework to hold the gears together; the placement of the gears in an unbalanced arrangement, the scattered dark accents they create, and the suggestion of motion given by the repetition of the small teeth of the gears, make this one of the few machine drawings by Picabia to simulate the effect of motion, though the disassembled condition of the clock-works renders it incapable of actual motion.

Picabia's working procedure for making this drawing is described by Hans Arp: "I made Picabia's acquaintance when he visited Zurich in 1917...Tristan Tzara and I both curious and excited went to his hotel. We found him very busy pulling a clock to pieces. I couldn't help recalling the 'Anatomy Lesson' by Rembrandt...All the same it was a step nearer to abstraction. He attacked his alarm clock ruthlessly till he got to the spring which he pulled out triumphantly. He stopped working to greet us, then taking the wheels, the spring, the hands and other secret parts of the clock, he immediately impressed them on paper. He connected these imprints together by lines and added to the drawing sentences full of wit. Remote from the world of mechanical stupidity he created anti-mechanical machines...From these gratuitious machines blossomed an entire flora. 'La fille née sans mère' a thin book of verse that moved us deeply was written at that time. In that book there is no trace any more of the dried up sponges of rhetoric, 189
not a single sparkling sentence, no more 'Trompe l'oeil in a bra.'"

A more sensational "ready-made" of 1920 is the stuffed monkey pulling at his tail which sticks out from between his legs, labelled by

Picabia Portrait de Cezanne, Portrait de Rembrandt, Portrait de Renoir, Nature mort (pl.14,fig.43). He had originally wanted a live monkey for this Nature Mort, but finally settled for the stuffed one when a live one proved too difficult to locate.[190] This is, of course, a blasphemy aimed against the values of "High Art", while the ink blot labelled La Sainte Vierge (pl.14,fig.44), printed in 391, March, 1920, is a grand gesture of anti-religion, anti-sentiment iconoclasm.

The social symbolism of Duchamp is seen at its most obvious in the conception of the first drawing, made in 1913, for the Bachelors of La Mariée mise à nu..., called Cimetière de uniforms et livrées (pl.19,fig.60). In this drawing there were eight elements (a ninth was added in the 1914 study painted on glass.) These elements are malic moulds - industrial containers of acids. The forms of the molds may have their origin, in a general way, in chess pieces, as did his "King" and "Queen", for the molds in this drawing recall those of the "King" and "Queen" in the studies for Le Roi et La Reine entouré de Nus vites.[191] Duchamp also thought of the molds as empty hoods - "hoods without motors beneath" - and which he made analogous to persons who wear uniforms symbolic of their occupations: Constable, Dragoon, Priest, Bellhop, Department Store Delivery Boy, Flunkey, Undertaker's Assistant, Station Master. Kuh interprets this drawing as implying a relationship between the uniforms of officialdom and the sterility of a cemetery.[192] Perhaps in view of the rather lowly stations occupied by the uniformed men named "officialdom" is too specific, and Duchamp is commenting on the hollowness of uniforms in a general sense.

The arrangement of La Mariée mise à nu par ses célibataires, même, resembles an Assumption of the Virgin: The Virgin - the Bride - in the upper panel, and the secular world - the Bachelors - below. Actually, Duchamp considered it an apotheosis of virginity, and as embodying a number of different aspects to the state of virginity.

In 1935 Duchamp published a book of notes and drawings made during the course of the years, ca. 1912 - 1925, that he worked on the preliminary studies and on the final version of the painting. These notes are not those of a painter describing what he will do or has done to the work itself, but rather they exist in their own right as a separate work, - a work of literature that embodies some of the same ideas as the painting. Duchamp credits another work of literature as the main influence on him in this work: "It was fundamentally Roussel[193] who was responsible for my glass La Mariée mise à nu..." "From his play 'Impressions d'Afrique', I got the general approach. This play... helped me greatly on one side of my expression."[194]

The following descriptions of the Bride and the Bachelors are reduced from Duchamp's notes.[195] The virgin - the Bride - still attached to her girl friends and parents, is made up of ignorant desire; she is a motor who contains a gasoline of love that is exposed to ignition from life and which serves her to reach the goal of her desire, which is only the string that binds the bridal bouquet. She remains aloof and untouchable; yet she is not a mere a-sensual icicle, she warmly reflects on the bachelors' rebuffed offers. Though she and the Bachelors will always remain separated, she is a desiring virgin, and in her imagination she sees herself being stripped by the bachelors.

The bachelors - also referred to as Nine malic moulds, Eros machine,

Bachelor machine, or Cimetière de uniforms et livrées - in the lower panel is a machine made up of nine malic moulds all united by an imaginary horizontal plane, the plane of sex that cuts each at the point of sex. The malic moulds contain a "lighting" gas that is to be transferred to the virgin. The bachelors are tormented by eroticism which creates a desire-part. The desire-part gets closest to the virgin, but remains separated from her, and the bachelors must resort to electrical means to strip the virgin. The presence of the chocolate grinder (an actual machine in the window of a chocolate manufacturer in Rouen remembered by Duchamp from his childhood),[196] as suggested by Breton, qualifies the bachelors by referring to the adage "a bachelor grinds his own chocolate."[197]

The anti-social implications of Duchamp's "Ready-mades" lies chiefly in the de-sacredization of the traditional artistic means of expression,[198] and in a number of instances the objects chosen are also rather blatant insults of bourgeois taste, as in the case of the famous urinal, or the moustache painted on the reproduction of Da Vinci's Mona Lisa. Duchamp's "ready-mades" are almost always products of mass production(the first was a Bottlerack, chosen in 1914) which are selected by the artist, and by virtue of this selection are elevated to an equal footing with the more traditional works produced by the artist. One or two details may be altered by the artist, his signature may be added, or the object may be left untouched. A particularly interesting "ready-made" of 1922 - '23 is the Unhappy ready-made, which was a treatise on geometry, opened face up and suspended in mid-air from the corners of a porch for a period of time.

"Thus exposed to the weather, 'the treatise seriously got the facts of life'. ('What is the solution?' Duchamp proceeds to ask. 'There is no solution because there is no problem. Problem is the invention of man - it is nonsensical.')."[199]

Jean Arp spoke of the "ready-mades" as follows: "Dada objects are formed of elements found or manufactured, simple or heteroclite. The Chinese several thousand years ago, Duchamp, Picabia in the United States, Schwitters and myself during the war of 1914 were the first to invent and disseminate these games of wisdom and clairvoyance which were to cure human beings of the raging madness of genius and return them modestly to their rightful place in nature."[200]

PICABIA'S PAINTINGS OF 1920 - 1930

By 1920 Picabia was returning to painting as his chief means of self-expression. During the next two and a half decades he experimented with painting in a number of different directions. Only two generalizations can be made of all his painting up to the end of World War II: none are abstract, that is, composed entirely of invented forms, as were those of 1913, and none are concerned with the machine age. Around 1945 he resumed abstract painting in a series of canvases of brightly colored dots placed on black backgrounds which suggest a visualization of the universe.

However, though a cohesive unity of style is lacking in Picabia's work after 1920, there are certain related works, done at scattered intervals, which when isolated and grouped, reveal several distinct trends. Most pertinent to this study are those trends in his work from 1920 - 1930 which are variations on the means of suggesting motion. One variant makes use of a frenetic pictorial rhythm set up by an exaggeration of the expressionist technique using thick, wriggling streamers of paint, as in Mi Carême (pl.16,fig.49), where the employment of this technique suggests to the spectator that he is catching a fleeting glimpse of a flirtation between a man and woman in the midst of the swirling movement of a carnival. Another variant uses the repetition of elements, an example of which are the two sets of eyes given to each of the faces in Sous les Oliviers (pl.17,fig.52). Here Picabia toys with the possibilities of suggesting movement. While the cat stares fixedly ahead, having only one set of eyes, the woman shifts her eyes coquettishly from one glance to another, the man opens and shuts his eyes, that is, if the observer succeeds in placing these two sets of glances in chronological sequence and doesn't merely persist in seeing two faces with eight eyes between them.

A third variant uses the play between positive and negative areas, solids and shadows, as in La Nuit Espagnole (pl.15,fig.47). Both figures exist as flat silhouetted shapes that seem cut out of either black or white board, and at very first glance, one figure seems to be the hole left in the board when the positive shape was lifted out of it. The white female figure is a shooting-target on which two brightly colored bulls-eyes are painted, and bullet holes are indicated. The black male figure seems at first to be indicated as real, three-dimensional, for his left arm is drawn in foreshortened view, but he too must be a shooting target as bullet holes through his body are also indicated. What feeling of movement that is generated comes primarily from the mental attempts of the spectator to fit the black shape into the white hole or the white into the black, but as the two shapes are not identical, the spectator is left frustrated.

The most significant variation on the means of suggesting motion is that in which the pictorial elements are rendered as transparent. In the "transparencies" (Picabia's own term), two or more images are placed one over the other without apparent compositional regard for how they affect one another, and the spectator's eye and mind are obliged to experience the plurality of images, to shift from one to another. Changes of subject, or scene, or the location of the spectator are implied.

The proto-types of Picabia's "transparencies" are to be found in his own Caoutchouc of 1909, and among Marcel Duchamp's work of 1911, most particularly in the four versions of Les joueurs d'échecs, the two drawings (pl.18,figs. 54 and 55), an oil sketch (pl.18,fig.56), and the final (unfinished) oil painting (pl.18,fig.57). Though the pictorial elements of Duchamp's work are far from the academic realism employed by Picabia in his of the 1920's and 1930's.

In the visual appearance of such works, the influence of photography is quite apparent. The "transparencies" distinctly resemble the effect to be had by superimposing several transparent glass or acetate photographic plates, each bearing a separate image. In the preface of the catalog for the 1934 exhibition of Picabia's "transparencies" held in New York, Gertrude Stein wrote: "When Picabia came to see us in the country we talked about a great many things; we told each other a great many things. Among other things he told me that his grandfather who brought him up and with whom he lived, was one of the inventors of photography. He was a friend and companion of Daguerre who invented the daguerreotype. Picabia, when he as a young boy always visited museums and his grandfather, who was doing experiments in coloured photography at that time, being a well-known savant, was always given permission to photograph. So they photographed all day and developed all night, and this his early experience, so Picabia believes, and I am not sure he is not right, has had a good deal to do with the development of modern painting. Picabia got from the constant contact with photography, which gradually bored him very much in spite of his admiration and affection for his grandfather, got something which did give him the idea of transparence and four dimensional painting, and this through him certainly has a great deal to do with everything. Even now in his later painting and certainly in his drawing he has achieved a transparence which is peculiarly a thing that has nothing to do with the surface seen."[201]

Both versions of Duchamp's Nu descendant un escalier, the first of 1911, the second of 1912, as well as his Jeune Homme mélancolique dans un Train, 1912, undeniably resemble stroboscopic photography: a fact about which Duchamp said in 1946, referring back to the period of 1911: "Chromo-photography was at the time in vogue. Studies of horses in movement and of fencers in different positions as in Muybridge's albums were well known to me. But my interest in painting the Nude was closer to the Cubists' interest in decomposing forms than to the Futurists' interest in suggesting movement, or even to Delaunay's Simultaneist suggestions of it. My aim was a static representation of movement - a static composition of indications of various positions taken by a form in movement - with no attempt to give Cinema effects through painting."[202]

In the book Physio-logic Artistique by Hans Richer,[203] there are linear diagrams based on chrono-photographs of the human figure in motion. In these diagrams the human body and its limbs are reduced to single lines - "stick figures". In certain diagrams "stick figures" of positions of the body in the different stages of an act are superimposed, and one such diagram, Fig.115, page 299, of a figure descending a staircase is remarkably similar to Duchamp's version of the subject. Duchamp, too, thought of the forms of the body in motion in terms of single lines: "The reduction of a head in movement to a bare line seemed to me defensible. A form passing through space would traverse a line; and as the form moved the line it traversed it would be replaced by another line - and another and another. Therefore I felt justified in reducing a figure in movement to a line rather than to a skeleton. Reduce, reduce, reduce was my thought..." 204

Perhaps the first of Picabia's "transparencies" is *Femme aux Allumettes*, 1920 (pl.15,fig.46), a portrait of a woman. That this is still a Dada product is seen in the use of "found" materials to form the drawing; string outlines the face and neck, her eyebrows are of ridged coated wire, her nose is a piece of bent, smooth wire, her eyes are two small "bobby" hair-pins, her mouth is outlined with flat paper matches, the texture of her hair is given by small wooden matches, her necklace and one ear ring are of coins. The objects are all pasted on canvas and exist as a line drawing placed over a painted background which is divided into separately colored halves by a wavy diagonal line running from top left to lower right; a central part of the right-hand area is overlapped by a light colored area whose right-hand edge follows the contour of the woman's hair, and whose left-hand edge is the wavy diagonal line; another wavy light colored line painted on the left-hand area creates the contour of the other side of the woman's hair.

Le Beau Charcutier, 1921 (pl.15,fig.45), is more typical of the literary character of most of Picabia's "transparencies", though it tells its story more directly than do many of the later ones. *Le Beau Charcutier* has two superimposed images painted on a black background. One image is of the butcher who is bald-headed and has a flushed red face, beady eyes with pouches under them, and a small puckered mouth with a cat-whisker moustache; he wears a white shirt with a bow tie and black suit; all these elements are painted as flat areas of color. The image of the woman exists entirely in line, drawn in an academic manner. The area of her face is superimposed over the red-pink of the butcher's face; she is sensuous, has large languid eyes, a straight nose, and very full dark shaded lips. Two hands, presumably the woman's, caress the butcher, but the woman's spatial position in relation to the man is confused, she exists as a separate image, simply superimposed on him, perhaps as an indication of what occupies his thoughts. Ivory combs are attached to the canvas alongside and above the man's bald head, but overlapping the woman's forehead - they are a last Dada gesture.

Myrte, 1924 (pl.17,fig.51), is a very clear example of Picabia's pictorial aims in the transparency technique. It has several images superimposed, each drawn in a classical-academic manner, with great elegance. Each image of a face may, or may not be, of the same woman, but if not they are all of the same type: beautiful, fashionable, sophisticated, detached. And this is the figure type, male or female, most often encountered in Picabia's transparencies, and in most of his work throughout the 1920's and 1930's. One image dominates the composition by virtue of its size and the darkness of its lines; it is the head of a woman who is turning and is glancing over her left shoulder. She is viewed from the back. The faces of two other figures, of smaller size, and rendered in lighter tones appear behind the dominant one. One of these is viewed full-front; she is looking down, and her hands are placed on the shoulders of the other, who is seen in three-quarter view glancing upward. The contours of these figures are not materialized with equal definition all over. The bottom contour lines of the breasts of the figure who glances upward are beneath the shoulder of the dominating head. The face of a smaller third figure appears in the lower left of the picture, tilted at a strange angle. Her eyes look out at the observer; her right arm, painted in very light lines, is extended forward holding a twig in her tiny hand. Drawn even more faintly still, and in finer lines, is a full length standing figure, who stands along the central vertical axis of the painting. This figure is viewed from the back, and the large buttocks reveal it as a female form; superimposed along her right buttock and thigh is the drawing of a quiver containing arrows, and the strap by which it is attached. There is also a clearly indicated hand in the lower left of the composition that may be the left hand of the dominating figure, twisted in a mannered gesture, or it may be simply a detached hand, floating in space as are the flowers. All the lines of the composition float in space; there is no real architecture to the composition, only a very loose spotting of pictorial accents and the repetition of certain lines of direction gives it a unity and relates it to the four edges of the canvas. The thin washes of colors over which the lines float create a thick, under-water atmosphere; the drawing of the different images in lines ranging from bold to very faint emphasizes the sense of depth in this atmosphere.

The "transparency" Côte d'Azure (pl.17,fig.53), reproduced in an exhibition catalog of 1928, shows three nude young men, drawn in line in the classical-academic manner, superimposed over a scene of sail-boats and yachts and houses along the sea coast. Another, Antibes, reproduced in an exhibition catalog of 1934,[205] is of the head and hand of a girl in ballet pose, drawn in line, and superimposed over a conventional rendering of a bay with boats on the water. Both of these are simple cinematic "montage" effects, in which the observer is shown the "close-up" of young people and then a panoramic view of the scene they are part of.

The drawing Transparence, of 1932 (pl.16,fig.50), represents the "transparence" idea at its simplest. It is of a profile superimposed on a frontal view of the same face, which is an idea also found in those paintings, done at the turn of the decade, by Braque and Picasso, which combine profile and front views of heads, in which the line indicating the nose, lips and chin of the full face view also serves the purpose of being the contour of the profile.

The standing figure in Myrte, described above, suggests a statue, and in a number of Picabia's "transparencies", both drawings and paintings, antique statues as well as Renaissance paintings served as the models for certain figures. Among a group of drawings published in 1930,[206] is a drawing of the huge-muscled Farnese Hercules statue which is superimposed on drawings of nude female bodies. Among paintings reproduced in a catalog of 1934,[207] are Sagess et Resignation, whose drawings of nude male and female figures resemble similar figures by Botticelli and Signorelli, and Maternité, a drawing of a mother and child quite like sketches by Da Vinci and Raphael of the same subject. The head, and the hands in the gesture of prayer in Melibee (pl.16,fig.48), are those of the Madonna of Pierro della

Francesca's <u>Madonna and Child with Saints and Angels Adored by Federigo Da Montefettro</u>.

In 1924 Picabia devised the ballet <u>Relâche</u> for Les Ballets suédois, the music for which was composed by Eric Satie. There were two acts; one consisted of a film, <u>Entr'acte</u>, considered a prototype for later Surrealist films, written by Picabia and directed by Rene Clair. Picabia's aims in this ballet may be taken as also being the aims of the "transparencies": "<u>Relâche</u> itself...is perpetual motion, life, it is the minute in which we seek happiness; it is light, wealth, luxury, love, far removed from the conventions of the modest; without moral for the stupid, without artistic depths for the snobs: Relache is as good as alchohol, opium, sports, strength, holiness; it is baccara or mathematics..."[208]

SUMMARY

The paintings of Francis Picabia, made during the years 1908 through 1913, and certain of those made from 1920 to about 1930, embodied his conceptions of four ideas that were shared generally, knowingly or otherwise, by artists all through Europe who were experimenting and searching for new forms of expression. The four ideas concerned the expression of motion, from the movement of a human body to the movement of the universe; the expression of an awareness of simultaneous happenings or the simultaneous existence of many things; abstract painting which is the painting of forms entirely invented by the artist; and the use of machinery as a subject for painting.

Picabia, who from 1911 to 1913, moved in the orbit of the Cubist painters, by virtue of his insistence on the presence in his paintings of extra-painterly concepts, seems closer to the intentions of the Futurist painters than to the Cubists' (Picasso and Braque) concentration on problems of painting per se. Picabia, as he stated his aims in 1913, shared with the Futurists the intention to project the artist's emotional experiences in life to the spectator, and to use abstract forms and colors in paintings chiefly as an aid in projecting these experiences, relying in this on the concept of correspondences. Picabia, however, went further than the Futurists, and conceived of the possibility of making abstract painting a language of visual symbols capable of conveying the artist's thoughts, a conception shared by Marcel Duchamp. Led by their own attitudes towards their contemporary society, Picabia and Duchamp came to use machine forms, or forms derived from machinery, which they saw as most representative of modern society, as the chief element in their language of visual symbols. There were two aspects to their machine symbolism; the earlier one depended upon visual ambiguities between machine forms and the forms of the human anatomy, and most often made references to human sexual matters; in the later aspect specific machine elements were portrayed which the artists arbitrarily endowed with mocking references to society.

The expression of motion in painting played a role in both Cubist and Futurist painting, though it was an unique role in each case. Picabia, in his work from 1909 through the first half of 1913, was closer to the Futurists' concern with motion when he showed figures in motion and the dynamism of city life. But after the second half of 1913 Picabia, again in company with Duchamp, evolved from the simple idea of showing bodies in motion to other, less orthodox concepts of motion, including the psychological interchange between figures represented in a painting, and the Dadaist "gestures" defying the values set by society. Both Picabia and Duchamp made complex use of the expressive means of simultaneity, that is the rendering of painted forms as transparent. After 1920, Picabia's concern with motion found expression in the series of paintings he called "transparencies", paintings in which several separate realistic drawings are superimposed without apparent relationship to one another, and in which there is little concern shown for the 20th century world.

FOOTNOTES

1. Gabrielle Buffet-Picabia, "Some Memories of Pre-Dada: Picabia and Duchamp," The Dada Painters and Poets, an anthology, ed. Robert Motherwell, Wittenborn and Schultz, Inc., N. Y., 1951, pp. 253 - 268

2. Marcel Duchamp, "Marcel Ducahamp (an informal interview)," Bulletin of the Museum of Modern Art, N. Y., 13 no. 4 - 5, 1946, J. J. Sweeny, compiler and bibl., pp. 19 - 21, 47

3. For example, Picabia's poem "Dans une Eglisse," in K, revue de la poesie, Paris, no. 3, Mai, 1949, p. 23

4. Guillaume Apollinaire, The Cubist Painters, Documents of Modern Art, Wittenborn & CO., trans. Lionel Abel, N. Y., 1944, p. 14

5. Gabrielle Buffet-Picabia, "Apollinaire," Transition Fifty, no. 6, Oct. 20, 1950, pp. 110 - 125. In this article Gabrielle Buffet-Picabia gives a lengthy account of the friendship between Picabia and Apollinaire, including an account of the "Section d'Or" exhibition held at the Floury Gallery, Oct. 1912, and "organised under the auspices of Picabia."

6. Daniel-Henry Kahnweiler, Juan Gris, His Life and Work, trans. Douglas Cooper, N. Y., Curt Valentine, 1947, p. 71. An instance of Kahnweiler's criticism of those who participated in the "Section d'Or" exhibition occurs in this book: "I should add that the same (the concentration on the flat surface of the painting rather than on the representation of the volume of solids) applies to a number of the earliest followers of Picasso and Braque, also to almost all those who subsequently exhibited at the Section d'Or and to every exponent of 'Abstract Art' in

whatever form." "This type of painter has only perpetuated the errors of the symbolists, and also of the Fauves. They have merely produced stylization, for they are completely ignorant of the real problem which Cezanne considered fundamental and which later became the Cubists' main preoccupation, namely the representation on a canvas with only two dimensions of solid bodies which have three."

7. Gabrielle Buffet-Picabia, "La Section d'Or," Art d'Aujourd'hui, mai - juin, 1953, p. 74. In this article Buffet-Picabia gives an account of the "Section d'Or" exhibition.

8. Gabrielle Buffet-Picabia is guilty of giving two different versions as to the date of this trip, and the discussion that took place. In her article "Apollinaire", she states that it was shortly after the "Section d'Or" exhibition when the trip to Etival, in Jura, took place and during the course of which Picabia, Duchamp, and Apollinaire first discussed the publication of the book that was to become The Cubist Painters. In her article "La Section d'Or" she states that during the trip to Jura, "not only the exhibition of the Section d'Or, but also Apollinaire's sensational book on the new painting 'The esthetic meditations' (The Cubist Painters)...." were germinated. This would place the date of the trip in August or September of 1912.

9. Buffet-Picabia, "La Section d'Or"

10. Milton Brown, American Painting (1913 - 1929): From the Armory Show to the Depression, Thesis (Ph. D), New York University, Institute of Fine Arts, 1949. On pages 14 and 15, Brown further

defines Bohemianism as "basically an intellectual revolt against the confines of bourgeois society and the establishment of an intellectual community within the framework of that society but with a different set of mores and an antagonism toward those outside the community. The cause of this growth of a society within a society is basically the failure of the intellectual class to equate its own activities with social ends." "...since the revolt is mainly cultural and lacking a coherent program of social, political or economic action, even is anti social, it creates a condition where revolt for revolt's sake or art for art's sake becomes dominant."

11. Rosa Trillo Clough, Looking Back at Futurism, Ph D Thesis, Columbia University, N. Y., 1942, pp. 55 - 67. Especially in their theatrical activities and attempts to bring the audience into participation by the use of such devices as glue on the chairs and alarm signals, the Futurists anticipated the Dadaists. (Note: Rosa Trillo Clough's thesis was used as the basic source of material on the Futurists because of its English translations from the Italian of much of the most important writings by the Futurists, and because of her excellent interpretation and orderly presentation of that material.

12. Buffet-Picabia, "Some Memories of Pre-Dada"

13. ibid

14. The Armory show of 1913 was an exhibition organized by American artists to introduce the modern art of Europe to the till then provincial New York (and all the rest of the United States) art

world. An excellent account of the exhibition is given by Brown, op. cit..

15. Ezra Pound, article in Literary Review of New York Evening Post, Aug. 13, 1921

16. James Thrall Soby, "Marcel Duchamp in the Arensberg Collection," View, Marcel Duchamp Number, series V, no. 1, March, 1945, N. Y. "Duchamp belonged to an aristocratic and extraordinarily gifted family and it seems likely that his love of the enigma, and sense of private fantasy spring from an atmosphere of family secrecy and devotion. Moreover, the family life of his youth may provide a clue to his later withdrawel from the raucous traffic of the art markets...he may somewhere have felt that the most satisfying audience for his works would include only his brothers and sisters. His art may unconsciously have been intended as a symbol of family pact -a treasure trove which he still revisites and guards."

17. Albert Gleizes and Jean Metzinger, Cubism, trans. T. Fischer, London, 1913, p. 24

18. Clough, op. cit., quoting Soffici in an article in Lacerba, reprinted in Soffici, A., Scoperte e massacri, Fierenzi, Valecchi, 1919, p. 231

19. Brown, op. cit., p. 56

20. Walter Arensberg, in conversation with the writer, June 20, 1952, Los Angeles, Calif.

21. Brown, op. cit., p. 173

22. Buffet-Picabia, "Some Memories of Pre-Dada"

23. The actual date of the meeting is confused. Hans Arp in the catalog to the New York Picabia show of 1950 says they met in 1917. Gabrielle Buffet-Picabia in "Some memories of Pre-Dada" places this meeting in Feb., 1918. Georges Hugnet, in "The Dada Spirit in Painting," printed in The Dada Painters and Poets, says: "Dada no. 3, published Dec., 1918, introduced new names, including Picabia's. David Gascoyne, in A Short Survey of Surrealism, London, 1935, p. 29, states that Picabia brought out the eighth number of 391, a completely Dada number containing contributions by Tzara and Arp, in Feb., 1919.

24. Richard Huelsenbeck, in "En Avant Dada: A History of Dadaism," printed in The Dada Painters and Poets, pp. 21 - 49, discusses the ties the Dadaists had with the leading modern artists in Germany, Italy and France, and how their attitude towards the "newest" in art changed from admiration to burlesque.

25. Georges Ribemont-Dessaignes, "History of Dada," The Dada Painters and Poets, pp. 99 - 123

26. George Hugnet, "The Dada Spirit in Painting," The Dada Painters and Poets, pp. 123 - 197

27. Hulsenbeck, op. cit.

28. Robert Motherwell, introduction to The Dada Painters and Poets, p. xxvii

29. Francis Picabia, "Francis Picabia et Dada," L'Esprit Nouveau, v. 1, no. 9, 1921, pp. 1059 - 1060

30. The cover Picabia designed for Litterature, new series, no. 7, in

1927, is reproduced in <u>The Dada Painters and Poets</u>, p. 193

31. Rose Fried, Picabia's New York gallery dealer, in conversation with the writer, Nov. 25, 1952, N. Y.

32. Robert Motherwell, op. cit., p. xxxi

33. Duchamp, with the exception of <u>Nu descendant un escalier</u>, no. 2, never strongly emphasised such divisions.

34. Christian Zervos, <u>Histoire de l'art contemporain</u>, Paris, 1938, p. 311

35. Robert J. Goldwater, <u>Primitivism in Modern Painting</u>, Harper & Bros., N. Y. & London, 1938, p. 51. "In his book of 1907, which may be considered as embodying the principles of Art Nouveau, Van de Velde, its chief architectural exponent, tries to find an abstract aesthetic basis upon which all of the new art may be built, thus freeing it from the purely constructive origin it hitherto had had, and which demeaned it, and also establishing a further bond for the axiomatic unification of all the arts. This basis he finds in the screw, from which he thinks all ornament can be elaborated, since he cannot conceive of any particular ornamental motive 'whose life and logic one cannot derive from the screw'."

36. Brown, <u>American Painting (1913 - 1929): From the Armory Show to the Depression</u>, p. 192

37. Duchamp exploited this same evoking of the world of machinery in the final version of <u>Les joueurs d'échecs</u>, 1911, <u>Nu descendant un escalier, no. 2</u>, 1912, <u>Jeune Homme mélancolique dans un Train</u>, 1912, <u>Passage de la vierge à la mariée</u>, 1912.

38. Gertrude Stein, "Autobiography of Alice B. Toklas," <u>Selected Writings of Gertrude Stein</u>, ed. Carl Van Vechten, N. Y., 1946, p. 174

39. Gabrielle Buffet-Picabia, in Camera Work, special Picabia number, 1913, N. Y., p. 11 et seq.

40. Clough, op. cit., p. 121, quoting Boccioni, Pittura, Scultura futuriste, Milano, Edizioni Futuriste di "Poesia", 1914, p. 365

41. Daniel-Henry Kahnweiler, Juan Gris, p. 106, footnote no. 1. Kahnweiler quotes Cezanne on the inherent abstract character of line drawing. Of Cezanne's statement, quoted by Gasquet, "Drawing is complete abstraction...," Kahnweiler says: "Cezanne doubtless referred mainly to the absence of color in drawing, which involves a 'transcription' in black or red chalk and is thus a first 'abstraction.' However, he certainly had in mind also the strange faculty of pure line drawing to 'make an abstraction' of volume by discarding chiaroscuro. Cezanne put his finger on the non-illusionist character of drawing, which exists directly it is no longer the simple transcription of a picture in black and white; that is to say directly it is a strict line drawing..."

42. ibid, p. 106. Kahnweiler says of Gris' use of line in his work after 1920: "Line drawing within an oil painting thus became possible and the way was open to a form of representation capable of signifying objects without artifice... The position of objects was made clear by simple intersections. When it was important to give a complete view of an object in the background, the intersection was marked by drawing only the outline of the foremost object, so that the object behind is 'situated' without dissembling. As we have seen, the beginnings of this invention appeared in the Open Windows, in which the walls often do not conceal what appears essential in the landscape."

43. Clough, op. cit., pp. 110 - 11. The Futurists' use of line is described in this summary by Clough of part of a lecture given by Boccioni before Circolo Artistico of Rome, May, 1911: "Boccioni proclaimed 'the absolute and complete abolition of the finite and finished line.' The artist was to 'tear open the contour of a thing and push the enveloping milieu into it' ...with the aid of force-lines...the painter can represent an open window as a 'variable, irregular opening into which the bodies of the external world insert themselves, borne in by a conducting vehicle (the atmosphere) which penetrates the room in the form imprinted upon it by the potentialities of the external objects themselves.' The Futurist painter thus saw and depicted, 'a stupendous spectacle enacted by the influence of both the force-lines of the external objects and the force-lines of the window and the conducting body (the atmosphere), with the latter gradually creeping in, in a verying density of straight thrusts and forshortenings'."

Again, Clough quotes Boccioni, on page 211: A "force-line" was a "direction of color-form" which in turn was the "representation of movements of matter along the trajectory determined by the structure of the object and its section," and these force-lines were the paths by which finite things reach infinity.

44. In a more thorough investigation of the subject, comparisons with similar ideas held by other artists including Leger, Delaunay, Kandinsky, Klee and Mondrian would have to be included.

45. Daniel-Henry Kahnweiler, <u>The Rise of Cubism</u>, trans. Henry Aronson,

Documents of Modern Art, Wittenborn, Schultz, Inc., N. Y., 1949, and Daniel -Henry Kahnweiler, Juan Gris, His Life and Work

46. Robert Melville and E. L. T. Mesens, The Cubist Spirit in its Time, London Gallery Editions, 1947 (Exhibition catalog), p. 15. E. L. T. Mesens states this warning against considering the Cubist painters as united in aim: "The Cubist epoch has not been a school unless one excludes from it all its most important personalities. Neither has it been an 'aesthetic' unless one values its bad and late consequences in architecture and interior decoration.

"Cubism has been neither 'the continuation of Cezanne's work,' as has so often been said, nor 'the logical consequences of it.' Cezanne's painting is entirely concerned with the physical transcription of nature, within the limits imposed by the canvas and the pictorial means. It denotes a bourgeois austerity and restriction compared with for instance, the sensuous attitude to life of the early Impressionists. There are certainly visual echoes of Cezanne in some Cubist paintings but not to a greater extent than there are mental agreements with Seurat's conceptions, and plastic lessons from African wood sculpture and Henri Rousseau's spiritualization of volume."

47. Christopher Gray, The Cubist Aesthetic Theories, Johns Hopkins Press, Baltimore, 1953

48. Clough, Looking Back on Futurism. Clough's warning about the basic contradiction in the thinking of the Futurists' must be kept in mind. On page 122 she says, "These artists like

most critics, persisted in discussing the irrelevant...they knew their rules, technical devices and new subject matter had little to do with what is essential in art. Soffici, Boccioni and Carra know this and yet wrote volumes to justify their plastic and literary creations in terms of perscriptions and content... They could see the paintings of Boccioni were beautiful and those of some of his disciples who used all his devices were miserable crusts. That they knew this is betrayed by the frequent reminder that a painting was a law unto itself, the warning that the 'sensation of dynamism' is nothing unless accompanied by 'creative intuition.' Sometimes they remarked that only a few possess 'feeling for dynamism'..."

49. Apollinaire, The Cubist Painters, p. 15

50. Gray, op. cit., pp. 65 - 70

51. ibid, pp. 36 - 37

52. ibid, p. 69, quoting H. Bergson, Creative Evolution, Modern Library, N. Y., 1944, p. 14

53. ibid, p. 86

54. ibid, p. 87, quoting H. Bergson, Introduction to Metaphysics, N. Y., 1912, pp. 7 - 9

55. ibid, p. 86, quoting Gleizes and Metzinger, Cubism, p. 44

56. ibid, p. 86, quoting Gleizes and Metzinger, Cubism, p. 16

57. Kahnweiler, Juan Gris, pp. 88 - 89. Kahnweiler says: "Apparently Gris' ideal of architectural grandeur can only be realized with a static subject. But during the summer of 1915 he produced a series of pictures which are full of movement. The most important of the series...is an oval inscribed on a

rectangular canvas. The objects no longer stand upright on the base of the rectangle, solid and motionless as usual, held in place by the frame; they have lost their footing on the slippery surface of the oval and are whirling around like mad things....was it that Gris played for a moment with the idea of so-called abstract painting and forced himself to create 'forms in movement'? If this last is the case he must have retreated from disaster very quickly for, in the works that followed, the objects found their feet again and stopped moving."

58. Balcomb Greene, Mechanistic Tendencies in Painting from 1901 to 1908, M. A. Thesis, New York University, Institute of Fine Arts, 1943

59. ibid. p. 41

60. Kahnweiler, The Rise of Cubism, pp. 10 - 12

61. ibid, p. 12. Kahnweiler says: "How the rhythmisation necessary for the coordination of the individual parts into the unity of the work....can take place without producing disturbing distortions, since the object in effect is no longer 'present' in the painting... In other words, there exists as well, but only in the mind of the spectator, the finished product of the assimilation, the human head for instance. There is no possibility of conflict here, and yet the object once 'recognized' in the painting is now 'seen' with a perspicasity of which no illusionistic art is capable."

62. Albert Skira, From Picasso to Surrealism, History of Modern Painting, v. 3, Skira, Geneva, 1950. Reproduction of Picasso's Harlequin and his family, p. 50. Reproduction of Braque's Houses at l'Estaque, p. 51.

63. Kahnweiler, The Rise of Cubism, p. 12

64. ibid, p. 96. Kahnweiler says: "I remember a conversation in about 1912 between Braque and a young German expressionist painter who criticized him for the absence in his pictures of that extra-plastic element... 'But that's all understood' Braque replied." "For at that time the Cubist painters were all agreed that the plastic element in painting was sufficient in itself and that the message transmitted thus was complete. Indeed, the Cubist felt that the 'expressionism' which the young German painter looked for in their works was foreign to painting; they condemned it as 'literary,' a word which had for them only a perjorative meaning..."

65. Clough, Looking Back on Futurism, p. 117, quoting Carra in Lacerba 1, p. 64

66. ibid, pp. 89 - 90, quoting Soffici in Lacerba 1, n. 3, p. 92

67. ibid, pp. 91 - 94, quoting Boccioni, Pittura, Scultura futuriste, pp. 118 et seq.

68. ibid, p. 103

69. ibid, pp. 100 - 101. A "pictorial object appears (to the Futurist) as the product of its surroundings and its atmosphere -it may be called the 'apparition' of a thing. The Impressionists were satisfied with this superficial 'apparition'. The Futurists wanted to go below the surface for 'knowledge' of the object (the asthetic joy in looking at the Parthenon depends upon the 'feeling' that the temple is made of marble and not of wood)."

70. ibid, p. 102, quoting Boccioni, Pittura, Scultura futuriste, p. 183

71. Clough, Looking Back on Futurism, p. 102, quoting Boccioni, Pittura, Scultura futuriste, p. 183

72. ibid, p. 84, quoting Boccioni, op. cit., p. 95

73. ibid, p. 114

74. ibid, p. 114, quoting Boccioni, op. cit.

75. ibid, pp. 99 - 100

76. ibid, p. 112, discussed by Boccioni, op. cit., pp. 202, 241, 298, 265, 381, etc.

77. ibid, p. 112, quoting Soffici, Primi principi di una estetica futurista, p. 80

78. A. J. Eddy, Cubists and Post-Impressionists, Chicago, 1914, p. 173, quoting from the 1st Futurist Manifesto

79. Clough, op. cit., p. 121, quoting from the Technical Manifesto

80. Eddy, op. cit., p. 173, quoting point 5 of the 1st Futurist Manifesto

81. Clough, op. cit., p. 120, no source noted

82. ibid, p. 109, quoting Boccioni, Pittura, Scultura futuriste, p. 211

83. ibid, p. 109, quoting from the preface of the catalog for the first Paris Futurist exhibition

84. ibid, p. 109

85. ibid, pp. 110 - 111, quoting Boccioni, from a lecture presented at the Circolo Artistico of Rome, May, 1911

86. G. Apollinaire, Les Peintres Cubistes, Pierre Cailler, Éditeur, Genève, 1950. Reproduction of Jeune Homme mélancolique dans un Train, 1912, pl. 40

87. 20th Century Art, Arensberg Collection, The Art Institute of Chicago, 1949. Reproduction of Le Roi et La Reine entourés de Nus vites, 1912, p. 61, fig. 67

88. *20th Century Art, Arensberg Collection*, p. 65, fig. 72. Reproduction of *Glissière Contenant un Moulin à Eau*, 1913 - 15.

89. ibid. p. 58, fig. 62. Reproduction of *Nu descendant un escalier, no. 1*, 1911.

90. ibid, p. 53, fig. 56. Reproduction of *Sonate*, 1911.

91. ibid, p. 54, fig. 57. Reproduction of *Yvonne et Magdeleine Déchiquetées*, 1911.

92. ibid, p. 55, fig. 58. Reproduction of *Portrait*, 1911.

93. *Passage de la vierge à la mariée*, 1912, collection of the Museum of Modern Art, N. Y.

94. *20th Century Art, Arensberg Collection*, p. 66, fig. 74. Reproduction of *Broyeuse de Chocolat, no. 2*, 1914.

95. These experiments are discussed at length by Harriet and Sidney Janis in "Marcel Duchamp, Anti-Artist", *The Dada Painters and Poets*, pp. 306 - 316, and by Gabrielle Buffet-Picabia in "Magic Circles", *View*, special Duchamp no., March, 1945.

96. Skira, *From Picasso to Surrealism*, p. 112. Reproduction of *Nine Malic Moulds*.

97. Julien Levy, "Duchampiana", *View*, special Duchamp Number. "The glass broke one day. Duchamp ...was gleeful. 'Do you think I should have made it on glass,' he said, 'if I had not expected it to break?' And he showed a sketch he had drawn, prophesying the shapes of the fragments so that the reconstructed glass could truly be said to have improved with the addition of these ineradicable cracks."

98. *Paysage de la Creuse*, 1908, owned by Mr. and Mrs. H. L. Winston, exhibited at the Rose Fried Gallery, N. Y., Nov. 1953.

99. Alfred H. Barr, Jr., Picasso, Fifty Years of His Art, The Museum of Modern Art, N. Y., 1946, p. 62. Reproduction of Landscape with Figures

100. J. T. Soby and Alfred H. Barr, Jr., Twentieth Century Italian Art, The Museum of Modern Art, N. Y., 1949, pl. 20. Reproduction of Severini's Boulevard, 1910 - 11

101. Gleizes and Metzinger, Cubism, p. 133. Reproduction of Port of Naples, 1911

102. Skira, From Picasso to Surrealism, p. 50. Reproduction of Picasso's Harlequin and His Family, p. 50

103. Art d'Aujourd'hui, Mai - Juin, 1953, p. 17. Reproduction of Moi aussi j'ai vecu en Amerique. Dr. Lopez-Rey suggested, in conversation with the writer, that the title of this painting is a play on the title of Poussin's painting, Moi aussi, j'ai vecu en Arcadia.

104. Clough, Looking Back on Futurism, pp. 76 - 77, quoting Soffici in a talk given at the Verdi Theater in Florence, Dec. 12, 1913.

105. Apollinaire, The Cubist Painters, p. 11

106. Hutchins Hapgood, "A Paris Painter," reprinted from the New York Globe in Camera Work, XLII - XLIII, 1913, pp. 49 - 51, quoting Picabia

107. Apollinaire, op. cit., p. 14

108. Clough, op. cit., p. 97, quoting Apollinaire in Lacerba, Aug. 1, 1913

109. ibid, pp. 97 - 98, quoting Apollinaire in Montjoie (Organ de l'imperialisme artistique Francais), 1913

110. ibid, p. 97

111. In the attempt to explain his art to the public at large, Picabia again stood closer to the Futurists who addressed lengthy

explanations of art to the people of Italy, than to the Cubists. Neither Gleizes' and Metzinger's book Cubism, nor Apollinaire's The Cubist Painters, nor his articles in the periodical Les Soirées de Paris, are addressed to the public at large, but rather to other intellectuals.

112. Samuel Swift, review of Picabia's exhibition, reprinted from the New York Sun in Camera Work, XLII - XLIII, 1913, pp. 46 - 49, quoting Picabia

113. Hapgood, op. cit., quoting Picabia. It is necessary to keep Hapgood's qualification in mind; he said, "He (Picabia) showed me some paintings which he had done since arriving in New York only a few weeks ago, and with these paintings as illustrations he talked of the art of painting, of what he was attempting to do. I shall not attempt to quote him exactly...but only to express the spirit of what he said."

114. Buffet-Picabia, statement in Camera Work, special Picabia number. 1913, p. 11

115. Francis Picabia, Cubism by a Cubist, the preface to the catalog of his New York exhibition at the Stieglitz Gallery, reprinted in Camera Work, XLII - XLIII, 1913, p. 19

116. Hapgood, op. cit., quoting Picabia

117. Eddy, Cubists and Post Impressionists, p. 96, quoting from an interview first published elsewhere, source not given

118. Maurice Aisen, "The latest evolution in art and Picabia," Camera Work, special Picabia number, 1913, pp. 15 - 20

119. Hapgood, op. cit.. Hapgood, in his review of Picabia's exhibition goes on to express his own opinion on the subject of how the

artist's "soul states" are rendered plastic, thereby showing how generally acceptable these ideas expressed by Picabia were in 1913. He says, "the writer believes that in any intense effort of expression in any art means that by means of a few simple devices we suggest, rather than state the spiritual picture of our soul and its wealth of unconscious detail. What William James calls the 'fringe of consciousness' is suggested by these simple devices. And it is this 'fringe' that gives expression."

Hapgood's ideas and the reference to James' "fringe of consciousness" and its role in artistic creation may be taken as indication that the seeds which were to reach full flower in Surrealism were "in the air".

120. Buffet-Picabia, statement in Camera Work, special Picabia number

121. Eddy, op. cit., p. 91, quoting Picabia

122. Buffet-Picabia, "Apollinaire," pp. 110 - 125

123. Apollinaire, The Cubist Painters, p. 11

124. ibid, p. 30

125. Gray, The Cubist Aesthetic Theories, pp. 14, 15, 16, 17, 89, 90

126. ibid, pp. 14 - 15

127. ibid, p. 17

128. Gray, op. cit., p. 88, quoting Charles Blanc, Grammaire des arts du dessin, Paris, 1867, pp. 500 - 501, 573, 559

129. ibid, p. 88

130. ibid, pp 89 - 90

131. ibid, p. 16, quoting Mallarmé, Propos sur la poésie, ed. H. Mondor, Editions du Rocher, 1946, p. 43 (Letter to Henri Cazalis, Oct. 1864)

132. Gray, op. cit., p. 112

133. ibid, p. 15

134. ibid, p. 97. Note about Juan Gris quoted from Kahnweiler's *Juan Gris*, p. 105

135. F. Picabia, *Cubism by a Cubist*

136. Swift, in *Camera Work*, XLII - XLIII, 1913

137. ibid

138. Francis Picabia, in *291*, no. 12, Feb., 1916

139. Duchamp, "Marcel Duchamp (an informal interview)"

140. Gabrielle Buffet-Picabia, "Magic Circles," *View*, Marcel Duchamp number, March, 1945

141. Eugene Jolas, "From jabberwocky to 'littrism'," *Transition Forty-Eight*, no. 1, Jan. 1948, pp. 104 - 120. Samuel Putnam, *The European Caravan*, Part 1, New York, 1931.
Jolas presents an excellent summary of the history of the search for new methods of literary expression. Putnam, on p. 101, in speaking of the Dadaists role in the search for new expressive means in writing, says: "As for the Dada poets...Tristan Tzara and Picabia are probably the best representatives...," and on p. 103 he states that Picabia's "influence upon the literature of the decade has been an appreciable one."

142. Kahnweiler, *Juan Gris*, p. 40

143. ibid, p. 127

144. Neither Kahnweiler nor Gris could tolerate nor understand the work of Picabia and Duchamp, neither in their earlier work done before 1913, as seen by Kahnweiler's dismissal of the "abstract"

art of those who participated in the Section d'Or exhibition (see footnote 6), or their Dada works. Gris condemned the Dadaists and Picabia in a letter to Kahnweiler, August 25, 1919 (Kahnweiler, Juan Gris, p. 93, footnote): "there is so much admiration for the flattest mediocrity; people rave about the products of disorder, but no one likes discipline and clarity. The exaggerations of the Dada movement and others like Picabia, makes us all look like classics... Those who believe in abstract painting are like weavers who think they can produce a material with only one set of threads and forget that there has to be another set to hold these together. Where there is no attempt at plasticity how can you control representational liberties? And where there is no concern for reality how can you limit and unite plastic liberties?"

And Kahnweiler made the flat statement (Kahnweiler, Juan Gris, p. 97) that "Dada contributed nothing: it was entirely nihilistic and destroyed even its own creators. Many is the time that I have heard Gris deplore Marcel Duchamp's waste of his considerable talents..."

145. Kahnweiler, Juan Gris, pp. 89 - 91

146. ibid, p. 84

147. Duchamp, op. cit.

148. Apollinaire, The Cubist Painters, p. 18 - 19

149. ibid, p. 30

150. ibid, pp. 30 - 31

151. Buffet-Picabia, "Apollinaire," quoting Apollinaire's review of the Salon d'auton, 1913

152. Apollinaire does not designate which versions of these paintings he

refers to. There are two paintings each that have "Edtaonisl" and "Udnie" in their titles.

153. Apollinaire, op. cit., pp. 12 - 13

154. Gray, The Cubist Aesthetic Theories, p. 64

155. Picabia, in 291, no. 12, Feb. 1916

156. Buffet-Picabia, "Apollinaire"

157. ibid. In this article Gabrielle Buffet-Picabia discusses the relationship between Picabia and Apollinaire at length.

158. Eddy, op. cit., p. 82, quoting from newspaper interviews

159. J. T. Soby and A. H. Barr, Twentieth Century Italian Art, Barr quoting Carra, pp. 9 - 10

160. ibid, pl. 18. Reproduction of Carra's Funeral of the Anarchist Galli

161. ibid, p. 9

162. Clough, Looking Back on Futurism, p. 108, quoting Boccioni, Pittura, Scultura futuriste, p. 319

163. ibid, p. 107

164. ibid, pp. 106 - 108

165. ibid, p. 109, quoting Carra's explanation of the principle of "color-form" in Manifesto sulla pittura dei suoni, rumori, odori: in Lacerba 1, p. 185

166. Hapgood, in Camera Work, XLII - XLIII, quoting Picabia

167. Clough, op. cit., p. 78

168. ibid, p. 82

169. ibid, p. 55

170. ibid, p. 54, quoting Marinetti in his Supplement al Manifesto (to the Poetical Manifesto of 1912)

171. Katharine Kuh, "Marcel Duchamp," in <u>20th Century Art, the Arensberg Collection</u>, Chicago, 1949, pp. 11 - 18. An interesting example of Picabia's and Duchamp's "working procedure" in creating verbal puns is the following: "In 1915 Duchamp came to the United States for the first time. Five years later in New York City the enigmatic Rrose Sélavy was born, a pseudonym particularly useful for signing ready-mades and for increasing anonymity. Duchamp tells "The name evolved from a pun on French words: C'est la vie, Sélavy, Rose being the most commonplace feminine name I could think of (French taste of the period)." The double 'r' in the first name, Duchamp reports, came from a painting by Picabia which incorporated the signatures of his Parisian artist friends and which Duchamp signed using two 'r's' for the first time. He says, "The end of the sentence on that painting by Picabia was as follows: pi qu'habilla rrose Sélavy.'

Pi ca bia

The 'a' of 'habilla' gave me the idea to continue punning: arrose (the verb 'arroser' takes two 'r's') and then I thought it very clever to begin a word, a name, with two 'r's', like the two 'L's' in 'Lloyd'."

172. A similar interpretation of the relation of the machine to man is made by Paul B. Haviland in <u>291</u>, nos. 7 - 8, Sept. - Oct., 1915. "We are living in the age of the machine." "Man made the machine in his own image. She has limbs which act; lungs which breath; a heart which beats; a nervous system through which runs electricity... The machine is his 'Daughter born without a mother.' That is why he loves her. He has made the machine superior to himself, he endows the superior beings which he conceives in his poetry

and in his plastique with the qualities of machines. After making the machine in his own image he has made his human ideal machinomorphic. But the machine is yet at a dependent stage. Man gave her every qualification except thought. She submits to his will but he must direct her activities. Without him she remains a wonderful being, but without aim or autonomy. Through their mating they complete one another. She brings forth according to his conceptions..."

173. Buffet-Picabia, "Some Memories of Pre-Dada"

174. Kuh, "Marcel Duchamp"

175. 20th Century Art, Arensberg Collection, p. 58, fig. 62. Reproduction of Nu descendant un escalier, no. 1, 1911

176. J. T. Soby and Alfred H. Barr, Twentieth Century Italian Art, pl. 22, Reproduction of Severini's Dynamic Hieroglyphic of the Bal Tabarin, 1912

177. Melville and Mesens, The Cubist Spirit in its Time, p. 23, catalog note 18: "This somewhat Chinese landscape belongs to the world of Lear's 'Upsidownia'; the canvas has been reversed for the addition of the signature, date and title, leaving no doubt that the painter wants us to see an inverted image. The picture and its title combine delicate poetry and physical humour, presaging surrealist images: this remark made, one wonders why Apollinaire 'urges' him, in his book, 'to address himself to the subject (poetry), which is the essence of plastic art'."

178. George Isarlov, "Picabia peintre," in Orbes, No. 2, 1929, pp. 85 - 108, "Picabia's eye penetrates the subject to extract the most explicite essentials from it, its nervous system. In observing

a transatlantic liner, the ocean, a dancer, a clergyman with furtive regard, Picabia represents them in their eternal relationships, human, extracts the tragic basis in order to present it in 'un relanti condensé.' The rhythm of the dancer, the beating heart of the clergyman, the deck of the liner next to the immense ocean, clashing with each other, confused, howling. This linking up of nerves, by strength of being studied, opposed, stated precisely, is presented as an interweaving of metallic forms..."

Isarlov, in a footnote, identifies the painting of this description as Edtaonisl.

179. Buffet-Picabia, "Apollinaire"

180. A subject that is discussed at length by Balcomb Greene in his thesis, Mechanistic Tendencies in Painting from 1901 to 1908.

181. Greene op. cit., p. 34

182. Eugene Delacroix, The Journal of Eugene Delacroix, Phaidon Press, London, 1951, trans. Lucy Norton, p. 185 - 186

183. John I. H. Baur, "Dada in America: the machine and the subconscious," Magazine of Art, no. 6, Oct. 1951, p. 44, quoting from Van Wyck Brooks

184. Hans Richer, Physio-logic artistique, Paris, 1895

185. Baur, op. cit., discusses this.

186. Clough, op. cit., quoting and paraphrasing the Futurist Manifesto published in Figaro, Feb. 20, 1909

187. One of the most accessible of the poems is Wireless Telegraphy:

"My sickness listens to my heart
Closed bud of lost joys

(cont.)

I wish mischievously to be sad in the arms
Of my nice mother
To remember the blue sky
Where I had browsed huddling
One must try to forget all
The agony of the earth in the dizziness
Of heroes who spin in
The hideous waltzes of the war
In the inigmatic and masked
Atmosphere."

188. Kahnweiler, Juan Gris, p. 46. Kahnweiler speaks of Apollinaire's calligrams as "an attempt...made to endow French poetry with powers similar to the Chinese (Kahnweiler refers to the Chinese system of ideographic writing in which the eye sees an image as well as receives a signal to make a particular vocal sound)... When he (Apollinaire) revived in his poems what, in the seventeenth century had merely been fanciful decoration - a typographical arrangement forming one or more graphic signs - he intended to restore to French phonetic writing the 'power to solicit or compel.' At the same time Apollinaire came near to painting by his attempt to arrive directly at the image, for in phonetic writings the massage normally has to cross the no-man's land of abstractions (vocal sign, idea) before becoming an image. His experiment was confined to a small number of poems of his own and of the few disciples who copied him, for it is impossible deliberately to alter the nature of a language. But this enrichment had its limitations, for it then became impossible to read

the poems aloud and so they were deprived of the musical quality which all western poetry possesses. Apollinaire used a trick of typography: it seems that there is no way for the occidental poet to create new graphic signs."

In a footnote Kahnweiler adds: "There is no doubt that Mallarmé's Coup de Dés (as published in Cosmopolis in 1897) was the immediate starting point for Apollinaire's experiment." "Apollinaire...was acquainted with the baroque poems in the form of a tree, a flower, and a lyre, and perhaps even the graphic conceits of musical manuscripts, the cruciform and heart-shaped canons of the Renaissance; but without Coup de Dés he would not have thought of reviving them. Mallarmé, however, only created an atmosphere. He let a little air into the printed page; but he thought only of the typographical effect and had no pictorial tendency."

The Futurists and the proto-Dada publications 291 and 391, and almost all Dada publications, announcements etc. experimented wildly with typographical arrangements. Even those Cubist paintings by Picasso, Braque and Gris which use typographical elements share in this trend - it was another idea that "was in the air" of Europe at the time.

189. Hans Arp, "Francis Picabia, Exposition Galerie de deux iles," Art d'Aujourd'hui, Paris, no. 6, jan. 1950, p. 4

190. Hugnet, "The Dada Spirit in Painting"

191. 20th Century Art, Arensberg Collection, p. 60, figs. 65, 66. Reproductions of studies for La Roi et La Reine entourés de Nus vites, 1912

192. Kuh, "Marcel Duchamp"

193. David Gascoyne, A Short Survey of Surrealism, London, 1935, p. 21, Gascoyne speaks of Raymond Roussel, "Who was so rich that he could gratify if he so desired the least whim of his phenominally fertile imagination,..died in 1933. First published work in 1897...works full of strange (things)...nothing has ever rivalled in complexity or novelty the astounding invention of Roussel..."

194. Duchamp, "Marcel Duchamp (an informal interview)"

195. Andre Breton, "The Lighthouse of the Bride," View, Marcel Duchamp number, 1945. Breton quotes the "erotic commentary" written by Duchamp; the same translation of Duchamp's commentary is reprinted in The Dada Painters and Poets.

Sidney and Harriet Janis, Katharine Kuh, Andre Breton and Catherine Dryor have all writtem at length about this painting exploring a number of its aspects.

196. Man Ray, "Bilingual Biography," View, Marcel Duchamp number, 1945. "The demi-spheres aux mots exquis continue to rotate. But you have never told me about the Broyeuse de Chocolat. I had to find out by myself. It was a pleasure, a much greater pleasure to find out by myself. Would it be an indiscretion on my part to relate that, walking down the streets of Rouen with my back to the lop-sided steeples of the cathedral, I was overcome by a most delicious odor of chocolate which grew stronger as I advanced? And then, there they were, in a window, those beautifully polished steel drums churning around in the soft brown yielding mass of exquisite aroma. Later when questioned, you admitted your pure school-boy love. Ton amour-propre. I translate freely..."

197. Breton, op. cit.

198. The "ready-made" is closely related to the collage of the Cubists, the earliest of which seems to be Picasso's <u>Still Life with Chair Caning</u>, 1911 - 12, (reproduced, Barr, <u>Picasso</u>, p. 79).

Of the Cubist collage method Kahnweiler says, in <u>Juan Gris</u>, p. 86, that "this was no more than a new development of the 'real details', the introduction of which in the form of imitation wood and marble I have already discussed. Now these artists introduced into their pictures and drawings pieces of newspaper and wall paper, printed matter of one kind and another, engravings, oilcloths, etc., with the idea of abolishing more completely tricks of brushwork and of replacing the 'hand-painted' surface by the 'ready-made'. (Kahnweiler uses Duchamp's term "ready-made"). At the same time incorporation of the actual object in the picture was intended as an act of realism..." And on page 88, Kahnweiler adds, "Picasso's motives for using it (papier collé)... He was really concerned to be master of his means, to make his grip felt, to debunk the idea of 'noble means,' to prove that the painter can express his emotion just as well in terms of paper and cardboard...as in oil paint or gôuache. It was one of those romantic, ironic gestures calculated to display the pre-eminence of the creator's personality over his creation... (And for Gris, who hid behind his works) papier collé was...no more than another step towards anonymity..."

Picasso's motives in using papier collé were very close to Duchamp's and the Dadaist's. Duchamp, in addition to the assorted materials his various constructions were built from, and his "ready-mades," used string in Broyeuse de Chocolat, no. 2 to create all the straight lines, and all the lines of his paintings on glass are obtained by gluing wire onto the glass. His painting Tu M of 1919 includes a variety of attached objects, including a bottle-washing brush sticking straight out from the canvas, and a pointing hand painted directly on the canvas by a sign painter hired for the job.

Clough, in Looking Back on Futurism, p. 45, says of the Futurists' use of the collé technique, "The men who rebelled against the theory of reproduction in art...proceeded to bring bodily into their work the nature and reality with no modification except change of label and no excuse except alleged need of new modes of expression. Boccioni put nails and rags into his plastic work to be admired as artistic elements. Marinetti expected raw materials of sounds to be accepted as lyrical expressions. Russolo with his 'tone-tuner' brought into the theater street noises."

A. H. Barr, in Twentieth Century Italian Art, says of Severini's Dynamic Hieroglyphic of the Bal Tabarin, painted in Faenza in the summer of 1912, "The sequins glued to the canvas, Severini writes, had a respectable precedent in the jewel encrusted halo of a fourteenth century Saint Peter in the Brera, which Apollinaire mentioned to him. Severini's sequins themselves may have anticipated cubist collages by several months. Two years before, however, the cubists had begun to use isolated words and letters in their compositions. Severini, of course knew their work but with typically Futurist concern for subject matter he scatters such words as Valse, Bowling, Polka, through his Bal Tabarin, as integral and positive elements in the representation of the scene. Later words and images are used in almost equal balance by Severini and Carra in some of their war pictures and by Marinetti in his war poems."

199. Janis, op. cit.

200. Kuh, op. cit., quoting Hans Arp

201. Gertrude Stein, preface to exhibition catalog, Recent Paintings by Francis Picabia, Valentine Gallery, N. Y., Nov. 5 - 24, 1934

202. Duchamp, "Marcel Duchamp (an informal interview)"

203. Richer, Physio-logic artistique

204. Duchamp, op. cit.

205. Exhibition catalog, Catalog des aquaralles et dessins composant l'atelier de F. Picabia, vente aux enchere publique à Cannes, Galerie Alexander 111, Cannes, August, 1934

206. Jean van Heeckeren, Francis Picabia: seize dessins, 1930, Paris, 1946

207. Exhibition catalog, same as footnote 205

208. Francis Picabia, in Les Ballets suédois dans l'art contemporain, Paris, 1931

BIBLIOGRAPHY

Books by Picabia:

F. Picabia, <u>Jésus Christ rastaquouère</u>, dessins par Ribemont-Dessaignes, Paris, 1920

F. Picabia, <u>La loi d'accomodation chez les borgnes, "surzum Corda"</u>, (Film en 3 parties), Paris, Editions Th. Briant, 1928

F. Picabia, <u>Pensées sans langage</u>, Paris, Eugene Figuiere, 1919

F. Picabia, <u>Poèmes et dessins de la fille née sans mère</u>, 18 dessins, 51 poèmes, Lausanne, Imprimeries reuniee, 1918

F. Picabia, <u>Unique eunuque</u>, avec un portrait de l'auteur par lui-même et une préface par Tristan Tzara, Paris, du sans pareil, 1920

F. Picabia, contribution in <u>Die Schammade</u>, Max Ernst, ed., Cologne, 1920

F. Picabia, extracts from writinge, <u>Anthologie de l'humour noir</u>, Andre Breton, ed., Paris, ca. 1940, pp. 189 - 191

F. Picabia, contribution in <u>Les Ballets suédois dans l'art contemporain</u>, Paris, Editions du Trianon, 1931

F. Picabia, "Télégraphie sans fils"; "Anedocte"; "Hager"; "Chanson finale", in Bo, Carlo, <u>Antologia del surrealismo</u>, 1944, pp. 259 - 260

Articles by Picabia in Periodicals:

F. Picabia, "Anticoq", <u>Little Review</u>, New York, v. 8, no. 2, Spring 1922, Picabia Number, (issue also contains 18 reproductions of Picabia's work

F. Picabia, "Avenue Moche", Bifur, Paris, no. 2, Juillet 1929, pp. 24 - 29

F. Picabia, "Cubism by a Cubist", the preface to Picabia's New York exhibition of 1913, reprinted in Camera Work, XLII - XLIII, 1913, p. 19. Also reprinted in For and Against: view on the International exhibition, Association of American painters and sculptures, inc., N. Y., 1913, pp. 45 - 47

F. Picabia, "Dans une église", K, revue de la poesie, Paris, no. 3, Mai 1949, p. 23

F. Picabia, "Entr'act", Orbes, no. 3, 1932

F. Picabia, "Extraordinare", Dau Al Set, Barcelona, Agost - Setembre de 1952, Picabia Number, issue also contains 12 reproductions of Picabia's paintings

F. Picabia, "Fumigations", Little Review, New York, Autumn, 1921, pp. 12-14

F. Picabia, "Francis Picabia et Dada", L'Esprit Nouveau, 1921, v. 1, no. 9, p. 1059 - 1060

F. Picabia, "Francis Picabia in his latest moods" (Articles, exerpts from the artists writings, and reproductions), This Quarter, Monte Carlo, 1927, v.1, no. 3, p. 296 ff.

F. Picabia, "Good painting", Little Review, N. Y., Autumn, 1922, pp. 61 - 62

F. Picabia, "Ma main tremble", Little Review, N. Y., v. 9, no. 1, Autumn, 1922, p. 40

F. Picabia, "Monstres delicieux", Orbes, Paris, no. 3, Spring, 1932, pp. 129 - 132

F. Picabia, "Opinions et portraits", 391, Paris, no. 19, 1924, p. 2 - 3

F. Picabia, "Orgue de Barbarie", Little Review, New York, v. 8, no. 2, Spring, 1922, Picabia number

F. Picabia, "Manifeste cannibale dada," Dada (Dadaphone), no. 7 - 8, Mar. 1920

F. Picabia, "Manifeste dada", 391, no. 12, Mar. 1920

F. Picabia, "Petit Bobo", Mecano, Leiden, no. (1?), jaune, 1922

F. Picabia, "Plafonds creux", Rongwrong, New York, no. 1, 1917, p. 3

F. Picabia, "Soldats, Ascète, Elle, Hier", 391, New York, no. 7, Aug. 1917, p. 2

F. Picabia, contribution in Orbes, no. 1, 1928, p. 81

F. Picabia, contribution in Litterature, May, 1920, v. 2 no. 13, Dada number, pp. 1 - 23. Vingt-Trois manifestes du mouvement dada.

F. Picabia, contributions, Dada Documents (n.p., n. d.), Scrapbook of Dada documents, Museum of Modern Art Library

F. Picabia, contributions, 291, edited by Alfred Stieglitz, New York, 1915 - 16, nos. 4, 5 - 6, 9, 10 - 11, 12

F. Picabia, editor, Cannibale: revue mensuelle, no. 1 - 2, Apr. 25 - May 25, 1920, Paris, "Au sans pareil", 1920, 1 v. illus.

F. Picabia, editor, La Pomme de Pins, St. Raphael, Feb. 25, 1922, reproduced pp. 268 - 71 in The Dada Painters and Poets, R. Motherwell, ed., Wittenborn and Schultz, N. Y., 1951

F. Picabia, editor, 391, Barcelona, New York, Zurich, Paris, 1917 - 24

F. Picabia, six reproductions of paintings, Soirées de Paris, Paris, no. 22, 15 mars, 1914, pp. 137, 139, 149, 151, 169, 179

Books Devoted to Picabia:

André, Edouard, Picabia, Paris, 1908

Heeckeren, Jean van, Francis Picabia: seize dessins, 1930, Paris, "Les Presses rapides", 1946, 16 plates

La Hire, Marie de, Francis Picabia, Paris, Galerie La Cible, 1920, 11 plates

Books Containing Material on Picabia:

Apollinaire, Guillaume, The Cubist Painters, Documents of Modern Art, Wittenborn and Co., trans. Lionel Abel, N. Y., 1944

Barr, Alfred, Jr., ed., Fantastic Art, Dada, Surrealism, New York, 1947 (cop. 1936)

Breton, André, Les Pas Perdus, Paris, Gallimard, 1924 (Les documents blues. 6), pp. 159 - 65

Breton, André, Le Surréalisme et la Peinture, Paris, 1928, Gallimard Library

Eddy, A. J., Cubists and Post-Impressionists, Chicago, 1914

Guggenheim, Peggy, ed., Art of this Century, Art of this Century Gallery, New York, 1942. Biographical section on Picabia

Huyghe, René, ed. Histoire de l'art contemporaine: la peinture, Alcan, Paris, 1935. Originally published in L'Amour de l'art, March, 1934. Includes La nouvelle subjectivité by René Huyghe, Le dadaisme et la surréalisme by Jean Cassou, Notice historique sur dada et le surréalisme by Germain Bazin. Additional notices on Picabia and others.

Massot, Pierre de, De Mallarmé à 391, Paris, au Bel Exemplaire, 1922, F. Picabia pp. 95 - 122

Motherwell, Robert, editor, The Dada Painters and Poets, an anthology, Wittenborn and Schultz, Inc., N. Y., 1951. Includes:

Introduction and comments by Robert Motherwell

"En Avant Dada, A History of Dadaism," by Richard Huelsenbeck, 1920

"History of Dada," by Georges Ribemont-Dessaignes, 1931

"The Dada Spirit in Painting," by George Hugnet, 1932 and 1934

"Some Memories of Pre-Dada: Picabia and Duchamp," by Gabrielle Buffet-Picabia, 1949

"Marcel Duchamp: Anti-Artist," by Harriet and Sidney Janis, 1945

"Dada Fragments," by Hugo Ball, 1916 - 17

Seuphor, Michel, L'Art abstrait, Paris, Maeght, 1949. "Dada", p. 50 - 62, Biog. & bibl. note: Picabia, p. 308

Skira, Albert, ed., From Picasso to Surrealism, vol. 3, The History of Modern Painting, Geneva, 1950

Tharrats, Juan José, Artistas espanoles en el ballet, 1950, p. 42 - 44

Wilenski, R. H., Modern French Painters, Reynal and Hitchcock, N. Y., ca. 1941

Brooklyn Museum: International Exhibition of Modern Art, arranged by the Société Anonyme for the Brooklyn Museum, N. Y., Société Anonyme, Museum of Modern Art, 1926. Picabia, p. 22, Duchamp, p. 23

Catalog of Collection of the Société Anonyme: Museum of Modern Art, 1920, Yale University Art Gallery, New Haven, Conn., 1950

Picabia, biographical sketch by Marcel Duchamp and bibliography, p. 4 - 5

Type over

Material on Picabia in Periodicals:

Aisen, Maurice, "The latest evolution in Art and Picabia", *Camera Work*, Special Picabia Number, New York, 1913

Apollinaire, Guillaume, "Salon d'automne", *Soirées de Paris*, Paris, no. 18, 15 novembre 1913, p. 6 - 10; no. 19, 15 decembre 1913, p. 46 - 49

Arensberg, Walter Conrad, "Partie d'échecs entre Picabia et Roché", *391*, New York, no. 7, Aug. 1917, p. 3, illus.

Arp, Jean, "Francis Picabia" (Exposition Galerie des deux iles), *Art d'Aujourd'hui*, Paris, no. 6, janvier 1950, p. 4, illus. Also printed in catalog for Rose Fried Gallery, New York, Jan. 15, 1950

Bazin, Germain, "Notices Biographiques et bibliographiques", *L'Amour de l'art*, no. 3, March, 1934, p. 344. Note: Histoire de L'Art Contemporain. 1. Chapitre XII, La nouvelle subjectivité. Reprinted in Hughe, René, ed., *Histoire de l'art contemporaine: la peinture*, Paris, Alcan, 1935

Buffet-Picabia, Gabrielle, "Apollinaire", *Transition fifty*, no. 6, pp. 110 - 25, Oct. 20, 1950

ch, 1950

Buffet-Picabia, Gabrielle, "Barcelone 1916 - Berceau de '391'",
Buffet-Picabia, Gabrielle, "La Section d'Or", *Art d'Aujourd'hui*, mai -
Dau Al Set, Barcelona, Picabia number, Agost - Setembre de 1952
Juin, 1953, p. 74

Buffet-Picabia, Gabrielle, "Dada", *Art d'Aujourd'hui*, no. 7 - 8, pp. 26 - 29, Mar

Buffet-Picabia, Gabrielle, "On demand 'Pourquoi 391? Qu'est-ce que 391?'", Plastique, no. 2, pp. 2 - 8, Summer, 1937

Buffet-Picabia, Gabrielle, statement in Camera Work, Special Picabia Number, New York, 1913, p. 11

Cassou, Jean, "Le Dadaisme et le Surréalisme", L'Amour de l'art, no. 3, March, 1934, pp. 337 - 40

Duchamp, Marcel, "Francis Picabia", Dau Al Set, Barcelona, Pic bia Number, Agost - Setembre, 1952. (Biographical sketch, same as in Catalog of the Société Anonyme, Museum of Modern Art, 1920, Yale Univ. Art Gallery, New Haven, Conn., 1950, p. 4 - 5)

Du Mas, Vivian, "L'Occultisme dans l'art de Francis Picabia", Orbes, Paris, no. 3, Spring 1932, pp. 113 - 28

Gordon, Godfrey Jan, "Common sense and contemporary art", The Studio, v. 126, Jan., 1944, pp. 1 - 12

Hapgood, Hutchins, "A Paris Painter", reprinted from the "New York Globe", Camera Work, XLII - XLIII, 1913, pp. 49 - 51

Heeckeren, Jean Van, "Le picador de l'ennui", Dau Al Set, Barcelona, Picabia Number, Agost - Setembre, 1952

Isarlov, George, "Picabia peintre", Orbes, no. 2, 1929, pp. 85 - 108

This article contains what seems to be a complete list of exhibitions in which Picabia participated as well as of his one man shows, from 1899 until October, 1928, with the titles of the paintings exhibited, and also a large number of European and American newspaper and periodical references of the reviews of these exhibitions. There is also a list of owners of Picabia's works.

Lebel, Robert, "Picabia and Duchamp or Pro and Contre", Paru, Paris, Nov., 1949, p. 141

Lévesque, Jacques-Henri, "Picabia et Dada", Dau Al Set, Barcelona, Picabia Number, Agost - Setembre, 1952

Pound, Ezra, a discussion of Picabia's literature in an article in the "Literary Review" of the New York Evening Post, August 13, 1921

Ribemont-Dessaignes, G., "Francis Picabia", L'Esprit Nouveau, 1920, v. 1, pp. 108 - 10

Swift, Samuel, Review of Picabia's New York exhibition, 1913, reprinted from the New York Sun, Camera Work, XLII - XLIII, 1913, pp. 46 - 49

Thomas, Victor, "Les mois artistique", L'Art et les artistes, v. 1, le année, April, 1905, pp. 46 - 52

"A post-cubist's impressions of New York", New York Herald Tribune, Sunday, March 9, 1913, Part II, Miscellany and art. Three reproductions of watercolors framed in a line drawing by a staff artist.

"Picabia Self Portrait going to war", reproduction and review of Picabia exhibition at the Photo-Secession Gallery, New York Herald Tribune, Jan. 19, 1915

"5 Picabia works sold to satisfy debt", news item, New York Herald Tribune, May 24, 1951, p. 25

"Picabia sale at the Rose Fried gallery", Art Digest, July 4, 1951, p. 25

Exhibition Catalogs:

Arp, Hans, Francis Picabia, New York, Pinacotheca Gallery, Feb. 1950.

The same statement by Arp is in Art d'Aujourd'Hui, Paris, no. 6, janvier, 1950, p. 4

Basel Offentliche kunstsammlung (exhibition), Francis Picabia, v.a.; sammlung hell Walden; 12. Janvar - 3 Februar, 1946, Basel, Kunsthalle, 1946

Breton, André, Francis Picabia, Barcelona, 1922

Beaune Galerie, Paris, Francis Picabia, Nov. 4 - 17, 1938

Briant - Robert, galerie, Paris, Francis Picabia, Nov. 11 - 30, 1927, illus.

Briant, Th., galerie, Paris, Francis Picabia, Oct. 26 - Nov. 15, 1928, illus

Galerie de Beaune, Paris, Picabia exhibition, 19 Nov. - 2 Dec., 1937

(contains a collection of brief quotations from other statements)

Marcel Duchamp (Rrose Sélavy 8.3. 1926)

André Breton (preface to an exhibition, 1922)

Jan Van Heeckeren (La ligne de Vie - Orbes, 1931

Jean Cocteau (Le secret professionnel, 1922)

Ribemont Dessaignes (N. R. F. ier, Juin, 1931)

Vivian Du Mas (Orbes, printemps, 1932)

Jacques Henry Levesque (Les 20 ans de l'esprit Dada, conference à la Sorbonne, 4 mai, 1936)

Gertrude Stein

491, illus., Paris, Réné Drouin, 1949, catalog in newspaper format issued March 4, 1949, for Picabia exhibition of 136 works, dated 1879 - 1949. Edited by Michel Tapié. Includes the following contributions:

André Breton, "Doubles for bandaged eyes"

Michel Tapié, "50 Ans de plaisirs"

Michel Perrin, "Picabia Poète"

Picabia, "The painters and their effects from a distance"

Olga, "Francis"

Georges Charbonnier

"Foreshortened"

H. F. Roché, "Picabia seen at a galop"

Michel Seuphor, "Rebus"

Guiness, Meraud Michael, preface, Francis Picabia, The Intimate Gallery, New York, April 9 - May 11, 1928

Hotel Drout, Paris, Catalog des tableaux, aquarelles et dessins par Francis Picabia appartenant à M. Marcel Duchamp, illustrated catalog of an auction sale, March 8, 1926

Lévesque, Jacques-Henry, preface, Quelques oeuvres de Picabia, époque dada 1915 - 1925, Galerie Artiste et Artisain, Paris, 20 Nov. - 4 Dec., 1951

Mignon, Maurice, preface, Catalogue des aquarelles et dessins composant l'atelier de Francis Picabia, vente aux enchères publiques à Cannes, Galerie Alexandre III, Cannes, aout, 1934

Miles, Roger, preface, Exposition Picabia, Haussmann galerie, Paris, Feb. 10 - 25, 1905, Feb. 1 - 15, 1907

Petit, Georges, galeries, Paris, Exposition de tableaux par Francis Picabia, March 17 - 31, 1909

Picabia, Francis, preface, catalog of Picabia's exhibition at the "Little Gallery of the Photo Secession", March 17 - April 5, 1913

Picabia, Francis, preface, Picabia, recent paintings, Léonce Rosenberg, Galerie du Luxembourg, 11 avril - 8 mai, 1948

Picabia, Francis, and Rosenberg, Léonce, essays, Exposition Francis Picabia: trente ans de peinture, illustrated, Paris, decembre 9 - 31, 1930

Léonce Rosenberg Gallery, Francis Picabia, Dessins (99), Paris, decembre 1 - 24, 1932

Seuphor, Michel, preface, La fin de tout, Picabia Point, Galerie Des Deux Iles, Paris, 12 - 31 decembre, 1949

Stein, Gertrude, preface, Recent Paintings by Francis Picabia, Valentine Gallery, New York, Nov. 5 - 24, 1934

Tzara, Tristan, preface, Exposition Dada, Francis Picabia, Sans Pareil Galerie, Paris, April 16 - 30, 1920, illustrated

Exhibition Reviews:

"Exposition, Francis Picabia, Galerie Hauesman, Paris", The New York Herald, Paris edition, Dimanche 3 Fev., 1907, five reproductions

"Review of Picabia exhibition at 291", International Studio, May, 1913

"Les expositions à Paris et ailleurs", Cahiers d'art, v. 2, no. 7 - 8, 1927, p. 3 - 5

"Exposition, Francis Picabia", P. Berthelot, Beaux Arts, 9: 22 - 23, N. '31

"Retrospective Show, Francis Picabia", gallery of H. L. Rosenberg, P. Fierens, Art News, 29:30, Jan. 17, '31

"Portrait", Francis Picabia, Beaux Arts, pl., July, 1921

"Francis Picabia", R. Vitrac, Beaux Arts, p. 3, Nov. 17, 1933

"Exhibition, Francis Picabia", Valentine gallery, Art News, 33:16, Nov. 10, 1934

"Exposition, Francis Picabia", Valentine gallery, Parnassus, 6:25, Dec., 1934

"Exposition, Francis Picabia", Beaux Arts, p. 6, Nov. 2, 1934

"Might it not be called superimpositionalism?", illu., Art Digest 9:11, Nov. 15, 1934

"A Travers les galeries: Francis Picabia", L'Amour de l'art, v. 19, no. 10, Dec., 1938, p. 392

"Exposition galerie Colette Allendy, Francis Picabia", Arts, p. 5 O 18: p. 4 O 25 '46

"Exposition, Francis Picabia", galerie Denise René, D. Chevalier, Arts, p. 2, mai 10, 1946

"Abstraction" galerie du Luxembourg, Arts, p. 4, April 16, 1948

Stahly, F., "Francis Picabia, Galerie René Drouin", Werk, Zurich, 36. Jahrg., hft. 5, mai 1949, sup. p. 63

"Exhibition, Francis Picabia", Pinacotheca gallery, Art News, 49:10, March, 1950, illus.

"Le Musée d'art Moderne va exposer deux toiles anciens de Picabia", Arts, p. 5, illus., March, 1950

"Picabia's heart still belongs to Dada", exhibition at Rose Fried gallery, Art Digest, 24:14, March 1, 1950

Davay, Paul, "Picabia d'hier d'aujourd'hui", Beaux Arts, Brussels, 15e année, no. 505, 27, Oct., 195-, p. 3, review of exhibition, Galerie Apollo

Material on Marcel Duchamp:

Buffet-Picabia, Gabrielle, "Some Memories of Pre-Dada: Picabia and Duchamp", The Dada Painters and Poets, R. Motherwell, ed. Wittenborn and Schultz, Inc., N. Y., 1951

Duchamp, Marcel, "The bride stripped bare by her own bachelors," This Quarter, 5, no. 1, pp. 189 - 92, Sept., 1932. Extracts introduced by Breton

Duchamp, Marcel, La Mariée Mise à nu par ses célibataires, même, Paris, Editions Rrose Sélavy, 1934

Duchamp, Marcel, "Marcel Duchamp" (an informal interview), Bulletin of the Museum of Modern Art, New York, 13, no. 4 - 5, pp. 19 - 21, 47, 1946, J. J. Sweeney compiler and Bibli.

Kuh, Katherine, "Marcel Duchamp in Chicago Art Institute", 20th Century Art, Arensberg Collection, The Chicago Art Institute, 1949, pp. 11 - 18

View, New York, Marcel Duchamp Number, series V, no. 1, March, 1945

Contents:

André Breton, "The point of View: Testimony 45"

André Breton, "Lighthouse of the Bride"

James Thrall Soby, "Marcel Duchamp in the Arensberg Collection"

Gabrielle Buffet (Pic bia), "Magic Circles"

Robert Desnos, "Rrose Selavy" (1921-23), a collection of puns

Harriet and Sidney Duchamp, "Marcel Duchamp, Anti-Artist" (same appears in The Dada Painters and Poets, R. Motherwell, ed., Wittenborn and Schultz, Inc., N. Y., 1951)

Nicolas Calas, "Cheat to Chest"

Fredrick J. Kiesler, "Les Larves D'Imagie D' Henty Robert Marcel Duchamp", a photographic triptych

Man Ray, "Bilingual Biography"

Mina Loy, "Oh Marcel -Otherwise: I also have been to Louise's",

monologue transcribed

Julien Levy, "Duchampiana"

Henrie Waste, "A Portrait"

Robert Allerton Parker, "America Discovers Marcel"

Leon Kochnitsshy, "Marcel Duchamp and the Futurists"

INDEX OF PHOTOS

Fig. 9, Pl. 3 - Picabia, Danses à la source, oil, 47½ x 47½, 1912. Arensberg Collection, Philadelphia Museum of Art. Photo, 20th Century Art, Arensberg Collection, The Art Institute of Chicago, 1949, p. 91

Fig. 10, Pl. 4 - Picabia, Chanson Nègre, water-color, 21 5/8 x 29 5/8", 1913. Alfred Stieglitz collection, The Metropolitan Museum of Art, on loan to the Museum of Modern Art, New York. Photo, Museum of Modern Art

Fig. 11, Pl. 4 - Picabia, Fille née sans mère, ink drawing, 10 3/8 x 8 1/2", 1913. Alfred Stieglitz collection, The Metropolitan Museum of Art. Reproduced in 291, no. 4, June, 1915. Photo, The Metropolitan Museum of Art

Fig. 12, Pl. 4 - Picabia, Udnie, Jeune fille américaine, oil, 1913. Photo, R. Motherwell, ed., The Dada Painters and Poets, Wittenborn and Schultz, Inc. N. Y., 1951, p. 1

Fig. 13, Pl. 5 - Picabia, Je revois en souvenir ma chere Udnie, oil, 93 x 79", 1913. Collection the Museum of Modern Art, N. Y., Photo, Sidney Janis Gallery

Fig. 14, Pl. 5 - Duchamp, Mariée, oil, 34 3/4 x 21 1/2", August, 1912. Arensberg Collection, Philadelphia Museum of Art. Photo, New York University, Institute of Fine Arts slide collection

Fig. 15, Pl. 6 - Picabia, Danseuse etoile sur un transatlantique, water-color, 21 5/8 x 29 5/8", 1913. Photo, Metropolitan Museum of Art slide collection

Fig. 16, Pl. 6 - Picabia, Edtaonisl, Ecclésiastique, oil, 9' 10 3/8" x 9' 10 1/4", 1913. Anonymous loan to The Art Institute of Chicago. Photo, The Art Institute of Chicago

Fig. 17, Pl. 7 - Picabia, La ville de New York aperçue à travers le corps, water-color, 21 5/8 x 29 5/8", 1913. Collection of Benjamin Péret. Photo, Robert Melville and E. L. T. Messens, The Cubist Spirit in its Time, London Gallery Editions, 1947 (Exhibition catalog), p. 22

Fig. 18, Pl. 7 - Picabia, Danseuse étoil et son école de danse, water-color, 21 7/8 x 29 7/8 ", 1913. Alfred Stieglitz collection, The Metropolitan Museum of Art, on loan to the Museum of Modern Art, N. Y.. Photo, Museum of Modern Art

Fig. 19, Pl. 7 - Picabia, Culture Physique, oil, 35 1/8 x 45 3/4", 1913. Arensberg Collection, Philadelphia Museum of Art. Photo, 20th Century Art, Arensberg Collection, The Art Institute of Chicago, 1949, p. 92

Fig. 20, Pl. 8 - Picabia, Edtaonisl, Catch as Catch Can, oil, 39 1/4 x 32", 1913. Arensberg Collection, Philadephia Museum of Art. Photo, The Metropolitan Museum of Art slide collection

Fig. 21, Pl. 8 - Picabia, Very Rare Picture on the Earth, oil, gilt and silver, and collage, 1915 or 16. Photo, New York University, Institute of Fine Arts slide collection

Fig. 22, Pl. 9 - Picabia, Dedee d'Amerique, oil, gilt and silver paint, 1915. Saidie A. May Collection, Baltimore Museum of Art. Photo, Art Digest, Dec. 15, 1953

Fig. 23, Pl. 9 - Picabia, Four in Hand, watercolor, 1916. Photo, Dau Al Set, Barcelona, Picabia Number, Agost - Setembre de 1952

Fig. 24, Pl. 9 - Picabia, C'est clair comme le jour, oil, 1915 or 16. Photo, The Little Review, Picabia Number, Spring, 1922

Fig. 25, Pl. 9 - Picabia, Tableau peint pour raconter non pour prouver, drawing, 1915 or 16. Photo, Marie de La Hire, Francis Picabia, Paris, Galerie La Cible, 1920

Fig. 26, Pl. 10 - Picabia, ici, c'est ici Stieglitz, black ink and red water-color and collage, 29 7/8 x 20", 1915. Alfred Stieglitz Collection, The Metropolitan Museum of Art. Photo, The Metropolitan Museum of Art

Fig. 27, Pl. 10 - Picabia, Le Saint Des Saintes, black ink and red water-color. Illustration for 291, no. 5 - 6, July - August

Fig. 28, Pl. 10 - Picabia, Portrait d'une jeune fille américaine dans l'état de nudité, black ink, 1915. Illustration for 291, no. 5 -6, July - August, 1915

Fig. 29, Pl. 10 - Picabia, Voila Elle, 1915, black ink. Typographic calligram by M. De Zayas. Page from 291, no. 9, Nov., 1915. Photo, R. Motherwell, ed., The Dada Painters and Poets, Wittenborn and Schultz, Inc., N. Y., 1951, p. 343

Fig. 30, Pl. 11 - Picabia, Parade Amoureuse, oil on paper, 39 x 28 3/4", 1917. Private collection, New York. Photo, New York University, Institute of Fine Arts slide collection

Fig. 31, Pl. 11 - Picabia, L'enfant carburateur, oil, crayon, silver and gold on wood, 50 x 40", 1918. Collection of Lucien Lefebure-Foinet, Paris. Photo, Museum of Modern Art, N. Y.

Fig. 32, Pl. 12 - Picabia, Ballet mecanique, 1917. Photograph printed on cover of 391, no. 7, Aug., 1917

Fig. 33, Pl. 13 - Picabia, Mirroir de l'apparence, 1917. Retouched photograph printed on cover of 391, no. 2, Feb. 10, 1917

Fig. 34, Pl. 12 - Picabia, Réveil matin, black ink, 1919. Illustration for title page of Dada 4 - 5, May 15, 1919. Photo, R. Motherwell, ed., The Dada Painters and Poets, Wittenborn and Schultz, Inc., N. Y., 1951, p. 130

Fig. 35, Pl. 12 - Picabia, Flamenca, black and gold ink, 1917. Cover of 391, No. 3, March 1, 1917

Fig. 36, Pl. 12 - Picabia, Marie, black ink, 1917. Illustration in 391, no. 3, March, 1917

Fig. 37, Pl. 13 - Picabia, Hermaphrodisme, black ink, 1918. Illustration, Francis Picabia, Poèmes et dessins de la fille née sans mère, Laussanne, Imprimeries réunies, 1918

Fig. 38, Pl. 13 - G. Apollinaire, Calligrams, 1917. From a catalog of an exhibition of paintings by Leopold Survage, with preface and calligrams by Apollinaire. Photo, <u>Art d'Aujourd'hui</u>, Mai - Juin, 1953, p. 32

Fig. 39, Pl. 13 - Picabia, <u>Égoïste</u>, ink, 1918. Illustration, Francis Picabia, <u>Poèmes et dessins de la fille née sans mère</u>, Lausanne, Imprimeries réunies, 1918

Fig. 40, Pl. 13 - Picabia, Exhibition catalog, Galerie au sans pareil, Paris, April 16 - 30, 1920. Photo, R.Motherwell, ed., <u>The Dada Painters and Poets</u>, Wittenborn and Schultz, Inc., N. Y., 1951, p. 90

Fig. 41, Pl. 14 - Picabia, <u>Portrait de Tristan Tzara</u>, 1918. From <u>Cannibale</u>, no. 1, Paris, April 25, 1920. Photo, R. Motherwell, ed.,<u>The Dada Painters and Poets</u>, Wittenborn and Schultz, Inc. N. Y., 1951, p. 249

Fig. 42, Pl. 14 - Picabia, <u>Les Yeux Chauds</u>, ca. 1918. Photo, <u>The Little Review</u>, Picabia Number, Spring, 1922

Fig. 43, Pl. 14 - Picabia, <u>Portrait de Cezanne</u>, collage with stuffed monkey, 1920. Photo, R. Motherwell, ed., <u>The Dada Painters and Poets</u>, Wittenborn and Schultz, Inc., N. Y., 1951, p. 175

Fig. 44, Pl. 14 - Picabia, <u>La Sainte Vierge</u>, ink blot. Illustration in <u>391</u>, No. 12, March, 1920

Fig. 45, Pl. 15 - Picabia, <u>Le beau charcutier</u>, oil and collage, 36 x 30", 1921. Photo, Sidney Janis Gallery, N. Y.

Fig. 46, Pl. 15 - Picabia, <u>Femme aux allumettes</u>, oil and collage, 36 x 29", 1920. Photo, Sidney Janis Gallery, N. Y.

Fig. 47, Pl. 15 - Picabi , <u>La Nuit Espagnole</u>, oil, 65 x 51", 1922. Photo, Sidney Janis Gallery, N. Y.

Fig. 48, Pl. 16 - Picabia, Melibee, gouache, ca. 1924. Photo, New York University, Institute of Fine Arts slide collection

Fig. 49, Pl. 16 - Picabia, Mi Carême, oil, ca. 1926. Photo, This Quarter, Monte Carlo, 1927, v.1, no. 3, p. 296 ff

Fig. 50, Pl. 16 - Picabia, Transparence, drawing, 1932. Photo, Dau Al Set, Barcelona, Picabia Number, Agost - Setembre de 1952

Fig. 51, Pl. 17 - Picabia, Myrte, gouache, 48 x 39", ca. 1924. Photo, Sidney Janis Gallery, N. Y.

Fig. 52, Pl, 17 - Picabia, Sous les oliviers, 1924. Photo, This Quarter, Monte Carlo, 1927, v.1, no. 3, p. 296 ff

Fig. 53, Pl. 17 - Picabia, Cote d'Azur, water-color. Photo, exhibition catalog of works by Picabia, Th. Briant galerie, Paris, Oct. 26 - Nov. 15, 1928

Fig. 54, Pl. 18 - Duchamp, Les joueurs d'échecs, charcoal and ink, 1911. Collection of Mr. and Mrs. Edgar Varese. Photo, Museum of Modern Art

Fig. 55, Pl. 18 - Duchamp, Les joueurs d'échecs, charcoal and ink, 13 x 15 3/8", 1911. Arensberg Collection, Philadelphia Museum of Art. Photo, 20th Century Art, Arensberg Collection, The Art Institute of Chicago, 1949, p. 56

Fig. 56, Pl. 18 - Duchamp, Les joueurs d'échecs, oil, m. 50 x m. 61, December, 1911. Collection of Jacques Villon, Puteaux, Photo, Le Cubisme (1907 - 1914), Musée National d'Art Moderne, Paris, 30 Janvier - 9 Avril, 1953, catalog of exhibition, pl. XX

Fig. 57, Pl. 18 - Duchamp, Les joueurs d'échecs, oil, 39 1/4 x 39 1/4", 1911. Arensberg Collection, Philadelphia Museum of Art. Photo, 20th Century Art, Arensberg Collection, The Art Institute of Chicago, 1949, p. 57

Fig. 58, Pl. 19 - Duchamp, Nu descendant un escalier, No. 2, oil, 58 5/8 x 35 3/8", 1912. Arensberg Collection, Philadelphia Museum of Art. Photo, New York University, Institute of Fine Arts slide collection

Fig. 59, Pl. 19 - Duchamp, Moulin à café, oil, 1911. Collection of Maria Martins, Rio, Brasel. Photo, New York University, Institute of Fine Arts slide collection.

Fig. 60, Pl. 19 - Duchamp, Cimetière des uniforms et liverées, pencil, 12 5/8 x 15 3/4, 1915. Arensberg Collection, Philadelphia Museum of Art. Photo, 20th Century Art, Arensberg Collection, The Art Institute of Chicago, 1949, p. 64

Fig. 61, Pl. 19 - Duchamp, La Mariée mise à nu par ses célibataires, même, oil, and wire on glass, 1915 - 1923. Collection of Katherine S. Dreier, New Haven, Conn.. Photo, Museum of Modern Art

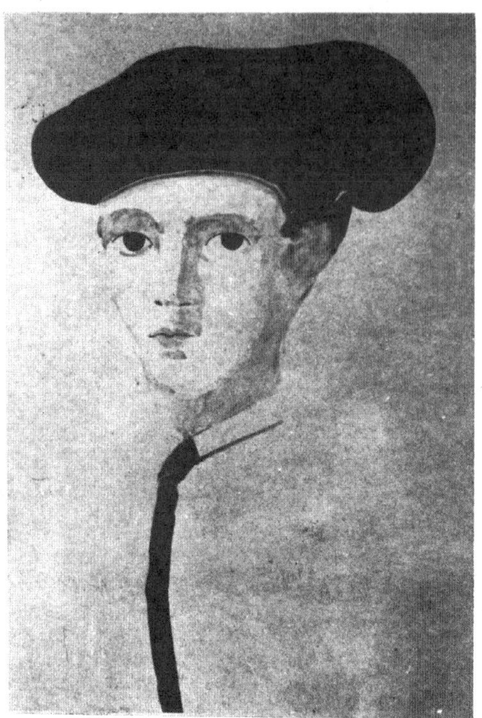

Fig. 1 Picabia, Portrait, 1902

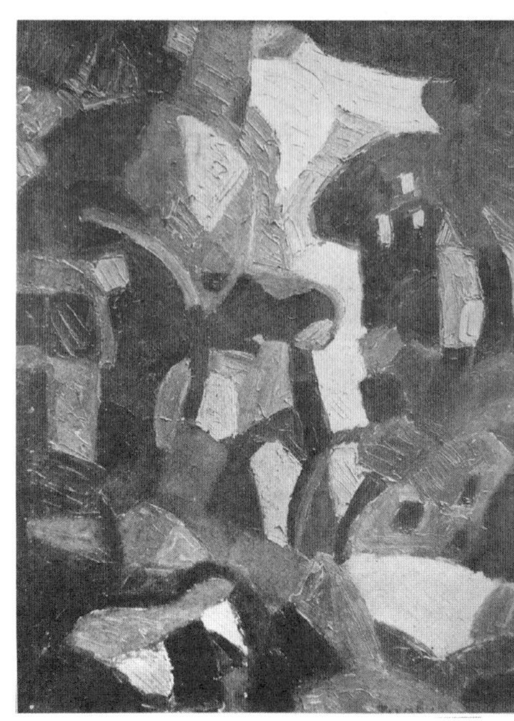

Fig. 2 Picabia, Paysage, 1911

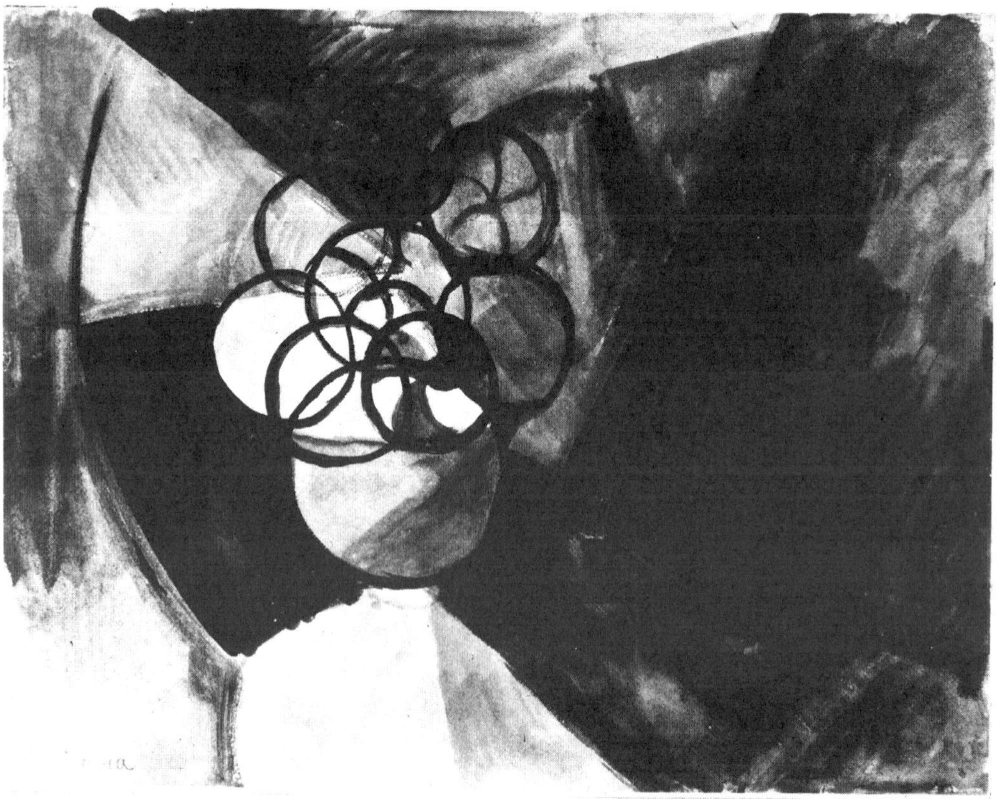

Fig. 3 Picabia, Caoutchouc, water-color, 1909

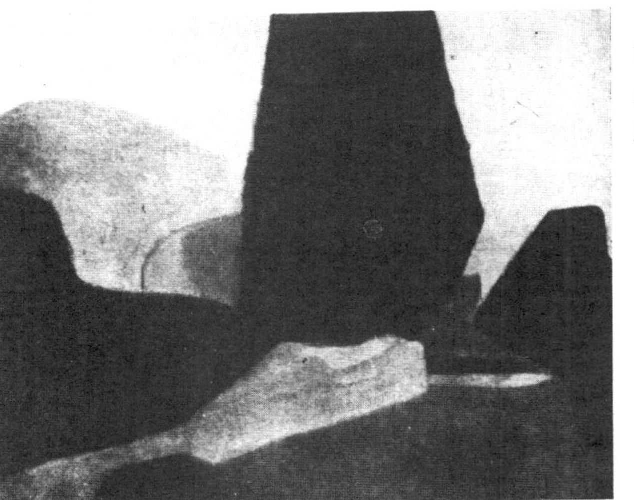

Fig. 4

Picabia, Paysage, 1908

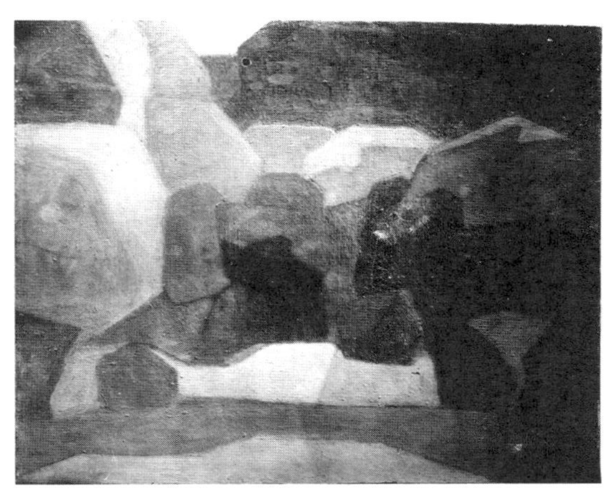

Fig. 5

Picabia, Paysage de Cassis, 1909

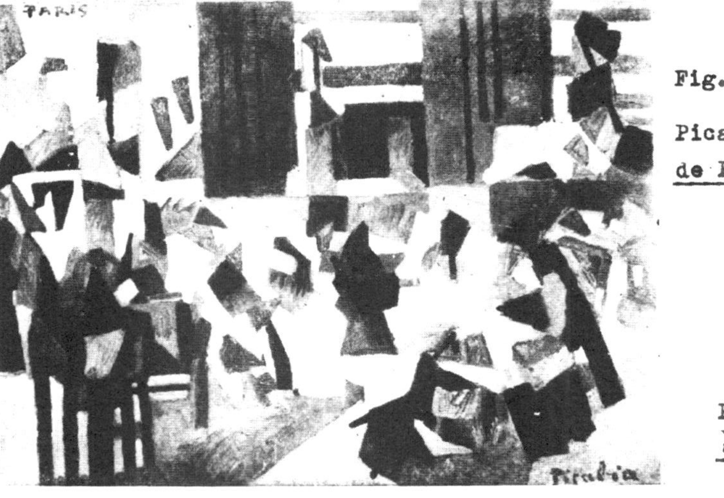

Fig. 6

Picabia, La ville de Paris, 1911

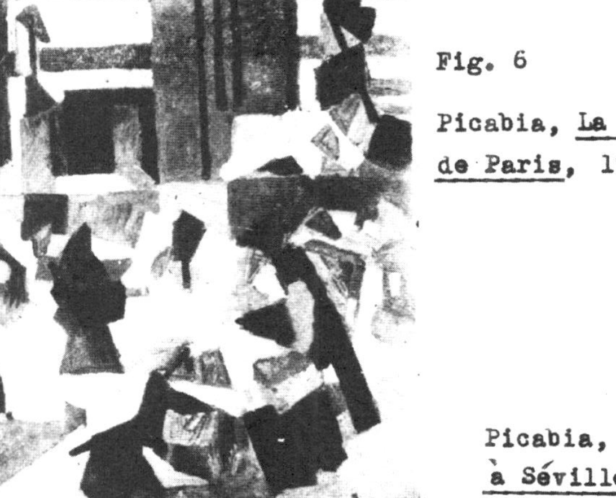

Fig. 7

Picabia, La Procession à Séville, 1912

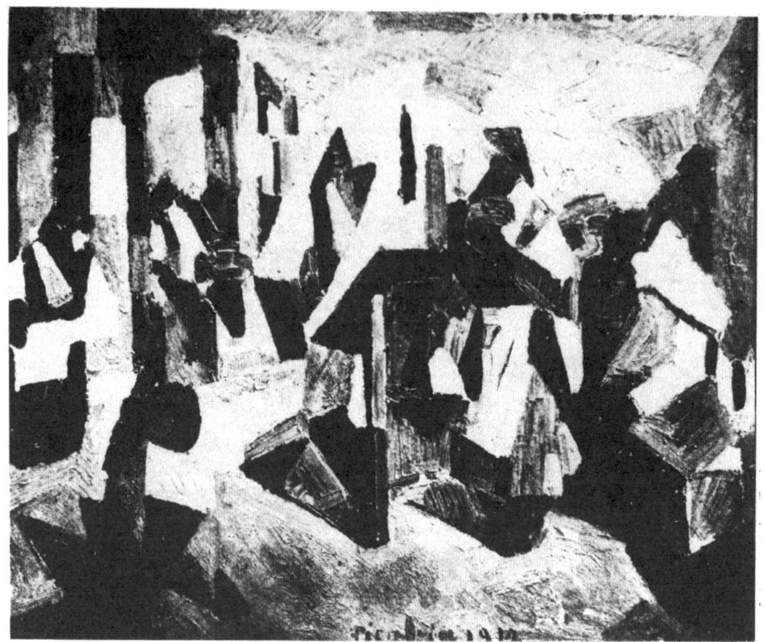

Fig. 8 Picabia, Tarentella, 1912

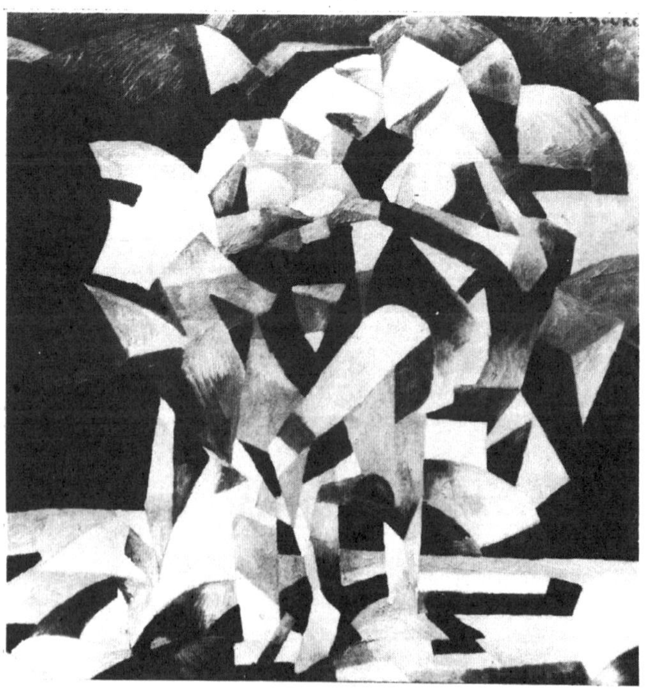

Fig. 9 Picabia, Danses à la source, 1912

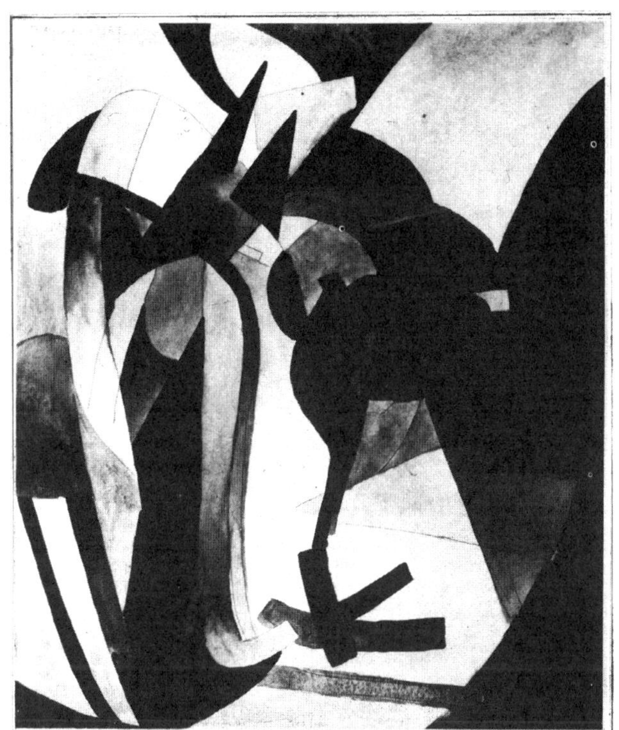

Fig. 10

Picabia, *Chanson Nègre*, 1913

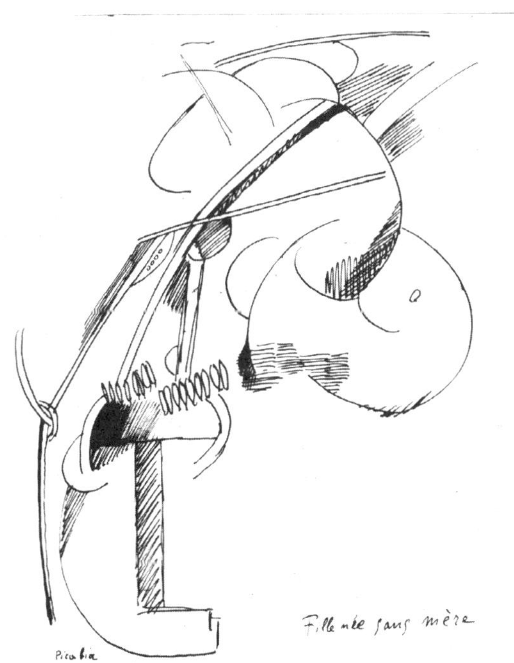

Fig. 11 Picabia, *Fille née sans mère*, 1913

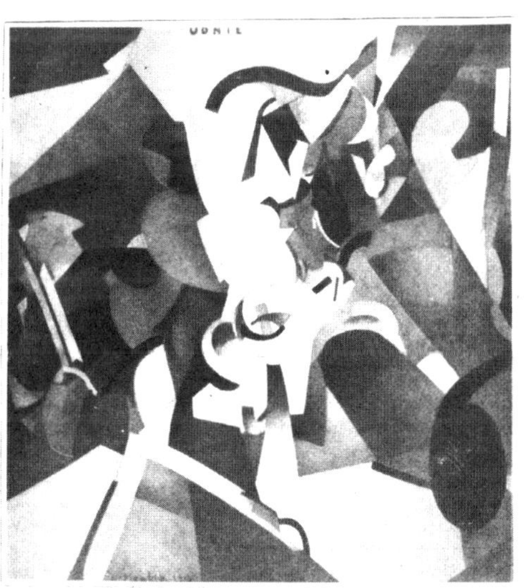

Fig. 12 Picabia, *Udnie, Jeune fille américaine*, 1913

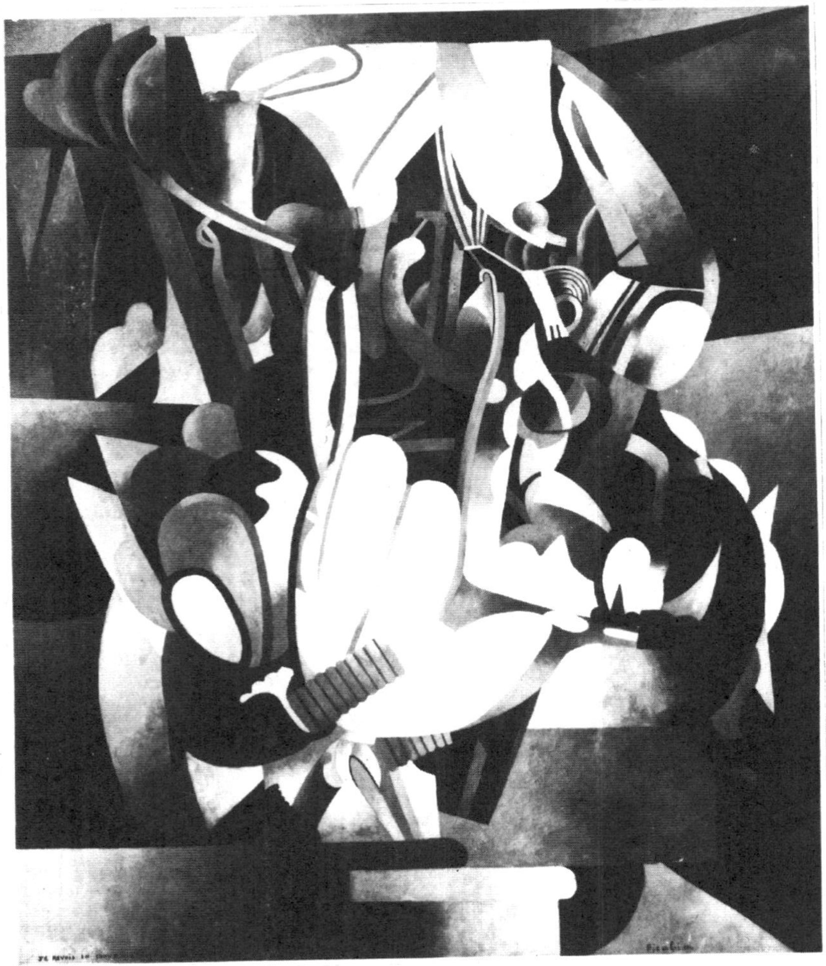

Fig. 13 Picabia, *Je revois en souvenir ma chere Udnie*, 1913

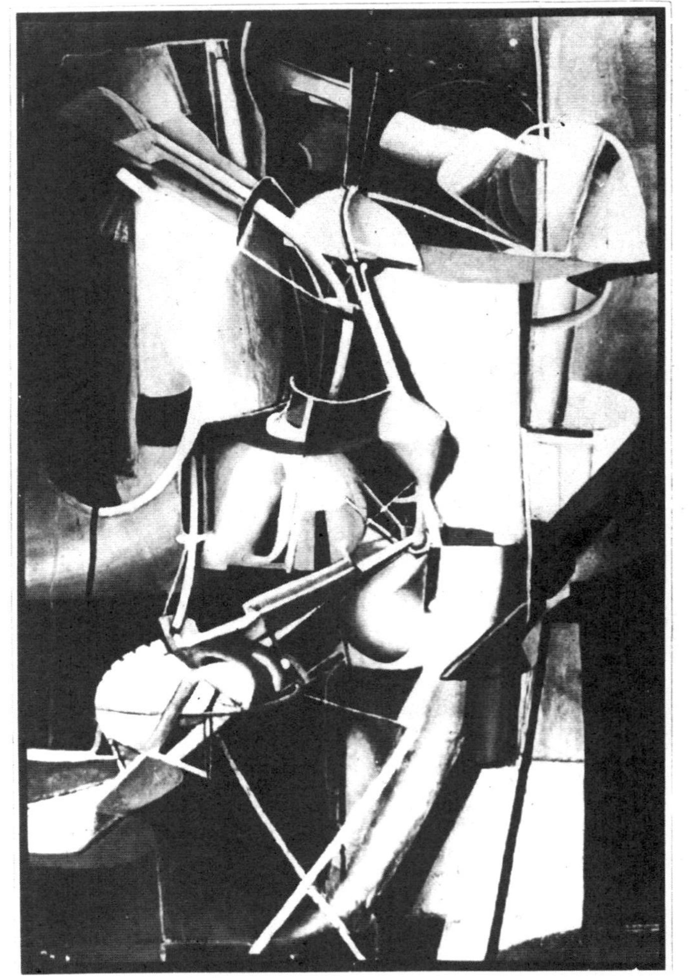

Fig. 14 Duchamp, *Mariée*, 1912

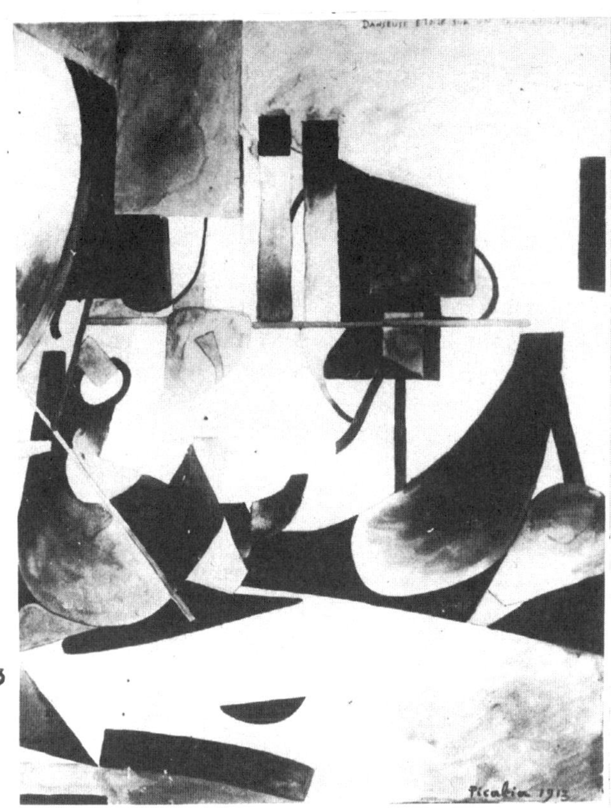

Fig. 15

Picabia, *Danseuse étoile sur un transatlantique*, 1913

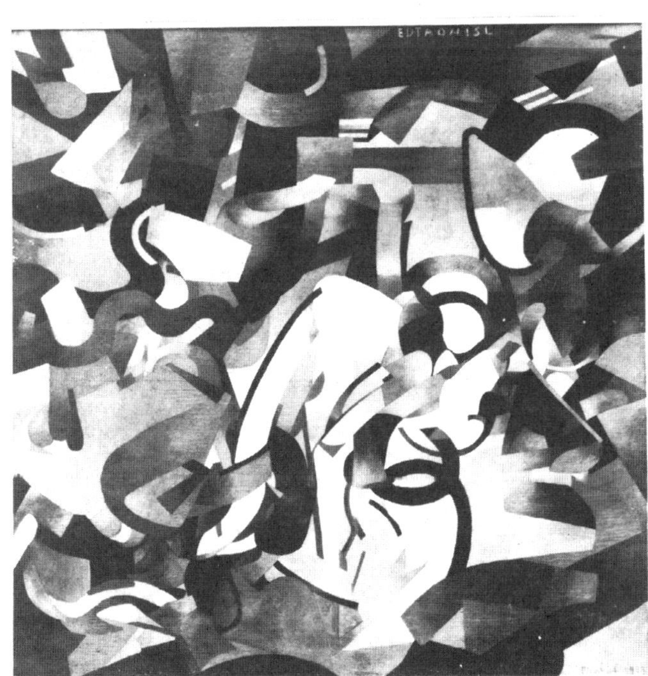

Fig. 16

Picabia, *Edtaonisl, Ecclésiastique*, 1913

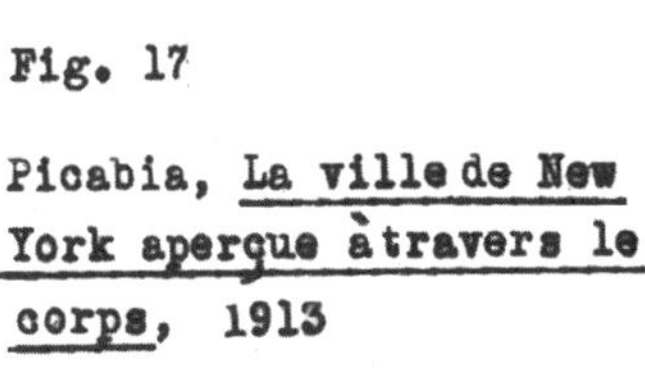

Fig. 17

Picabia, <u>La ville de New York aperçue à travers le corps</u>, 1913

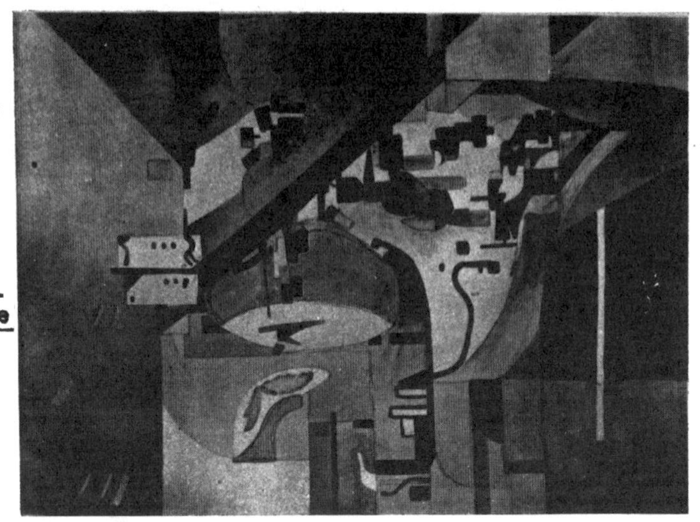

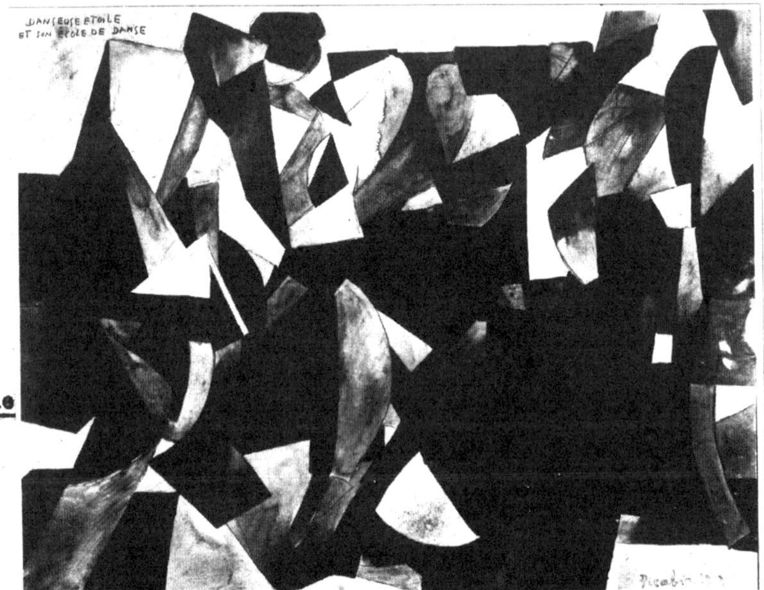

Fig. 18

Picabia, <u>Danseuse étoile et son école de danse</u>, 1913

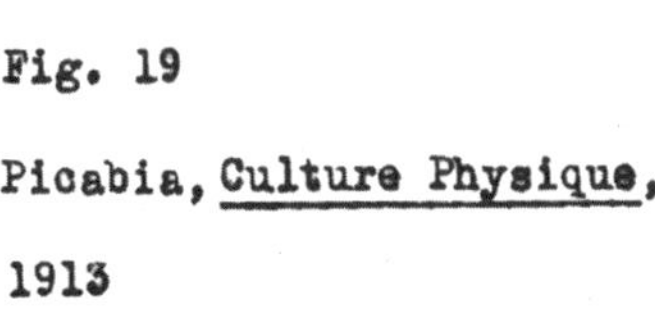

Fig. 19

Picabia, <u>Culture Physique</u>, 1913

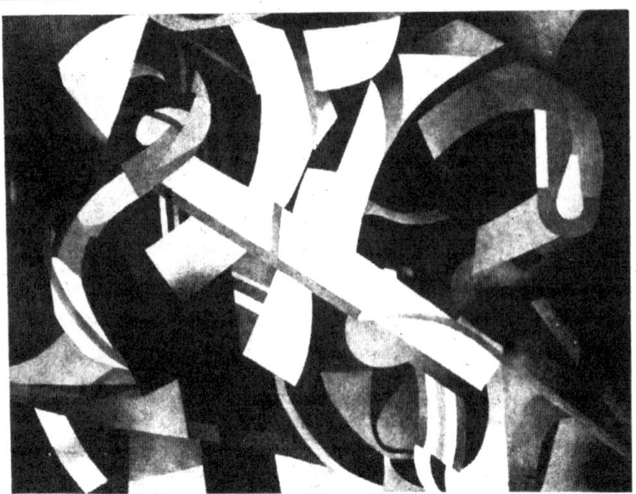

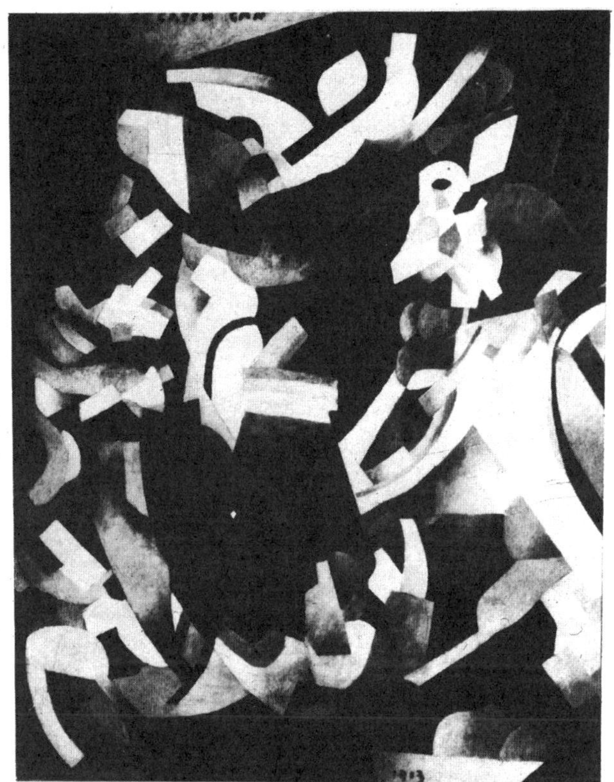

Fig. 20

Picabia, Edtaonisl, Catch as Catch Can, 1913

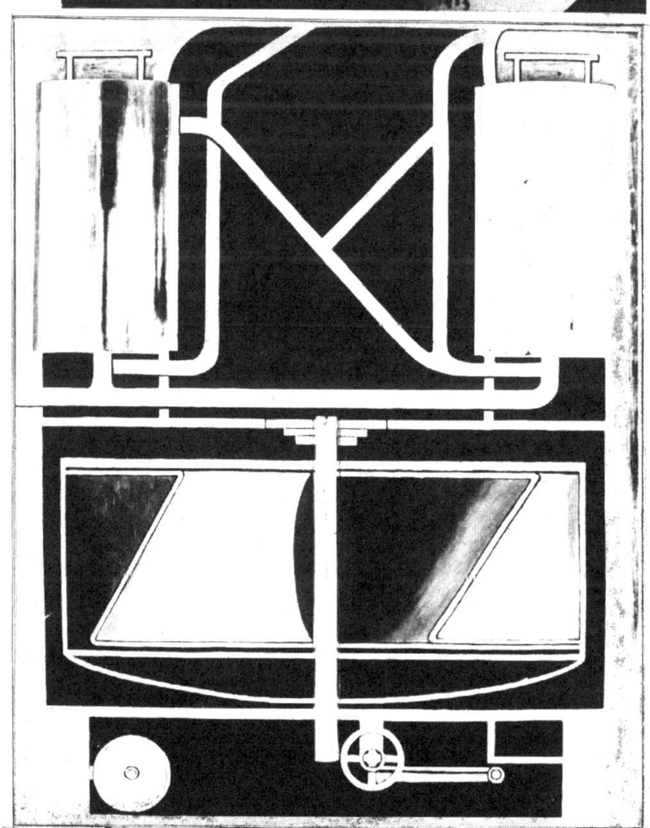

Fig. 21

Picabia, Very rare picture on the earth, 1915 or '16

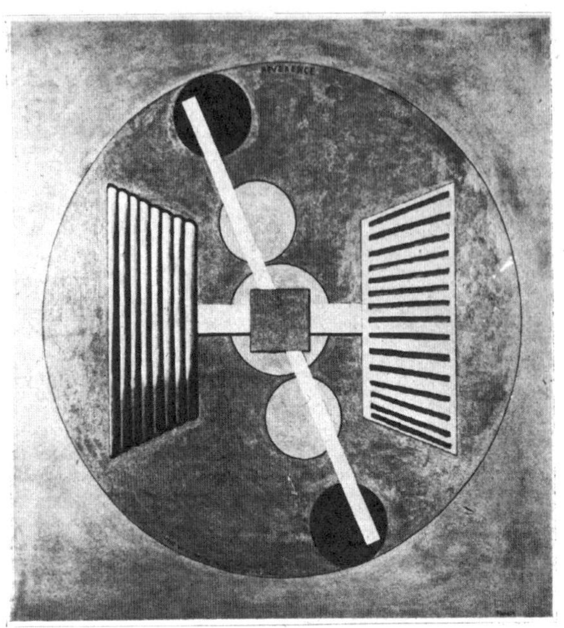

Fig. 22

Picabia, Dedee d'Amerique, 1915

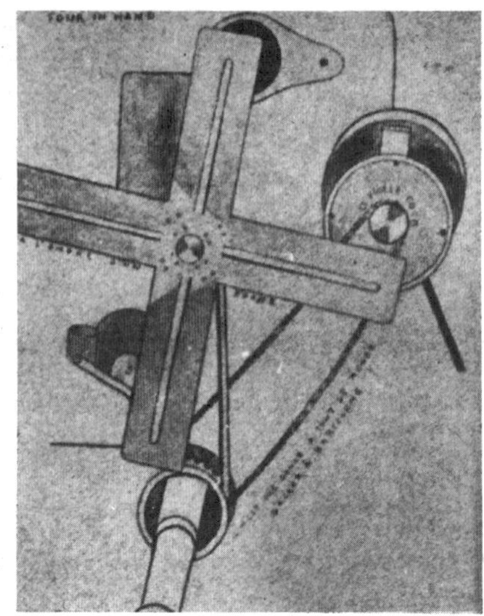

Fig. 23

Picabia, ~~Four in hand~~ Portrait de Marie Laurencin, 1916

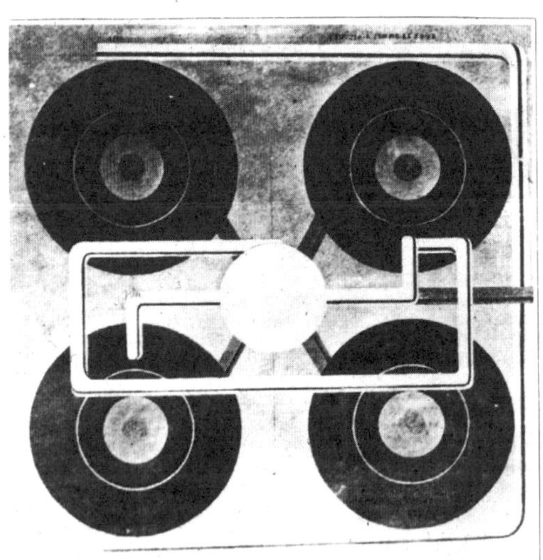

Fig. 24

Picabia, C'est clair comme le jour, 1915 or '16

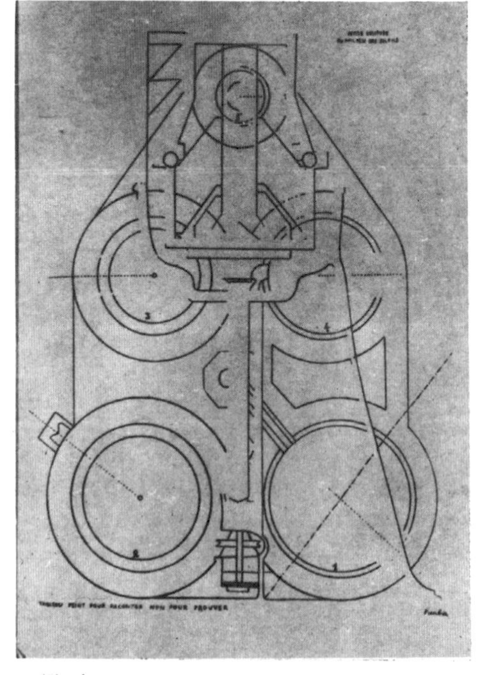

Fig. 25

Picabia, Tableau peint pour raconter non pour prouver, 1915 or '16

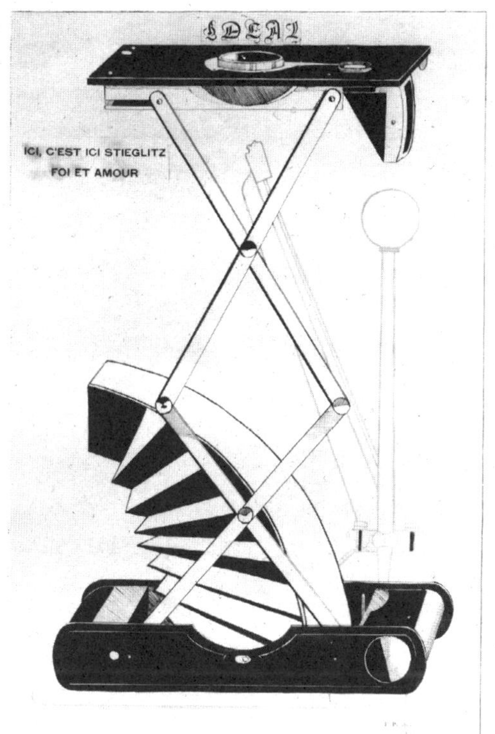

Fig. 26 Picabia, *ici, c'est ici Stieglitz*, 1915

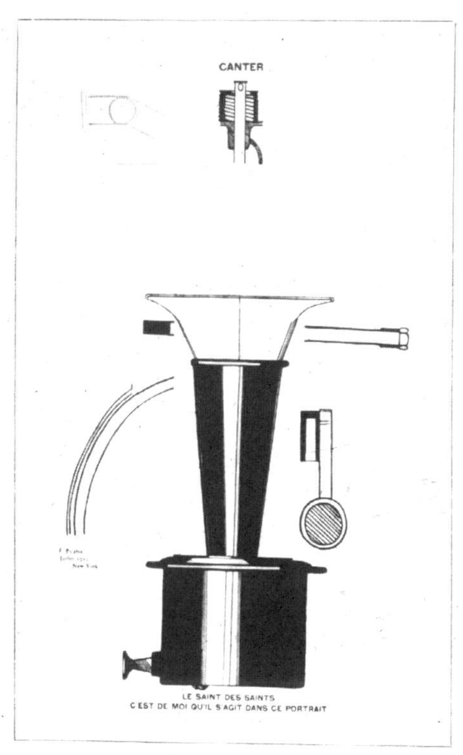

Fig. 27 Picabia, *Le Saint Des Saints*, 1915

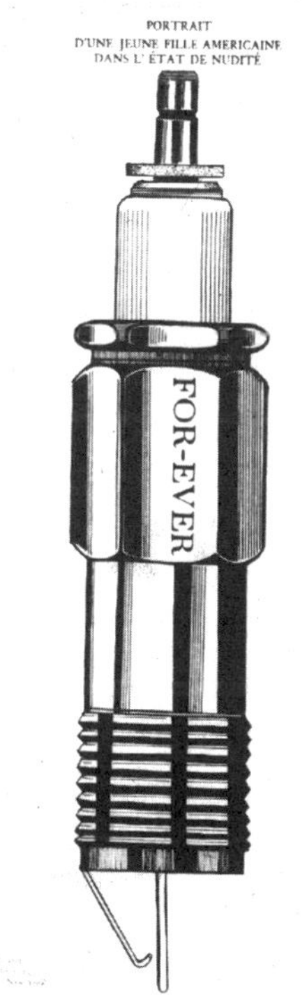

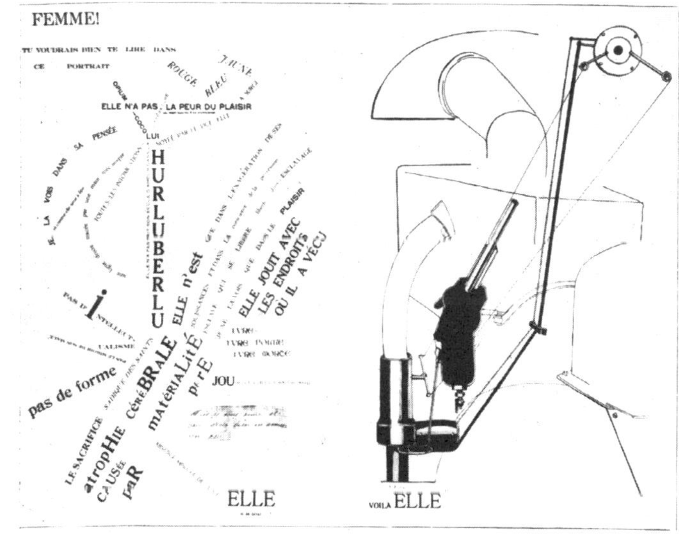

Fig. 29 Picabia, *Voila Elle*, 1915

Fig. 28 Picabia, *Portrait d'une jeune fille américaine dans l'état de nudité*, 1915

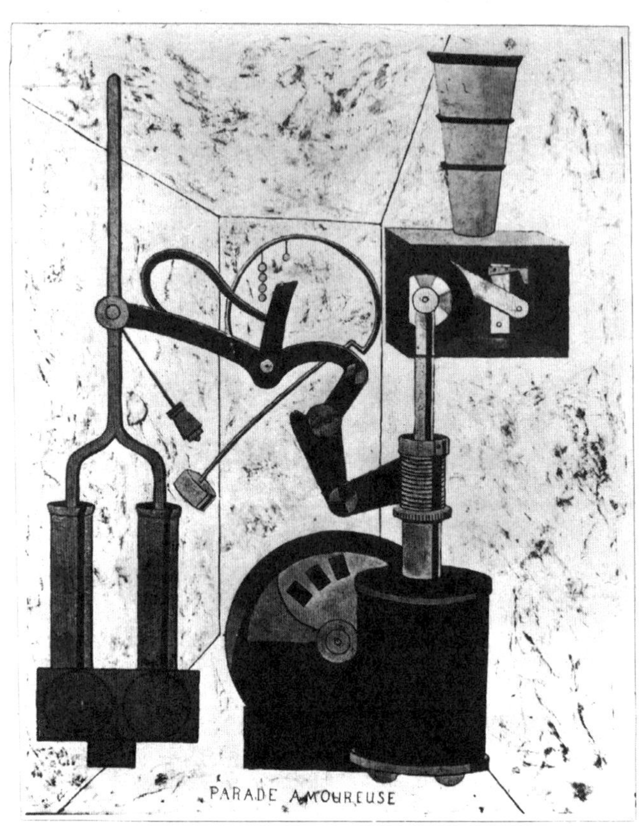

Fig. 30

Picabia, Parade Amoureuse, 1917

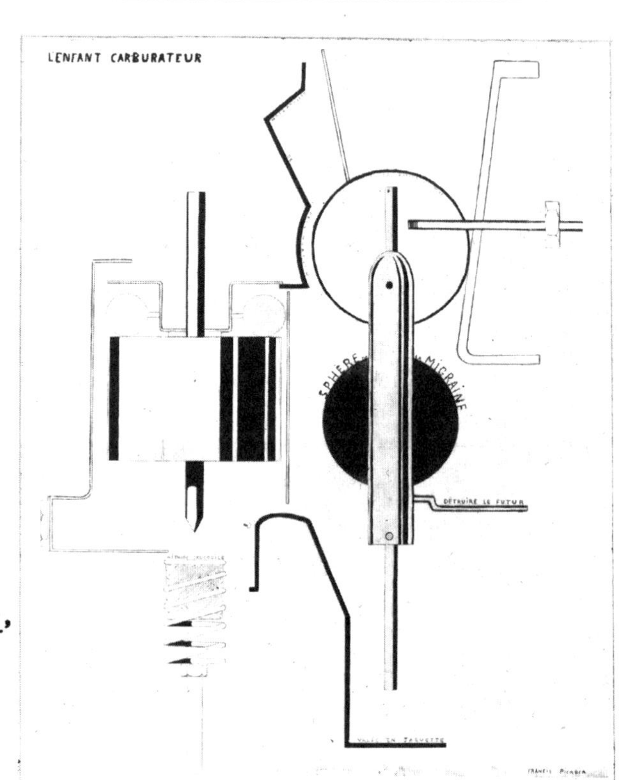

Fig. 31

Picabia, L'enfant carburateur, 1918

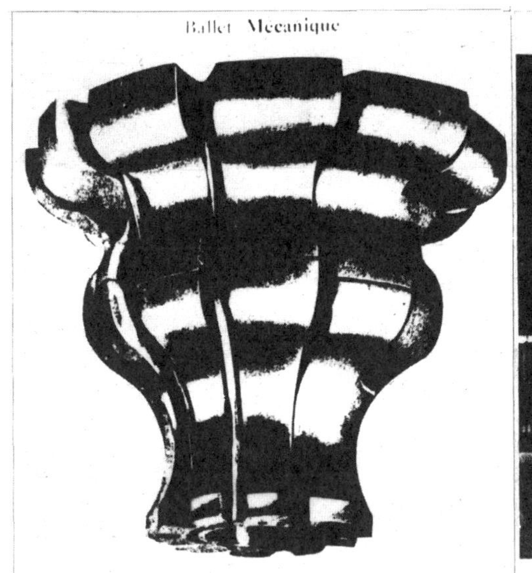

Fig. 32
Picabia, Ballet mecanique, 1917

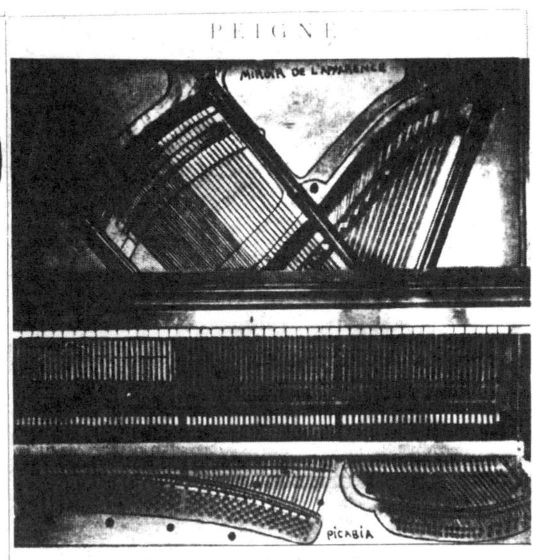

Fig. 33
Picabia, Mirroir de l'apparence, 1917

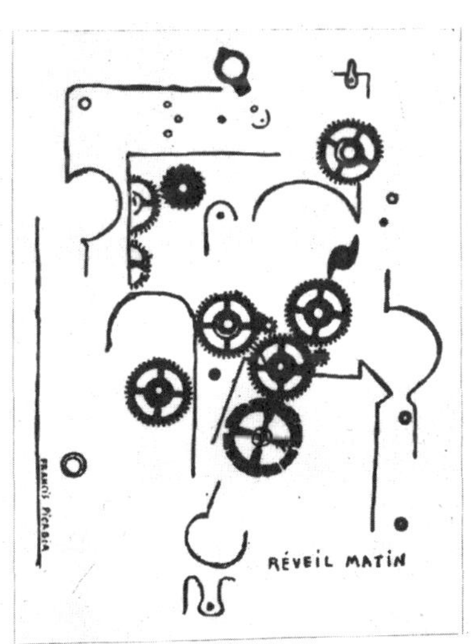

Fig. 34
Picabia, Réveil matin, 1919

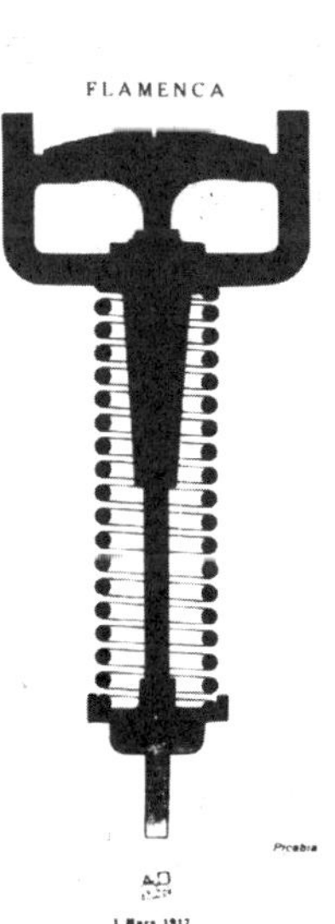

Fig. 35
Picabia, Flamenca, 1917

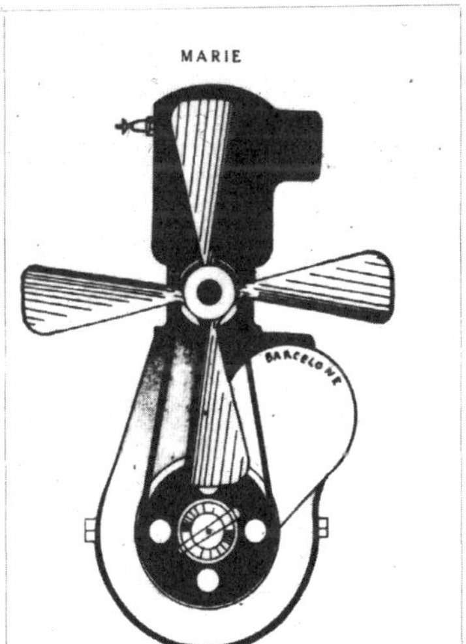

Fig. 36
Picabia, Marie, 1917

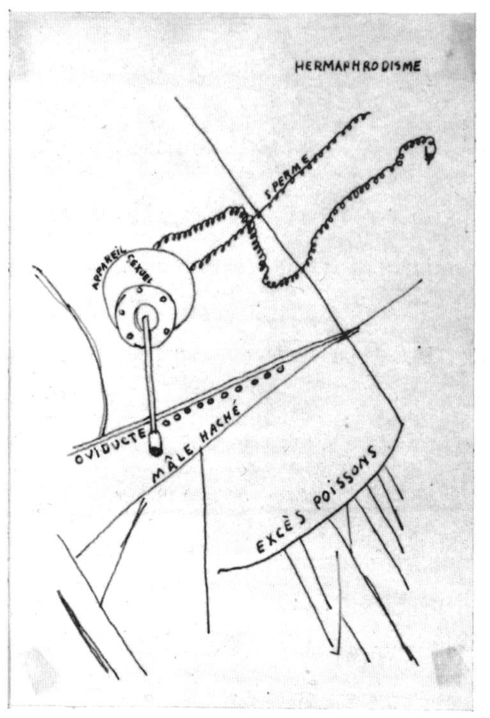

Fig. 37 Picabia, <u>Hermaphrodisme</u>, 1918

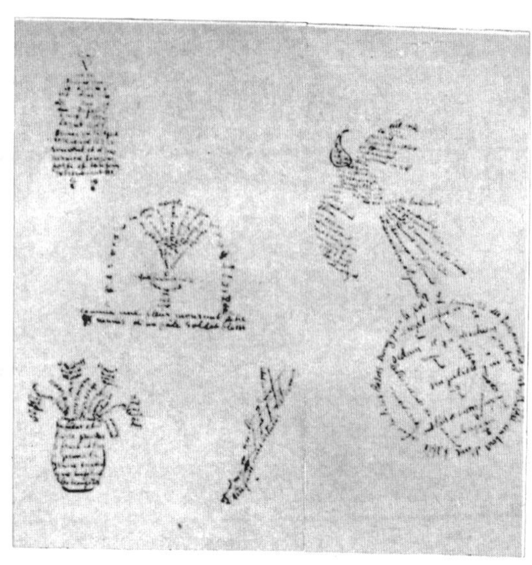

Fig. 38 Apollinaire, <u>Calligrams</u>

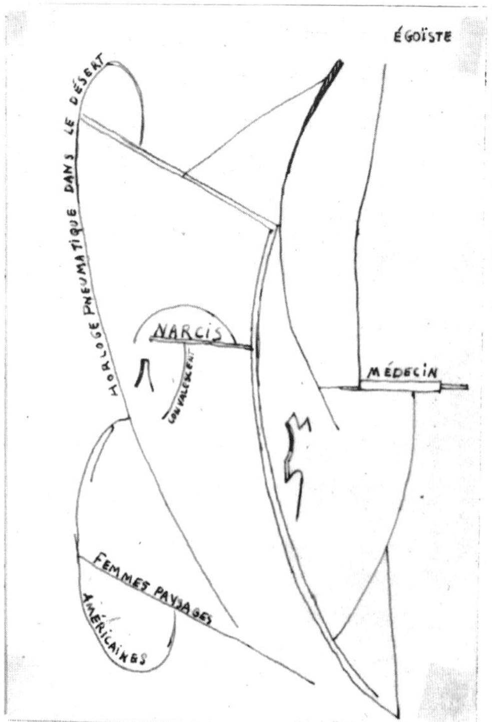

Fig. 39 Picabia, <u>Égoïste</u>, 1918

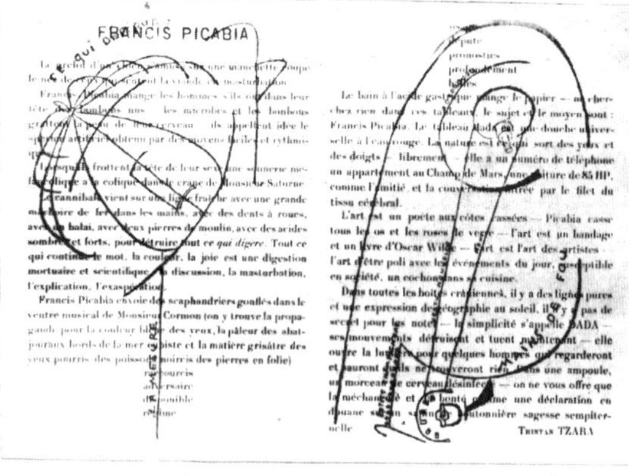

FRANCIS PICABIA

[illegible] une manchette coupe le nez [illegible] la viande en masturbation.

Francis Picabia mange les hommes s'ils ont dans leur tête des bonbons nus — les microbes et les bonbons grattent la peau de leur cerveau — ils appellent idée le sperme artificiel obtenu par des moyens faciles et rythmiques.

Lorsqu'ils frottent la tête de leur sexe une sonnerie mélancolique a la colique dans le crane de Monsieur Saturne.

Le cannibale vient sur une ligne fraîche avec une grande mâchoire de fer dans les mains, avec des dents à roues, avec un balai, avec deux pierres de moulin, avec des acides sombres et forts, pour détruire tout *ce qui digère*. Tout ce qui continue le mot, la couleur, la joie est une digestion mortuaire et scientifique, la discussion, la masturbation, l'explication, l'exaspération.

Francis Picabia envoie des scaphandriers gonflés dans le ventre musical de Monsieur Cormon (on y trouve la propagande pour la couleur bleue des yeux, la pâleur des abat-jour aux bords de la mer cubiste et la matière grisâtre des yeux pourris des poissons noircis des pierres en folie)

raccourcis
adversaire
disponible
régime

[illegible]
dispute
[illegible]
profondément
[illegible]

Le bain à l'acide gastrique mange le papier — ne cherchez rien dans ces tableaux, le sujet et le moyen sont : Francis Picabia. Le tableau Dada est une douche universelle à l'eau rouge. La nature est ce qui sort des yeux et des doigts — librement — elle a un numéro de téléphone un appartement au Champ de Mars, une voiture de 85 HP, comme l'amitié, et la conversation entrée par le filet du tissu cérébral.

L'art est un poète aux côtes cassées — Picabia casse tous les os et les roses de verre — l'art est un bandage et un livre d'Oscar Wilde — l'art est l'art des artistes — l'art d'être poli avec les événements du jour, susceptible en société, un cochon dans sa cuisine.

Dans toutes les boîtes crâniennes, il y a des lignes pures et une expression de géographie au soleil, il n'y a pas de secret pour les notes — la simplicité s'appelle DADA — ses mouvements détruisent et tuent maintenant — elle ouvre la lumière pour quelques hommes qui regarderont et sauront qu'ils ne trouveront rien dans une ampoule, un morceau de cerveau désinfecté — on ne vous offre que la méchanceté et la bonté comme une déclaration en douane selon son [illegible] boutonnière sagesse sempiternelle

TRISTAN TZARA

Fig. 40 Picabia, Exhibition catalog, 1920

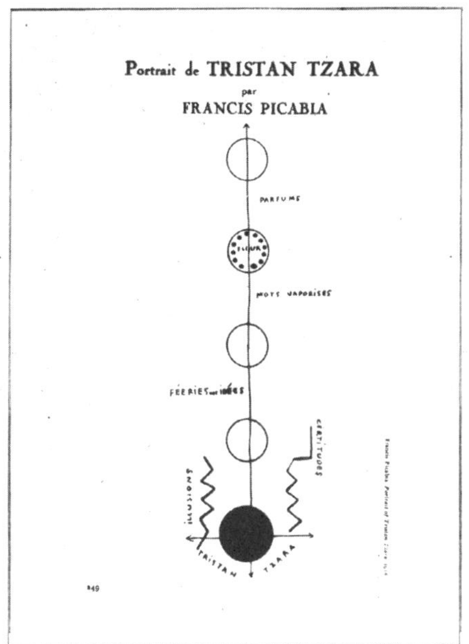

Fig. 41 Picabia, Portrait de Tristan Tzara, 1918

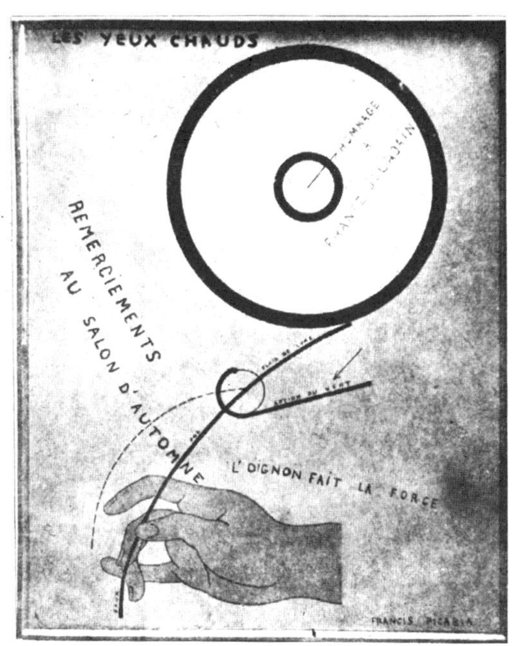

Fig. 42 Picabia, Les Yeux Chauds, ca. 1918

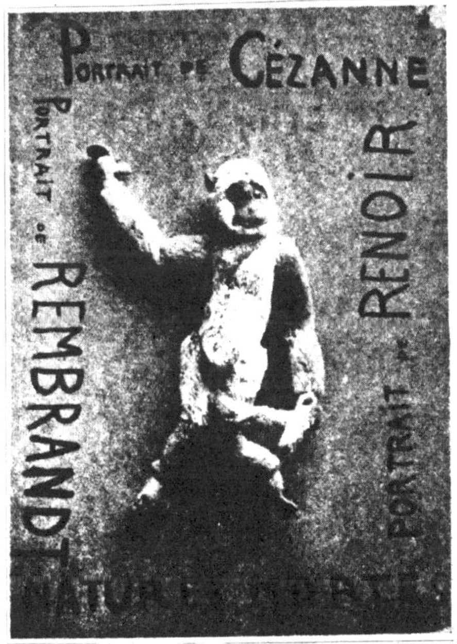

Fig. 43 Picabia, Portrait de Cézanne, 1920

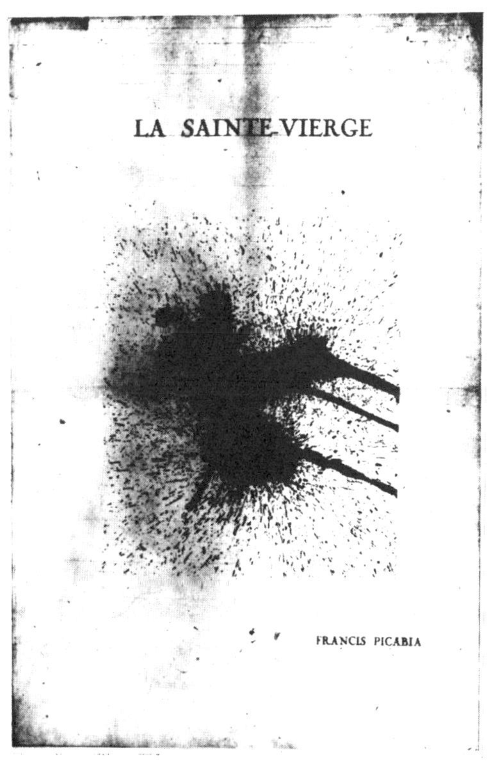

Fig. 44. Picabia, La Sainte Vierge, 1920

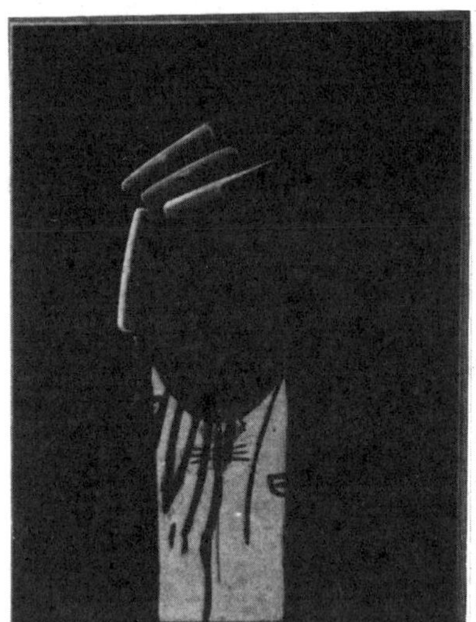

Fig. 45 Picabia, *Le beau charcutier*, 1921

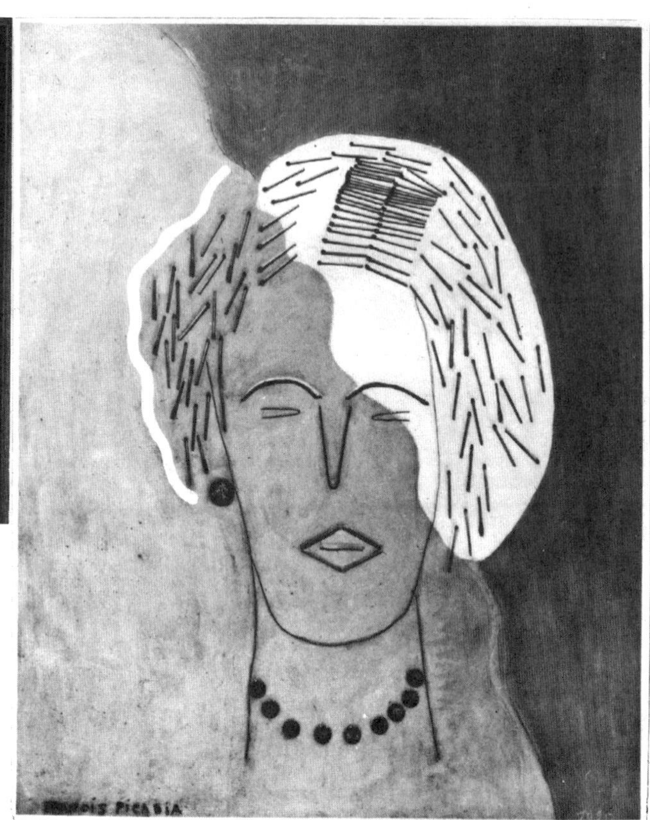

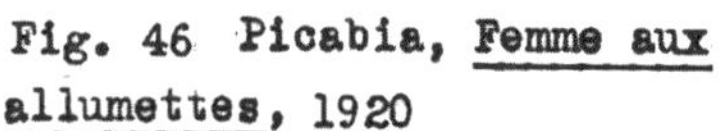

Fig. 46 Picabia, *Femme aux allumettes*, 1920

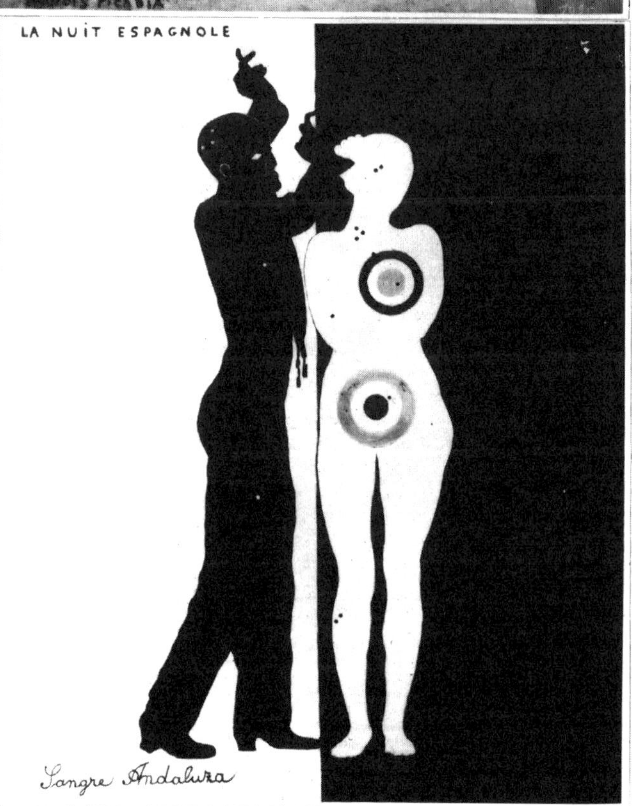

Fig. 47 Picabia, *La Nuit Espagnole*, 1922

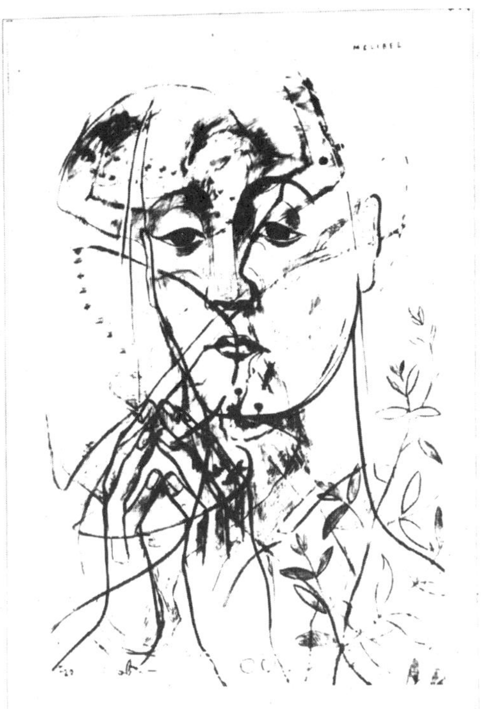

Fig. 48 Picabia, Melibee, ca. 1924

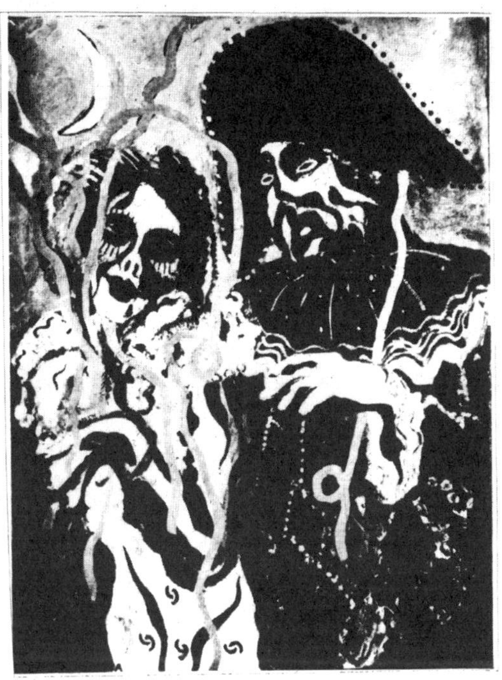

Fig. 49 Picabia, Mi Carême, ca. 1926

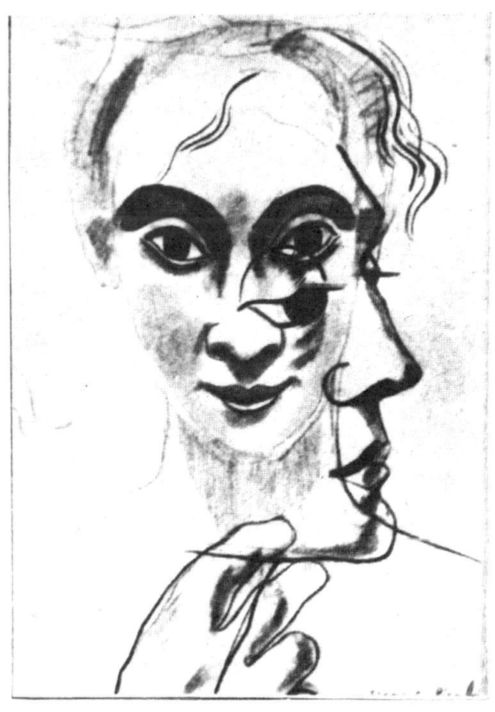

Fig. 50 Picabia, Transparence, 1932

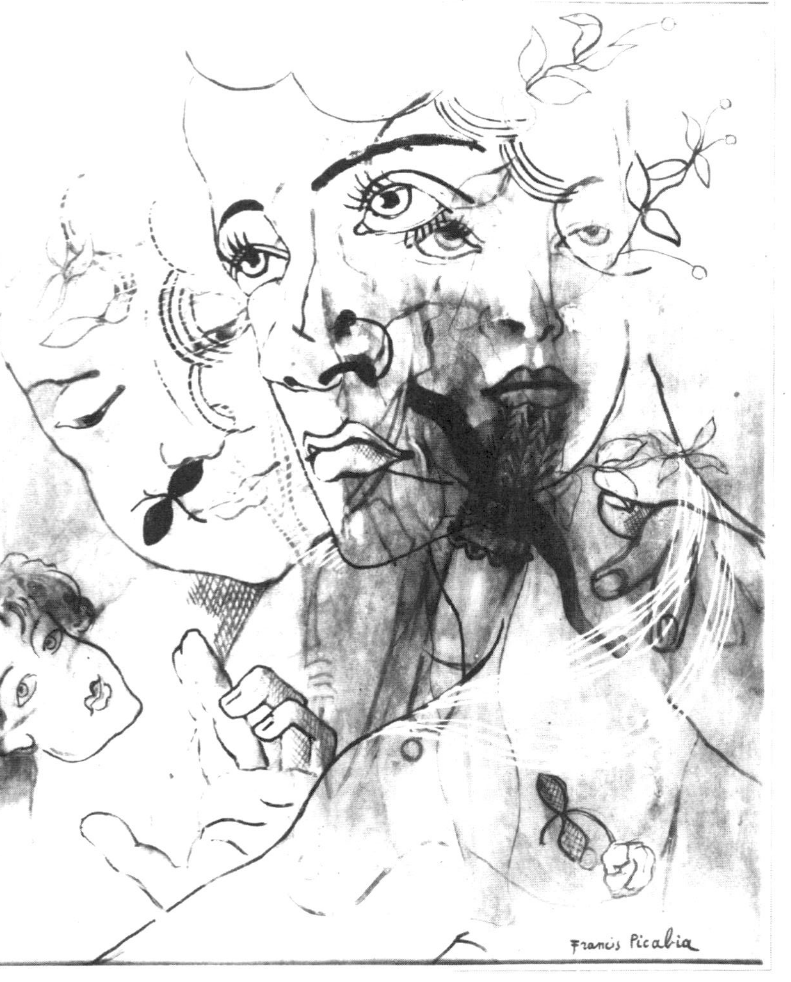

Fig. 51 Picabia, Myrte, ca. 1924

Fig. 52 Picabia, Sous les oliviers, 1924

Fig. 53 Picabia, Cote d'Azur, ca. 1928

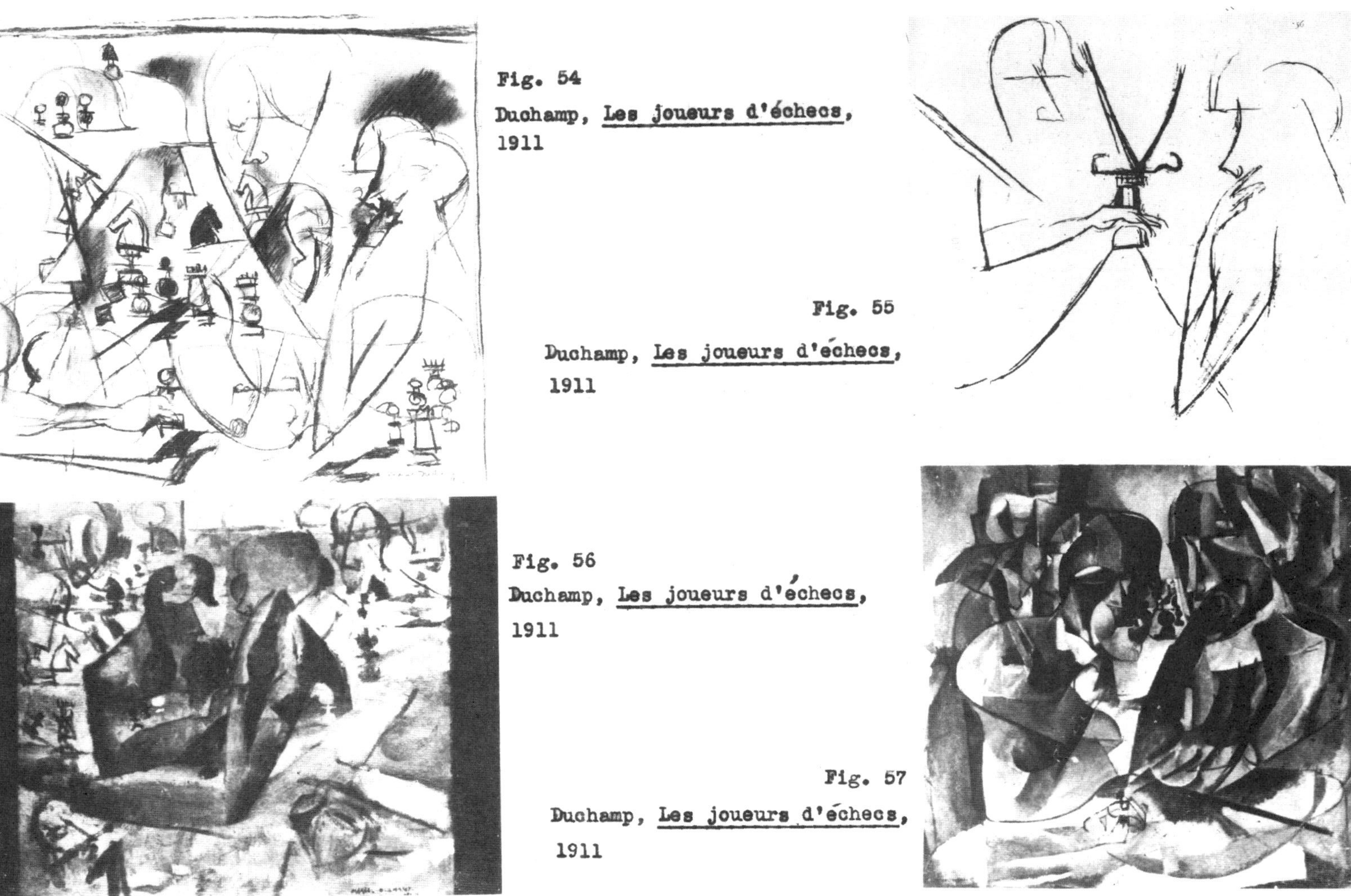

Fig. 54
Duchamp, _Les joueurs d'échecs_, 1911

Fig. 55
Duchamp, _Les joueurs d'échecs_, 1911

Fig. 56
Duchamp, _Les joueurs d'échecs_, 1911

Fig. 57
Duchamp, _Les joueurs d'échecs_, 1911

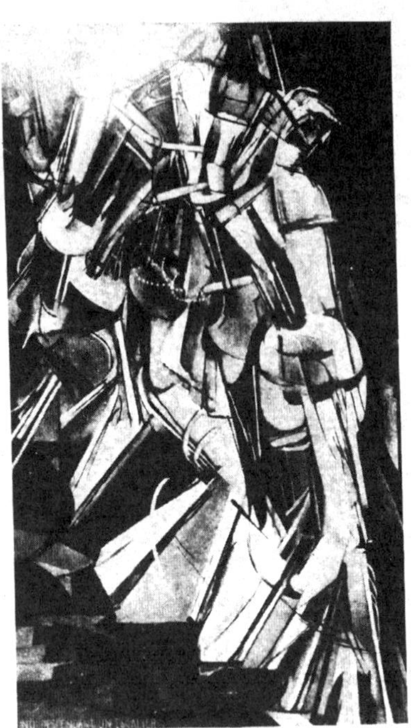

Fig. 58 Duchamp, <u>Nu descendant un escalier</u>, 1912

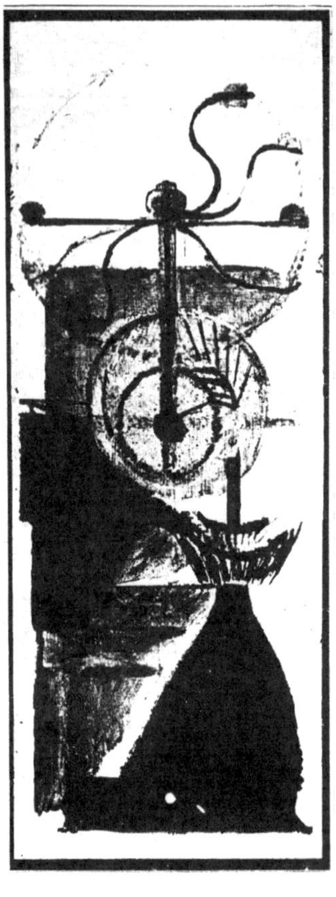

Fig. 59 Duchamp, <u>Moulin à café</u>, 1911

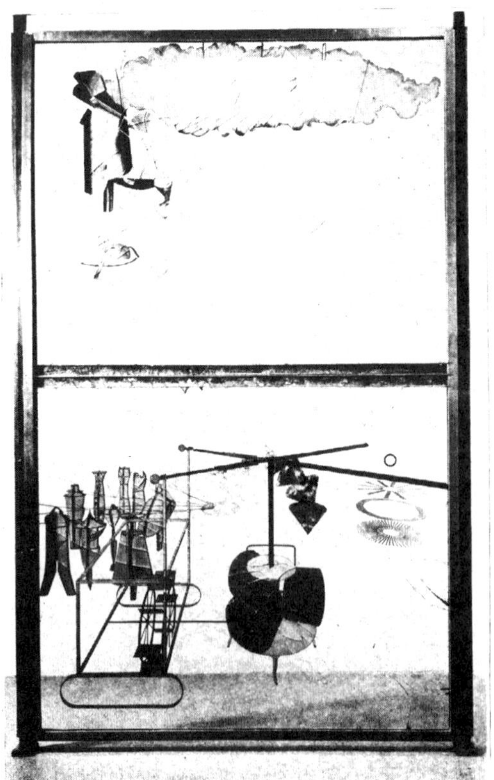

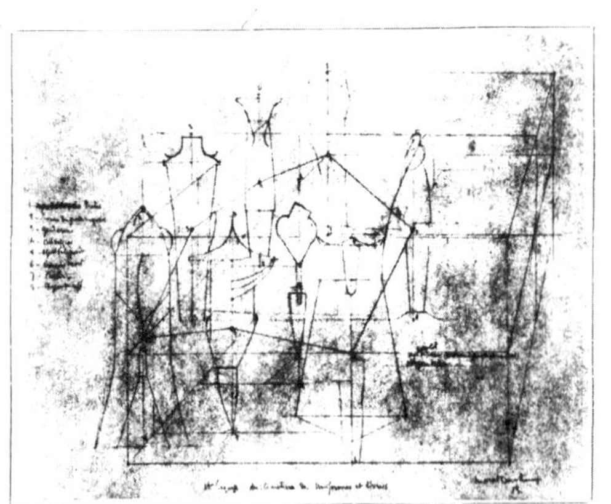

Fig. 60 Duchamp, <u>Cimetiere de uniforms et livrées</u>, 1913

Fig. 61 Duchamp, <u>La Mariée mise à nu par ses célibataires, même</u>, 1915 - 1923